SCOTT WALKER

Paid for by Friends of Scott Walker, Kate Lind, Treasurer

UNINTIMIDATED

UNINTIMIDATED

A Governor's Story and a Nation's Challenge

Scott Walker

with Marc Thiessen

Sentinel

SENTINEL

Published by the Penguin Group
Penguin Group (USA) LLC
375 Hudson Street
New York, New York 10014

USA | Canada | UK | Ireland | Australia | New Zealand | India | South Africa | China
penguin.com
A Penguin Random House Company

First published by Sentinel, a member of Penguin Group (USA) LLC, 2013

ISBN 978-1-59523-107-9

Printed in the United States of America
10   9   8   7   6   5   4

Set in Adobe Garamond Pro
Designed by Spring Hoteling

For Tonette, whom I've been infatuated with for more than two decades, and for Matt and Alex, because I want them to live in an America as great as the one I grew up in

CONTENTS

INTRODUCTION

Ⅲ

"If It Can Happen in Wisconsin, It Can Happen Anywhere"

If you are like me, the view from Washington, D.C., these days is pretty grim.

Barack Obama has been elected to a second term. Obamacare will not be repealed anytime soon. Congress has approved massive tax increases. The national debt is on track to double during Obama's presidency. We are experiencing the worst economic recovery America has ever had.[1] Family income has plummeted, and more than three quarters of Americans are living from paycheck to paycheck.[2] Over twenty million Americans still cannot find work or have simply given up trying. And the Congressional Budget Office projects that we won't return to full employment until the end of 2017[3]—a year after President Obama leaves office.

Worse, a recent study by Rutgers University found that six in ten Americans believe that the nation's economy has "undergone a permanent change" and that today's dismal economic situation is the "new normal."[4]

Think about that: Our citizens are poorer, our debt is larger, our growth is slower, and our people are less hopeful than at any time in recent memory—and a majority of Americans have come to expect and accept this sorry situation as "normal."

Yet President Obama has laid out a second term agenda that doubles down on the failures of his first. And Republicans are being warned that they should not even try to stop him. The GOP, we are told, is increasingly out of touch with the American people. Our once center-right country is moving center-left. We are told that the only way for Republicans to avoid electoral annihilation is to stop opposing President Obama, abandon our conservative principles, and make peace with big government.

Depressed yet? Don't be.

Things may look hopeless in Washington, D.C., but from where I sit in Wisconsin, the view is decidedly more hopeful and optimistic.

Here is a little-reported fact: Outside the Washington beltway, big-government liberals are on the ropes, while conservative reformers are winning elections and policy battles in state houses all across the country.

Consider some encouraging data:

- At the time of this writing, not one incumbent GOP governor has lost a general election since 2007.
- Quite the opposite: In the last four years, Republicans have picked up governorships from Democrats in Iowa, Michigan, Ohio, Pennsylvania, Kansas, New Mexico, Oklahoma, Tennessee, Wyoming, North Carolina, New Jersey, Virginia, Maine, and in Wisconsin.
- The number of GOP governors has risen since 2008 from twenty-one to thirty—just four short of the all-time high of thirty-four Republican governors in the 1920s.
- When Barack Obama was first elected in 2008, Republicans held just 3,220 seats in state legislatures across the country. Today, two election cycles later, the number is 3,826—a net gain of 606 seats.

- In the 2012 elections, when President Obama was overwhelmingly elected to a second term, Republicans saw net gains in thirty-four legislative chambers, including chambers in four states won by President Obama: New Mexico, Ohio, Washington, and Wisconsin.

- When President Obama first took office, Republicans controlled just sixteen state houses of representatives and twenty state senate chambers. Today they control twenty-eight and twenty-nine, respectively. And they hold veto-proof majorities in sixteen states—a gain of three during the 2012 election that sent Obama back to the White House.

- Four years ago, Republicans controlled both the legislature and governor's mansion in just eight states. Today, the number is twenty-three—and nearly half our citizens live in states where both the legislature and the governorship are in Republican hands.

Does this sound like the record of a party that is out of touch with the priorities of the American people?

So the question is: Why are so many Republican governors and state legislators winning elections at a time when national Republicans are faring so poorly?

The answer, in part, is that while Washington remains locked in endless battles that most Americans don't see as having much impact on their daily lives, Republican leaders at the state level are offering big, bold, positive reforms that are relevant to the lives of our citizens.

In Washington, politicians fight over "fiscal cliffs," "debt limits," and "sequesters." In the states, we are focused on improving education, caring for the poor, reforming government, lowering taxes, fixing entitlements, reducing dependency, and creating jobs and opportunity for the unemployed.

Just look at what some of our nation's Republican reformers have accomplished at the state level:

In Indiana, Governor Mitch Daniels inherited a two-year deficit of $800 million,[5] and left Indiana with a $500 million annual surplus and $2 billion in reserves, without raising taxes.[6] He ended collective bargaining for state employees, privatized Indiana's toll roads, and created the largest school choice program for low-income students in the country.

In Louisiana, Governor Bobby Jindal took on his state's long history of corruption and enacted comprehensive ethics reform that restored integrity to state government—while at the same time closing a $341 million budget shortfall and giving $1.1 billion back to the hardworking taxpayers across his state over five years.

In New Jersey, Governor Chris Christie enacted a 2 percent cap on property taxes, passed public employee pension and health benefit reforms that will save taxpayers more than $130 billion over the next thirty years, balanced four budgets without raising taxes,[7] and gave taxpayers $2.35 billion in job-creating tax cuts.[8]

In New Mexico, Susana Martinez became the first Latina governor in United States history, and turned a $450 million budget deficit into a $200 million surplus.[9] In Michigan, Governor Rick Synder closed a $1.5 billion deficit while lowering personal income taxes and eliminating the state's job-killing business tax.[10] In Idaho, Governor Butch Otter passed legislation in 2011 that restricts collective bargaining for Idaho schools, institutes merit pay, and eliminates teacher tenure.[11] And there are countless other examples.

Here in Wisconsin, we are doing our part as well. When I took office in January 2011, our state faced a massive $3.6 billion budget deficit and a stark choice: We could raise taxes or lay off more than ten thousand middle-class government workers to close the gap, or we could reform the corrupt system of political cronyism and collective bargaining—in which union bosses collected involuntary dues from every government employee, and had effective veto power over any changes to their pay, benefits, or working conditions—that was driving our state into fiscal ruin.

We chose reform. The state legislature passed my budget repair bill, known as Act 10, that requires public workers to contribute 5.8 percent of their salaries to their pensions (up from zero for most) and to pay 12.6 percent of their health insurance premiums (up from about 6 percent). We ended collective bargaining for everything except base wages. We ended compulsory union membership, and stopped the forced collection of union dues—allowing teachers and other public workers to choose for the first time whether they wanted to join the union and pay dues. And we freed school districts from the stranglehold of collective bargaining rules—allowing them, for example, to buy health insurance on the open market and hire and fire teachers based on merit for the first time.

Today, thanks to these reforms, the $3.6 billion deficit we inherited has turned into more than a half-billion-dollar surplus.[12] School districts across Wisconsin have saved tens of millions of dollars—money they have used to offset state spending cuts and improve education, instead of laying off teachers. Property taxes dropped for the first time in over a decade. Unemployment is down. Our bond rating is solid. For the first time in state history, we set aside money in two consecutive years for the rainy day fund. And Wisconsin's pension system is the only one in the country that is fully funded.

Seems like common sense, right?

Well, the union bosses in Washington and Madison didn't see it that way. They understood that our reforms were the leading edge of a national grassroots movement for fiscal reform—a movement that is flying below the radar of the mainstream media, but which holds the hope for a bold conservative resurgence across America.

They understood the threat this grassroots movement posed to their entrenched interests. So they decided to fight back.

And they made Wisconsin ground zero in their counteroffensive.

Why did they pick Wisconsin to draw their line in the sand? In part, it was because of our state's "progressive" history. Wisconsin was the birthplace of public sector unions in 1936, and the first state to allow collective bargaining for government employees in 1959. If the union bosses could not stop collective bargaining reform in the state where collective bargaining began, they had little hope of stopping it anywhere.

I suspect they also figured that Wisconsin was favorable political ground. The state has not voted for a Republican president since 1984, and Barack Obama won here in 2008 by a comfortable fourteen points. Moreover, our capital, Madison, is kind of the Berkeley of the Midwest (former governor Lee Dreyfus once called it "thirty square miles surrounded by reality"). In other words, there were plenty of students, teaching assistants, and leftover sixties radicals available for mass protests. It must have seemed like a natural place to push back, score an easy victory, and send a clear message to would-be reformers across the country: If you dare to take on the public sector union bosses, you will be writing your own political epitaph.

But ultimately, the unions took their stand in Wisconsin because of the unprecedented nature of our reforms. We did not simply go after the money—the lavish benefits the unions had extorted from taxpayers over the years. We dismantled the entire system of corruption and cronyism by which the unions perpetuated their political power and dictated spending decisions to state and local government. We took the reins of power from the union bosses and put the taxpayers back in charge.

The big-government union bosses knew that if they did not stop our reforms in Wisconsin, the floodgates of change would open across the land. Other political leaders, emboldened by our success, would summon the courage to enact similar changes in their home states—and eventually in Washington, D.C.

The unions could not allow that to happen. The precedent we were setting in Madison had to be stopped. As one protester lamented to the *Los Angeles Times*, "If it can happen in Wisconsin, it can happen anywhere."[13]

So they threw everything they had at us. They mobilized some one hundred thousand protesters to take over the Wisconsin State capitol in a sit-in that helped give birth to the Occupy movement.[14] They transported agitators from Illinois, New York, Nevada, and other states; banged drums and blasted horns day and night; harassed and spit on lawmakers as they made their way through the capitol; and turned our historic rotunda into a theater of the absurd. They picketed my home and those of Republican lawmakers, harassed our families at school and even at the grocery store, and shouted us down at county fairs and ceremonial events across Wisconsin—all in an effort to intimidate us.

When their intimidation tactics failed to deter us, fourteen Democratic state senators fled the state—abdicating their constitutional duties in an effort to deny us a quorum needed to even take up our reforms.

When we found a way around their obstructionist tactics, they turned to the courts to stop us—targeting a good and decent Wisconsin supreme court justice for defeat simply because they *thought* he would vote to sustain our reforms.

When that judicial coup failed, they tried to recall six Republican state senators, guilty of no official misconduct, simply because they voted for our reforms.

When that effort failed to put the senate back in Democratic hands, they tried to recall more Republican senators. They tried to recall our lieutenant governor. And they tried to recall me.

They failed.

Despite everything they threw our way, we pressed forward with our reforms. And the results are there for all to see: Wisconsin is back in the black. Our economy is growing. Business is expanding. Jobs are being created. Taxes are falling. Educational opportunities are improving. The legislature remains in Republican hands. The state supreme court has upheld our reforms. So have the federal courts.

And I became the first governor in American history to beat a recall. As my wife, Tonette, likes to point out, I'm the only governor elected *twice* in the same term.

This book tells the story of how we won the battle for Wisconsin—the reforms we put in place, the mistakes we made, and the lessons we learned. In the pages that follow, I will discuss how we almost lost the "fairness" fight in Madison—and how we turned it around on the Democrats and their union allies. I will explain how we reached into President Obama's base and won over the "Obama-Walker" voters in Wisconsin—and how conservatives can do it anywhere in the country. I will demonstrate how we balanced our budget while rejecting the dour politics of austerity—and found a way to make fiscal responsibility hopeful and optimistic. I will show why it is a myth that winning the center requires moving to the center—and why the path to a conservative comeback lies not in abandoning our principles, but in championing bold, conservative reforms . . . and having the courage to see them through.

I firmly believe that the lessons we learned in Wisconsin can help conservatives win the fight for fiscal reform in Washington, D.C., and lead the way to greater prosperity for people all across America.

Our opponents in Madison were right about one thing: If we can do it in Wisconsin, we *can* do it anywhere—even in our nation's capital.

CHAPTER 1

"This Is What Democracy Looks Like"

Governor, we've lost control of the capitol.

The call came from my deputy chief of staff, Eric Schutt. Amid the chaos, his voice was calm and matter-of-fact: Thousands of protesters had overrun the police, and were rampaging through the historic Wisconsin state capitol building.

It was March 9, 2011, and the state senate had just held a sudden, unexpected vote on our legislation to reform collective bargaining. The move had caught the unions and the protesters by surprise. With fourteen Democratic senators still hiding out across state lines in Illinois, everyone had thought that the senate could not act. Under our state constitution, a vote on any bill that includes fiscal measures requires a quorum of at least twenty senators. There were only nineteen Republicans. Without at least one Democratic senator present, we could not pass the bill.

Unbeknownst to them, we had found a way to overcome their obstruction. Several weeks earlier, we discovered that if we split the bill into two—removing the fiscal provisions that required a quorum—the senate could pass the collective bargaining reforms as a stand-alone measure, without the missing Democratic senators present.

It was a simple, clean solution, and we urged the senate to do it right away. But the Republican senators hesitated. They were afraid that if they passed collective bargaining provisions alone, without the fiscal savings, they would be accused of union-bashing.

Of course, they were accused of union-bashing anyway. And as the weeks went on, while the senate was wringing its hands, their inaction had given the union bosses time to organize protests and build pressure.

In February, first hundreds and then thousands of people began living inside the capitol building. Every hour the protesters held a massive rally under the capitol dome, with bullhorns, drum circles, bagpipes, and chanting and singing. The roar of the crowd was nearly constant. The sound sometimes reached more than 105 decibels—louder than a Packers game at Lambeau Field. It literally shook the building.

The protesters in the capitol accosted anyone in a suit, shoving cameras in their faces and demanding to know who they were. The building was strewn with garbage and empty pizza boxes. It was so packed with human bodies that there was no way to move around, much less clean. After a while, the floors became covered with a disgusting film, and the odor of unwashed humanity wafted through the hallways. The place smelled like a Port-a-John. When the protesters eventually left, work crews with power washers had to spend days scrubbing the building from floor to ceiling.

People were smoking pot inside the capitol. There were so many sleeping bags, inflatable mattresses, and tents that my staff often joked about how many "protest babies" there would be in nine months' time.

After weeks of this chaos, on March 3 a judge finally ordered the police to clear out the capitol and restore a semblance of order. Instead of thousands, they allowed between five hundred and seven hundred protesters inside at a time, and required them to leave each night. In normal times, several hundred protesters inside the capitol would have been disruptive. But after weeks of occupation, it seemed like a relief.

Unfortunately, the relative calm would only last a few short days.

Outside the capitol, the protesters continued to march and chant and accost legislators. After enduring weeks of abuse, the Republican senators' frustration with the protests and the Democrats' obstruction grew. When it finally became clear their Democratic colleagues were never coming back from Illinois, the senate Republicans finally decided they had had enough. Opposition to splitting the bill melted away. The senate decided to act.

On the morning of March 9, I met with the Republican caucuses in the senate and the assembly. We laid out an orderly plan to end the stand-off and pass the bill. Republican leaders would announce that they had scheduled a hearing of the conference committee for the following day. The committee would meet, split the bill, and send it to the full senate for a vote. The senate would act and then send it to the assembly for final passage. While this was going on, I would fly across the state to rally support for our plan. The whole process would take forty-eight hours.

I left the meetings and headed to the airport. I was both relieved that we were finally ending this impasse and energized that we would finally be enacting our reforms.

The capitol was quiet as I departed that morning. Since no one was expecting the senate to act until the following day, and the costs of security were soaring into the millions, at around 3:30 p.m. my secretary of administration, Mike Huebsch, sent home the two hundred or so reserve police officers in the basement of the capitol.

Big mistake.

At 4:10 p.m. Mike got an urgent call from Eric Schutt.

"The senate's going in at six p.m.," Eric told him.

"What the [EXPLETIVE] are you talking about?" Mike asked.

"They're going to pass the bill," Eric explained.

Senate Majority Leader Scott Fitzgerald had decided to throw our orderly plan out the window and vote on Act 10 that night. He was presiding over a skittish caucus, and did not know how long he would have the votes. He decided not to wait.

Mike's face blanched. "Oh God, I just let the police officers go."

There was no way to call them back.

Fitzgerald posted a notice on the bulletin board outside the senate publicly announcing that the Joint Finance Committee would meet at 6:00 p.m. At the appointed time, the committee met for four minutes, split the bill, and voted it out. (Senate President Mike Ellis could be heard whispering under his breath as assembly Democrats protested, "Call the roll . . . call the roll . . . call the [EXPLETIVE]-ing roll.") The senate then met, passed the bill, and adjourned. The whole process, from public notice to final passage, took about four hours.

As word about what the senate was doing spread, social media exploded. The unions and their supporters flooded Twitter and Facebook with urgent calls for protesters to rush the capitol.

Standing on the capitol steps at dusk, Mike Huebsch watched as an army of thousands formed on State Street and began marching toward him. Soon they had descended on the building, banging on the doors and windows, chanting, "Let us in! Let us in!"

The small contingent of capitol police was quickly overwhelmed. Protesters ripped the hinges off an antique oak door at the State Street entrance and streamed inside. Mike watched in disbelief as the window to Democratic Representative Cory Mason's office opened right in front of him and protesters began crawling into the building. Once inside, they began unlocking doors and bathroom windows until a sea of thousands had flooded the capitol.

Still standing outside, Mike called the deputy chief of the capitol police, Dan Blackdeer, to report what he was seeing.[1]

"We've lost the ground floor, we're dropping back to the first floor," Blackdeer told him from inside the besieged capitol.

A few moments later, his phone rang:

"We've lost the first floor, we're dropping back to the second."

A few minutes later: "We've lost the second floor."

"For God's sake, don't give up the third floor," Mike said. That was where our command center was located.

"I know, sir," Blackdeer said. "I've got to go."

The protesters ran amok, chanting "This is our house!" and "This is what democracy looks like!"

And they began searching for the Republican senators who had dared to defy the will of the unions.

As the mob combed the building for the offending legislators, the police snuck the senators and my staff out through an underground tunnel that took them beneath the square outside, and then up into the Risser Justice Center across the street. Incredibly, a Democratic representative put out on social media that the senators were in the tunnels. So when the senators came up into the Risser Center lobby, the protesters were there waiting for them.

The tall windows that framed the lobby were plastered with people yelling and banging on the glass.

They were trapped.

The senators hid under a stairwell, out of view, while the police ordered a city bus to pull up in front of the building. Officers then formed a human wall on the sidewalk, parting the sea of protesters and creating a pathway for the senators to reach the bus. The door opened and they rushed out past the screaming throng to the bus. Once they were on board, the mob on the street began punching the windows and shaking the vehicle. Some lay down in front of it, trying to prevent the bus from pulling away. The police told the senators and staff inside to keep their heads down in case a window shattered.

Eventually, they cleared a path and slowly the bus inched away. The police decided to divert to the Department of Military Affairs, a secure area where any protesters following the bus could not enter. From there, they drove the senators back to their cars, away from the capitol.

Eric Schutt and my chief of staff, Keith Gilkes, escaped from the Risser building in a car driven by a very large and imposing police officer. They decamped to Lucky's, a bar a couple of miles from the capitol, where they called and filled me in on the harrowing escape. From a booth in the corner, Keith got firsthand reports from Mike, who was still on the capitol steps watching everything unfold, while Eric relayed the reports to me.

Mike was new on the job, so at first the protesters did not recognize him. But he was wearing a suit and talking on a cell phone, which made him suspect in their eyes. Soon a group of protesters was in his face, demanding to know who he was. He told me later it was the first time he had truly felt frightened for his safety. He made a quick escape and joined the rest of our team at Lucky's.

By morning, the police had regained control of the capitol, which was now being protected by SWAT teams in full body armor from the Justice Department's Division of Criminal Investigation (DCI)—the attorney general's police. It was like a scene out of *Call of Duty*.

The assembly met at 12:30 p.m. As Representative Michelle Litjens tried to say an opening prayer, the Democrats shouted her down. They wanted the Reverend Jesse Jackson—the former Democratic presidential candidate who had come to Wisconsin along with other B-list celebrities to join the protest movement—to deliver it. Incredibly, he was allowed to do so. I will never forget the image of Reverend Jackson, smiling in the well of the assembly while Representative Bill Kramer, the speaker pro tempore, sat next to him with his head in his hands. The Democratic leader offered a motion to remove Speaker Jeff Fitzgerald, which failed. After three hours of debate, Act 10 was approved by a vote of 53 to 42.

We wanted to avoid a repeat of the previous day's security disaster, so Keith asked Ed Wall, the head of the DCI team, if there was any way to get the legislators out of the building in secret. Ed said there was, so long as no other police units knew the plan. Dane County Sheriff David Mahoney had already declared that his force would not be used as my "palace guards."[2] Ed feared other units might tip off the protesters.

So Ed arranged for a "decoy bus" to be parked outside the capitol and told the Madison Police Department to help block off the street. Without telling the Madison police, Ed then secretly arranged for eighteen vans driven by DCI SWAT officers to be parked in the garage under the Risser building. When the heavily guarded bus pulled up on the Capitol Square, all the protesters went streaming toward it, ready to accost the legislators.

As they did, Ed quietly snuck the assembly members through the underground tunnel and into the waiting vehicles, which sped away one by one out of the Risser building before most of the protesters could figure out what was going on. A few of them noticed the last few vans spinning out of the garage and yelled to the crowd, "Hey, they're over here!" But it was too late.

The next morning, on March 11, 2011, my legal counsel Brian Hagedorn sent the bill to me at the governor's residence. My initial reaction was to rush and sign it then and there. The protests had eaten up a good month of our time, and I was eager to get back to my number one priority: helping the people of Wisconsin create more jobs. But Scott Matejov, one of my top aides, suggested that we should at least take a picture or two first to mark the historic moment. I stood for a moment and took it all in. But since we did not want to take any chances, I signed Act 10 into law right there at my dining room table.

After all we had been through, I was not going to simply sign this law in private, as if hiding from the crowds. We would also hold a formal signing ceremony in the capitol later that day.

Soon, I headed back to the statehouse via the Risser building. Once parked, I made my way through the underground tunnel to my office in the capitol. Up above, throngs of protesters were chanting on the Capitol Square, but down here it was eerily quiet.

We passed beneath a bakery, which filled the tunnel with the smell of warm fresh bread. Then, turning the corner, I stared down the hundred-yard underground corridor dotted with emplacements of riot gear every fifteen yards or so. It was a grim reminder of how serious things had gotten in and around the capitol.

As I walked up the back stairs to my office, I was greeted by Scott

Fitzgerald and his brother, Assembly Speaker Jeff Fitzgerald; Assembly Majority Leader Scott Suder; Senate President Mike Ellis; joint finance committee cochairs Representative Robin Vos and Senator Alberta Darling; as well as other courageous legislators who had voted for this bill.

These individuals had withstood intense pressure, and protests unlike anything seen in Madison before, in order to pass our reforms. And now that the legislation was finally law, they were still being threatened. As he raced back to Madison from hiding out in Illinois, Democratic senator Chris Larson issued a stark warning: "Everyone who is a party to this travesty is writing their political obituary."[3]

So I would have understood if Act 10's supporters had decided to skip the ceremony. But they wanted to be there. They were proud of what we had accomplished, and I was proud to stand beside them. We had become like a family.

As protesters outside chanted "Shame!" I took a dozen pens, one by one, and signed Act 10 before the cameras. I might well have been signing my own political death warrant. But as I formally affixed my signature to the new law, politics was the furthest thing from my mind. We had done something important for our state, something I knew would put Wisconsin on the path to fiscal solvency and greater prosperity. And perhaps our actions would inspire politicians in other states, and even Washington, to do the same.

"Some have asked whether this is going to set a national precedent," I said after signing the law. "For us we're doing this to lead the way in our own state, to get Wisconsin working again." But if our actions ultimately inspired others "to stand up and make the tough decisions . . . so that our children in all states and across the country don't have to face the dire consequences we face because previous leaders have failed to stand up and lead, I think that is a good thing."

It was certainly my hope that others would eventually follow our lead. But at that particular moment, it was unlikely that anyone was looking to us as a model.

Since Election Day, my approval rating had dropped nearly ten points. One poll showed that if the 2010 gubernatorial race were held again, I would lose to my opponent, Milwaukee mayor Tom Barrett, by a margin of 50 to 43 percent.

Time magazine declared me "Dead Man Walker."[4] Writing in *National Journal*, Paul Maslin, pollster to former California governor Grey Davis (who was removed from office in a recall election), warned that the same would happen to me.[5] Democratic strategist Dean Debnam of Public Policy Polling said of my electoral prospects: "He'd be done if the vote was today, it's just a question of whether that desire to put him out can continue to be sustained in the coming months."

In fact, in the coming months, my approval would drop even further. In June 2011, a 53 percent majority of Wisconsinites said they either "very much" or "extremely disapproved" of the way I was handling the job of being governor of Wisconsin. At one point, my approval rating reached an all-time low of 37 percent.[6] To put that in perspective, President George W. Bush's average approval rating during his second term was 37 percent.[7]

Not good.

Support for our reforms was upside down as well. One poll showed that 74 percent of Wisconsin voters said that if public workers agreed to pay more for health care and pensions, they should be allowed to retain all their collective bargaining "rights." That included nearly half (47 percent) of all Republicans. Only 21 percent of voters agreed collective bargaining should be curtailed.[8]

The protests and union propaganda were taking their toll. But standing there in the governor's conference room, as the ink dried on Act 10, I was not the least bit worried.

That was for one reason: I knew our reforms were going to work.

CHAPTER 2

"Go Ahead and Do It!"

How could I be so sure our reforms would work? How could I be certain that, freed from the grip of collective bargaining, local officials could save millions, improve schools, and make government work better?

Because I had been a local official.

In 2002, I was elected to lead Milwaukee County, one of the most Democratic-leaning counties in the state. My predecessor as county executive, Tom Ament, had presided over a pension scandal in which county officials rewrote pension rules to give themselves six-figure lump-sum payments on retirement, on top of their already generous monthly pension checks.[1] Had he won reelection, Ament had stood to receive a lump-sum payment of $2.3 million when we retired, in addition to an annual pension of $136,000 a year for life.[2]

News of the payouts caused widespread public outrage and demands that Ament face a recall. Instead, he announced his retirement, and a few months later I won a special election to replace him with 55 percent of the vote.

When I took office in Milwaukee County, we inherited a fiscal mess. The cash payouts were only the beginning. Spiraling health care and pension costs had grown so out of control they were like a virus that was eating up more and more of our county budget. I had promised in my campaign not to raise property taxes, which were already astronomically high. And I did not want to have massive layoffs of county workers.

One of the things I spent the most time praying about when I was county executive was layoffs. I realized how such decisions affected people's lives. Collective bargaining rules protected workers with seniority, which meant those most likely to get a pink slip were the people who could least afford it—younger workers, just starting off, with low pay and families to support. When I sent out layoff notices, I knew they were often going to people trying to meet mortgage payments or feed and clothe their kids.

Moreover, I knew that mass layoffs would decimate public services. That is because under collective bargaining rules, decisions about whom to layoff have to be made without regard to merit. In the private sector, when managers downsize they can assess their operations, decide where people are most needed, and choose to retain the best and brightest while letting the least productive workers go.

Not in the public sector. The rules under collective bargaining are as simple as they are inane: If you're the last to be hired, you're the first to be fired. Period. That meant that if we were forced to hand out random pink slips, we would have to let go of some of our most productive workers. Meanwhile, many of the least productive would be able to hold on to their jobs only because of seniority. That is no way to run anything.

I was determined to shrink the size of government, but I wanted to do it through attrition and reform, not random pink slips. So I did everything in my power to avoid massive layoffs.

To get the county on sound fiscal ground, I decided that we would all have to tighten our belts—starting with me. Over the course of my eight-year tenure in Milwaukee County, I gave about $370,000 in salary back to Milwaukee County taxpayers. If I was going to ask other county workers to sacrifice, I had to be willing to sacrifice as well. Indeed, I took a bigger hit as a percentage of my salary than anything I asked of the rest of the county workforce.

Next, I proposed a series of alternatives to public-worker layoffs. I asked for modest increases to employee pension and health care contributions, which were the biggest driver of our debt. I proposed moving seasonal workers (such as snowplow drivers) into other jobs (such as cutting grass) in the off-season to save money. I proposed going to a thirty-five-hour workweek, to spread the pain around in order to keep people working. At one point, I even proposed going to a thirty-five-hour workweek one week a month for four months.

But thanks to collective bargaining, all the proposals I put forward required the unions to sign off. And the union bosses made clear to me under no uncertain terms that they were not giving up any of the lavish benefits they enjoyed in order to save somebody else's job.

I will never forget sitting at the conference table in my office across from Rich Abelson, the head of AFSCME Council 48, explaining to him that without some of these modest changes we would have to lay off hundreds of workers.

He looked me in the eye and said: "Go ahead and do it!"

I was stunned. I explained again how many jobs would be lost if he stood in the way of our reform. He told me he didn't care how many workers I laid off, he wasn't giving up any benefits.

Perhaps Abelson and the other union leaders didn't think I would go through with it and were calling my bluff. Or maybe they thought that I was a short-termer—a Republican elected in a heavily Democratic district in a special election, thanks only to a political scandal. Better to absorb the layoffs, protect their benefits, and wait until a new county executive beholden to the unions replaced me in the next election.

If that was their logic, they certainly miscalculated. In 2004, two years after my special election, I was elected to a full term with 57 percent of the vote. Then in 2008, the year President Obama won Milwaukee

County with 67.5 percent of the vote, I was reelected with nearly 60 percent of the vote—which meant there were at least some Obama-Walker voters. I won three elections in a row, with a larger percentage of the vote each time, proving that conservative reformers can prevail with a deep blue electorate if they make tough decisions on issues that are relevant to the voters. Americans reward politicians who keep their promises and get results. In times of crisis, we want leadership.

Despite the fact that voters repeatedly backed me at the polls, the unions would not give an inch during my time as county executive. They were perfectly willing to see hundreds, even thousands, of union workers lose their jobs in order to keep the prerogatives they had amassed for themselves.

So much for "solidarity."

With the unions unwilling to make changes under collective bargaining rules, I had no tools at my disposal to reduce spending and get our budget under control without layoffs. So we had no choice—we had to cut jobs.

When layoff notices went out, I remember people streaming into my office, usually young workers in tears, pleading for their own job or that of a coworker. They would beg me to reconsider, to try the thirty-five-hour workweek or some of these other ideas instead. It was heartbreaking, but I'd have to tell them, "It's not for me to reconsider—go talk to your union steward, go talk to your union leadership. They're the ones who blocked the reforms."

Sometimes an employee who had not received a notice would come to me and say, "I'd be willing to give up some time so that this coworker of mine could keep working." I'd have to tell them that collective bargaining rules would not allow it.

Other times, a supervisor would come to me and say, "Scott, I know you have to lay people off, but so-and-so is doing such a great job. I can give you ten other people who are not producing and ought to go before her." They knew that if productive workers were let go, the burden would fall on their backs to pick up the slack for the unproductive workers who stayed on. I had to explain that under collective bargaining, we could not take into account merit or effort in deciding who got laid off. The only thing that mattered was seniority.

We could not move seasonal workers from one job to another in the off-season, because people's job duties were locked in by union contract—and the union refused to change them. Heck, we could hardly move a clerical worker from one office to another within the *same agency* without union sign-off. There was no flexibility. None.

So we had to let people go.

Laying off good workers was an agonizing experience, and it taught me an important lesson: Reforming collective bargaining was not just about saving money. It was not just about saving jobs. It was about making government work better for the people.

I believe that smaller government is better government. I am sometimes asked if I hate government. I don't. I hate government that is too big and government that does not work. I believe that government at the federal, state, and local levels should be smaller. But in the areas where government has an appropriate role to play—be it local education or national defense—taxpayers not only deserve but should also expect and demand that government carry out its functions exceptionally well.

As conservatives, we believe that as many decisions as possible should be pushed down to the local level. This is not only a matter of efficiency, it is fundamental to our freedoms. As Milton Friedman explains in *Capitalism and Freedom*, "If government is to exercise power, better in the county than in the state, better in the state than in Washington. If I do not like what my local community does, be it in sewage disposal, or zoning, or schools, I can move to another local community. . . . If I do not like what my state does, I can move to another. If I do not like what Washington imposes, I have few alternatives in this world of jealous nations."

If we believe in local government, then the last thing we want to do is decimate the ability of local officials to effectively serve their citizens. We want local communities to keep our streets clean, keep our citizens safe, and give our children the best possible education.

Collective bargaining makes those legitimate tasks much harder. Government can't work when unions siphon off taxpayer dollars meant for public works and public schools into excessive and unsustainable benefit packages. Government can't work when local officials are denied the tools their private sector counterparts enjoy to reward good employees and fire bad ones. Government can't work when managers have little or no authority to consolidate agencies, streamline functions, set performance standards, or change people's duties without the permission of a union. And government can't work when 10 percent of the public workforce is suddenly eliminated in random layoffs—and when managers are forced to get rid of some of the most productive workers while retaining some of the least productive.

Giving local officials tools to be more efficient and effective is a fundamentally conservative idea. And freeing them from the grip of collective bargaining rules is the only way to let them do that.

For years, Americans have been presented with a false choice between raising taxes and cutting government services. If you own a business, you don't double the price of your product or cut its quality in half—at least not if you want to stay in business. You find ways to run your business more efficiently, and deliver a better product than your competitor at lower cost. I tried to do that as county executive, but it was next to impossible because I was tied down by the Lilliputian threads of collective bargaining.

Collective bargaining is the enemy of good government. Its supporters call it a "right," but the fact is it is not a right enshrined in the U.S. or Wisconsin constitution. For most of American history, collective bargaining did not exist for government employees. Until 1959, when Wisconsin became the first state to allow collective bargaining for government workers, the pay, benefits, and working conditions of public employees were determined by the legislatures overseeing them as part of the regular budget process.

Even labor advocates like President Franklin Delano Roosevelt and AFL-CIO president George Meany were suspicious of collective bargaining for government employees. And as our experience in Milwaukee County showed, their suspicions were well founded. Rather than a right, collective bargaining has turned out to be an expensive entitlement. It allows union bosses to dictate spending decisions to state and local governments, and collect compulsory union dues to perpetuate their political power. But collective bargaining denies hardworking taxpayers their "right" to the efficient delivery of public services. It denies children their "right" to a decent education. And it denies citizens their "right" to a government that lives within its means.

During my eight years as county executive, we cut the number of county workers by 20 percent, and turned a $3.5 million county deficit into a surplus. On one hand, that is an achievement because the county government needed to be smaller. But because of collective bargaining, we couldn't do it the best way. Being forced to get rid of productive workers while retaining slackers, and having my hands tied by union intransigence and collective bargaining rules, was a searing experience. That experience was the ultimate source of the reforms I enacted as governor.

I knew how many jobs I could have saved in Milwaukee County, how much more money I could have saved the taxpayers, how much more efficiently I could have run the county government if I had the tools we eventually enacted in Act 10. During my tenure, I can remember sharing that frustration often with Jim Villa, Linda Seemeyer, Bill Domina, and other key advisers. They understood that we easily could have avoided layoffs, balanced our budget, kept taxes low, and delivered better services. But those tools were not at my disposal.

Later, when I took the oath of office as governor in January 2011, I promised the people of Wisconsin in my inaugural address that, as we tackle our $3.6 billion deficit, "we will not abandon our fundamental responsibilities to protect our families and our property, provide for a high-quality education for our children, ensure care for the most vulnerable among us, and enhance the quality of life for our citizens.

"Our government will not only be smaller. It will be better. More responsive, more efficient, more effective," I declared.

That was a promise I intended to keep.

CHAPTER 3

III

"See What You've Gotten Yourself Into?"

The day after my election as governor, Mike Huebsch took me to the capitol for a briefing on the budget mess with the Legislative Fiscal Bureau to see just what kind of a fiscal disaster we had inherited.

Mike is a former speaker of the assembly who would soon become my secretary of the Department of Administration. He's been my friend since we served together in the state assembly in the 1990s. He understood the budget process inside out.

We knew going in that there were some real budget problems, but the crisis was far worse than we had first thought.

During Governor Jim Doyle's eight-year tenure, he borrowed vast sums of money and avoided making tough budget decisions while expanding government programs. In the three biennial budgets since he took office, new state bonding had exceeded new tax-revenue collections by $2.1 billion. Doyle had been borrowing money to underwrite expansions of health care, education, and environmental programs.

The fiscal bureau staff walked us through the accounting gimmicks the Doyle administration had been using to balance the budget on paper while digging Wisconsin into a deeper and deeper hole with each passing year. Doyle had raided $1.3 billion from the state's transportation fund.[1] He had also raided $200 million from the Patients Compensation Fund, a state fund set up for victims of medical malpractice. But the Wisconsin supreme court had ruled that the raid was unlawful and ordered the state to repay the money immediately, along with interest that was accumulating daily, eventually costing Wisconsin taxpayers an additional $35 million. The state also owed another $60 million or so to the state of Minnesota in unpaid IOUs under a tax reciprocity agreement—and Minnesota was tired of waiting for its money.

By 2009, Doyle had run out of accounting tricks and segregated funds to raid. Then, just as he was about to face the consequences of his fiscal irresponsibility, President Obama was elected and passed his stimulus spending bill. The federal stimulus funds were like manna from heaven for profligate politicians like Doyle, allowing them to put off tough decisions and go on spending—and even taking on new obligations—leading to even larger deficits down the road.

Like a gambler with a new line of credit, Doyle used the one-time stimulus money to cover the ongoing costs of Medicaid and education. Now, as he prepared to leave office, the one-time money had run out, and we were left with no way to cover these ongoing costs in the next budget.

As I looked at the numbers, I realized why Doyle had chosen not to run for reelection. If he had somehow managed to win, he would have had to clean up the fiscal mess that he had helped to create.

We were faced with two impending budget crises: In the short term, we had to close an immediate budget deficit of $137 million[2] before the end of the fiscal year on June 30, 2011. That meant we had to start cutting spending right away. And that was the easy part. The deficit for the biennial budget that started on July 1, 2011, was a whopping $3.6 billion—one of the largest per capita deficits in the country.[3]

We had just a few months to figure out how to close it.

After leaving the budget briefing, Mike turned to me and said with a smile, "See what you've gotten yourself into?"

"I've seen worse," I told him. "You've got to remember, I come from Milwaukee County."

That was a bit of bravado. Truth be told, the situation was far worse than anything I'd seen in Milwaukee County. And the more I learned, the more resolved I became to fix this once and for all.

As we began crunching the numbers, it became clear that the plan I had campaigned on to have state workers contribute 5.8 percent of their salaries to pensions and 12.6 percent of their health insurance premiums would not be enough to close the gap. Even when we expanded this policy to county and local public workers, the numbers still did not add up. It was a drop in the bucket.

We had to find the money somewhere. There were only a few limited options:

I could raise taxes, as the governor across the border in Illinois ended up doing. But I had promised on the campaign trail not to raise taxes. I knew that doing so would harm economic growth, reduce state revenues in the long run, and hurt job creation when I had pledged to jump-start it. So tax increases were off the table.

I could lay off thousands of public workers, as governors ended up doing in California, New York, and Connecticut. But that would devastate middle-class jobs in the midst of the worst economy in a generation. I had promised to protect them.

I could cut Medicaid, as other governors ended up doing. But absent fundamental Medicaid reform in Washington, that would hurt needy families, children, and seniors—the poorest and most vulnerable of our citizens. I was not going to do that.

That left cuts in aid to schools and local governments, which make up more than half of the state budget. But as a former local official, I knew that the kinds of cuts necessary to balance the budget, if not accompanied by structural reforms, would devastate public education and cripple public services.

We were in a bind and there seemed to be no way out.

This much I knew for certain: I was going to balance the budget. I was going to do it without relying on budget gimmicks and temporary fixes. I was going to keep my campaign promises. I was not going to lay off tens of thousands of workers. And I was not going to decimate public schools and local governments.

I didn't tell my staff, but it was then that I started thinking: What if we cut aid to schools and local governments, but gave them the freedom to replace the lost aid through efficiencies that collective bargaining had prevented? What if we increased health care and pension contributions for public workers, but allowed them to make up for part of the lost money by giving them a choice as to whether to pay their union dues? What if we could find a way to balance the budget—while protecting taxpayers, protecting the poor, protecting schools, protecting local governments, protecting teachers and public workers—by taking the money from the unions instead?

What if we got rid of collective bargaining?

CHAPTER 4

Super-Size It

On November 19, a few weeks after that eye-popping budget brief-ing, I traveled to San Diego for the annual meeting of the Repub-lican Governors Association. At that meeting, I spent a lot of time with Indiana governor Mitch Daniels. Our discussions proved to be a critical turning point in my thinking about how to address the budget crisis in Madison.

Since taking office in 2005, Mitch had been a whirlwind of reform. He made tough decisions to close an $800 million deficit, pushed through controversial plans to adopt daylight saving time, and privat-ized Indiana's toll roads. I was particularly interested in learning more about one of his first acts as governor, when he eliminated collective bargaining for state employees. I wanted to hear everything he had learned from his experience with collective bargaining in Indiana—how he did it, how his opponents responded, and what the results had been.

Mitch told me his reforms had been a huge success. Eliminating collective bargaining saved taxpayers buckets of money, he said, but those savings were only the secondary benefit. The primary benefit was the flexibility to make state government perform better.

None of the hundreds of operational reforms he enacted during his two terms in office—from consolidating state agencies to privatizing toll roads—would have been possible if he had been required to put each decision through excruciating negotiations and compromises with the unions. Getting rid of collective bargaining freed him to act—to downsize government offices, shift workers from one job to another, and to make dysfunctional agencies functional again.

By the time he faced reelection, Mitch said, he had dozens of examples of agencies that were working better. The Department of Motor Vehicles, which most everyone hated when he took office, was soon rated the best in the United States and Canada. The same was true of other government agencies. Collective bargaining reform had not only helped him balance Indiana's state budget, it had also freed him to deliver services more efficiently to the taxpayers. Indiana voters recognized it and overwhelmingly elected him to a second term. During the campaign, his opponents were able to say a lot of things about him, but nobody was able to say, "The state government's a mess."

Mitch told me that he really hesitated over his decision on collective bargaining—and he was not one to dally. He said he had a mental view of mass protests erupting, and major opposition from the public-worker unions—the kinds of things that neither of us at that moment could have imagined would soon grip Wisconsin.

When he finally issued his executive order, he said he was surprised that it had caused so little a stir. It ended up being one of the least controversial decisions he had made as governor. Putting Indiana on daylight savings time had sparked a far greater public uproar. I'd have to evaluate for myself what the reaction in Wisconsin would be if I went ahead, he told me.

I knew Mitch's situation was different from ours in several respects. For one thing, his reforms applied only to state workers. I knew I was not going to be able to save enough money if I only eliminated collective bargaining for state employees. We were going to have to cut over a billion dollars in aid to schools and local governments. If they were going to make up for the lost assistance from the state, we would have to take what Mitch did and super-size it. We would have to free not just the state, but also counties, municipalities, and school districts from collective bargaining rules as well.

Mitch was also blessed by the fact that Governor Evan Bayh had instituted collective bargaining in 1989 by executive order. That meant he could eliminate it simply by issuing a new executive order. The deed was done with one swift stroke, before his opponents had time to organize protests, order signs, or rent buses and trailers to encircle his state capitol. Later, when the unions did just that to the state capitol in Madison, I joked that if I could have opened a desk drawer and found an executive order to reverse as Mitch had, I would have done it in a heartbeat.

I knew that if I decided to move forward, I would have to pass legislation. And based on my experience with the unions in Milwaukee County, I knew I would probably face a bigger push back than Mitch had faced (though I never imagined how much bigger).

Mitch gave me some advice: First, he said, whatever you decide to do, go big, go bold, and strike fast. If you have hard things to do, he said, do them as soon as you think they're right—because the sooner you act, the more time your reforms will have to work. You want as much time as possible for good results to show themselves, and for people to put an event in perspective. If I thought I knew what the right thing to do was, he said, I should do it quickly.

Second, he told me to remember that political capital is not something you *spend*, it's something you *invest*—and properly invested, it brings a return. When you make bold reforms and people see that they worked, they will give your next big idea a little more credence.

Third, he said, always have that next big idea ready. Never stop reforming. Some of your proposals will stall out, and there will always be folks who will not agree with you on everything you do. But people will come to see you as an innovator—someone with good ideas who is constantly trying to make things better. Moreover, if you're constantly innovating, your opponents will constantly be responding. When people disagree or throw rocks, better that they are responding to your agenda rather than setting one for you.

That advice in particular resonated with me. I was in the Wisconsin legislature in the 1990s when Tommy Thompson was governor. Tommy was constantly putting forward the next reform—welfare reform, tax reform, education reform. He was always several steps ahead of the opposition, and they could never catch up. As soon as they organized to try to stop one of his reforms, he'd have passed it and would be on to the next big thing.

The more I spoke with Mitch over the course of the weekend, the more I learned about how his reforms had worked, and the more confident I became that similar reforms could succeed in Wisconsin.

Leaving that meeting in San Diego, I was ready to get rid of collective bargaining.

Then something happened that confirmed the need for bold action.

CHAPTER 5

"Bring It On"

As Milwaukee County executive, I had refused to submit a wish list to Governor Doyle for items in the federal "stimulus" package. Like other politicians, Doyle had lined up at the federal trough begging for billions in "free" money to cover budget deficits and to fuel new spending. He and others were outraged that I didn't join them—and that I didn't relent even after the president signed the stimulus bill into law.

My explanation was simple. The "free" money from Washington wasn't free. The stimulus was a classic bait and switch. Once the highways were built and social service caseloads had increased, the stimulus funds would disappear and Wisconsin taxpayers would be left with the bill to maintain the new roads and services. Moreover, the stimulus was also a bait and switch on employment. While stimulus spending might create a few construction jobs in the short term, when the federal money disappeared, so would the jobs.

Not only had I refused to submit a stimulus wish list, I had also campaigned for governor on a promise to cancel a stimulus-funded program to build an expensive high-speed rail line between Madison and Milwaukee. While the Obama administration was promising $810 million in federal funds for the project, I knew that the state would be on the hook for shortfalls, as well as the annual operating subsidies once the line was complete. We estimated that the project was going to cost Wisconsin taxpayers $110 million. We were broke and just could not afford it.

After my election, Governor Doyle canceled the project. "I could play brinksmanship with this issue and I could just plow forward and put people out at job sites," Doyle said. "We could spend or obligate hundreds of millions of dollars between now and the time I leave office. And while obviously part of me says, 'Just do that,' I really have to actually consider what the practical consequences of this are. . . . I don't think that's in anybody's best interest."[1]

It was a major victory. We had saved Wisconsin taxpayers more than $100 million before even taking office.

Doyle and the public union bosses did decide to play brinksmanship on another matter, however—one that nearly scuttled our chances for budget reform.

In December, the outgoing Democratic majorities in the state legislature called a lame-duck session and tried to pass a series of union contracts negotiated with the Doyle administration—contracts that, if approved, would have tied my hands in dealing with the state budget shortfall when I took office.

I had made clear during the campaign that I would be asking state workers to pay more for their health care and pensions. I ran a television ad on it.[2] It was a centerpiece of my campaign. And with the fiscal crisis we inherited much worse than we had expected, we could not wait until the following fiscal year to make those changes I had promised.

But now, in the final days of Democratic rule, the unions were trying a last-minute end run—attempting to lock the contracts in and force us to put off our promised reforms. The unions were transparent in their objectives. AFSCME president Robert McLinn and executive director Marty Beil had written a letter to their union members right after my election in November warning that it was "important that we have a contract in place before the incoming Walker administration takes over."[3]

Now they were trying to jam that contract through the legislature just before Democrats ceded control. It was a raw power play, and it demonstrated in no uncertain terms that the unions were not interested in working with me.

On December 7, I addressed the issue at a Milwaukee Press Club luncheon. I began by making clear my respect for public workers. "You are not going to hear me degrade state and local employees in the public sector," I said. "There are good people who work in government, and they are public servants. But we can no longer live in a society where the public employees are the haves and the taxpayers who foot the bill are the have-nots. Public employees can't be the untouchables."

The unions were having none of it. "State workers and other public workers aren't about to sacrifice their benefits for some political future of a tyrant," AFSCME leader Marty Beil declared. "This is all about Scott Walker kind of bringing back, instead of public service, it is public servitude. He's the master of the plantation and we're supposed to be his slaves; that's his philosophy here. So I think he'd be real happy if we were paid minimum wage and had no pension at all."[4]

I would face far worse from Beil and his cohorts in the months ahead, but let the record show: Union leaders like Beil were declaring me a "tyrant" and "plantation master" long before we introduced Act 10.

In my comments, I cautioned that if the unions refused to cooperate, I would have no choice but to use every tool at my disposal on taking office to rein them in. "The bottom line is we are going to look at every legal means we have to try and put that balance more on the side of taxpayers," I said, adding that we would consider "anything from [decertification] all the way through modifications of the current law in place. The bottom line is we want to have a better ability to control what we do when it comes to wages and benefits."[5]

To this, Beil responded: "Bring it on."[6]

We almost didn't have a chance to do so. The unions' contract ploy nearly succeeded. In the assembly, Democrats called an extraordinary session where they approved the contracts by a razor-thin 47-46 margin. They had been one vote short of victory. To ram the contracts through, they needed the vote of Representative Jeff Wood, who was serving time for his fourth operating while intoxicated offense.[7] According to the Milwaukee *Journal Sentinel,* Wood cast the deciding vote after he "was released from jail Wednesday so he could attend the legislative session."[8]

In other words, an assembly that had just been fired by the people of Wisconsin approved contracts negotiated by a lame-duck governor relying on a state representative who was let out of jail to cast the deciding vote. It was a remarkable display of political bravado.

It looked to everyone like the contracts were headed for approval in the senate. But then something remarkable happened. Two Democratic senators—Russ Decker and Jeff Plale—bucked their party and voted no. Their defections deadlocked the senate in a 16-16 tie—killing the contracts. It was a remarkable display of political courage.

Plale was a centrist Democrat who believed in bipartisan cooperation, and the end run the unions were trying to pull offended him. He had lost his seat to a liberal primary challenger, and had made clear from the start that he would be voting against the contracts. His "no" vote had been expected by both sides.

But Decker's vote took everyone by surprise. He was not just another Democratic senator—he was the Democrats' *majority leader.* It would be like Harry Reid casting the lone, deciding vote against his own party in the U.S. Senate—virtually unthinkable. Moreover, Decker had voted in favor of the contracts that morning during a meeting of the legislature's employee relations committee.

Then, just before the vote on the first contract, Decker rose and explained to his startled colleagues that he would be voting no with the Republican minority. Decker was a straightforward kind of speaker who usually spoke off the cuff. But on this occasion, when he rose to address the members of the senate, he pulled out prepared remarks. He had obviously given great thought to what he was about to say.

"[E]lections have consequences," Decker declared. "While I would obviously like to have seen a different outcome in the election, both for myself and my Democratic colleagues, the people of Wisconsin have spoken and they have said they want someone else to make these decisions for them."[9]

He pointed out that in 2002, when Republican governor Scott McCallum lost his election, he held over contracts for a new governor and legislature to act upon instead of trying to ram them through in a lame-duck session. Now, Decker said, Democrats should extend the same courtesy to me and the incoming Republican majority.

"Now that the election has been held and the voters have spoken, I do not feel comfortable casting a vote in favor of these contracts," Decker said.

Decker's Democratic colleagues were furious, and they exacted swift vengeance. In a closed-door meeting after the first deadlocked vote, they stripped him of his majority leader post. Decker had served in the senate for twenty years. He was a union bricklayer. But despite all the good he had done for his party and the union cause in the past, when he crossed the union bosses on a point of principle, they kicked him to the curb.

The move was largely symbolic. Decker had lost his seat to a Republican in November and was about to retire anyway. And it made no difference to the final outcome. When Democrats called another vote under their new majority leader, Senator Dave Hansen, the result was the same. Each of the contract votes was deadlocked 16-16.

The union scheme had been upended. The contracts were dead.

Democratic senator Bob Jauch called Decker's vote "the most disgusting behavior by any public official I have seen in twenty-eight years."[10] He compared Decker to a "three-year-old who is pouting"[11] and said he had "left a legacy of being a loser."[12]

In his typically understated manner, AFSCME chief Marty Beil declared Decker "a whore,"[13] adding, "He'll never ever hold a seat as a Democrat" again.[14]

The unions had been just one vote away from tying our hands before we even took office. Had they succeeded in pushing through the contracts and delaying implementation of our reforms for another year, they would not have had the immediate, positive impact they did—and I might never have survived a recall election. Public opinion in Wisconsin began to turn decisively in our favor only after it became clear that our reforms had worked—when voters saw that we had not decimated public education but rather had allowed local officials and school districts to balance their budgets, lower property taxes, save money, and add teachers to the classrooms. If our reforms had been put off, those improvements might never have happened in time for the voters to judge us on the merits during the recall election in 2012.

So Decker's courageous vote not only upended the public-worker unions' attempted legislative coup, it probably saved my job.

The entire episode was sad. The Democrats had relied on a man who had to be released from jail to cast the deciding vote in the assembly, only to see their own majority leader cast the deciding vote against them in the senate. Jeff Fitzgerald, the incoming Republican speaker of the state assembly, called it "the final act of a Greek tragedy."[15] He was right.

The spectacle was also revealing. It made clear that the Democrats and union bosses were not interested in cooperation or compromise. If we were to get our fiscal house in order, half measures would not suffice. We needed to do more than simply go after the money; we needed to restore fairness to the system by putting the hardworking taxpayers back in charge instead of the union bosses.

We would have to take on collective bargaining itself.

CHAPTER 6

∏

"Nuclear Lite"

In my inaugural address, I invoked the one part of the Wisconsin constitution that has never been altered or amended since it was first approved in May 1848—the Frugality Clause—declaring, "It is through frugality and moderation in government that we will see freedom and prosperity for our people." Now the time had come to begin restoring frugality to our government and prosperity for our people.

We began with prosperity. Immediately on taking office, we called a special session of the legislature to tackle my number one priority as governor: jobs. In my predecessor's last term, Wisconsin lost 134,000 jobs, and the state's unemployment rate had reached 9.2 percent. We needed to stop the hemorrhaging and start creating jobs again. So in our first three weeks in office, we cut taxes on health savings accounts (HSAs), cut taxes on job creators in Wisconsin, relieved unnecessary regulation so we could enforce common sense—not excessive red tape—and passed tort reform to stop frivolous, job-killing litigation. Nearly every measure was passed with bipartisan support in both the assembly and senate. We were off to a great start.

On January 28, 2011, I called my staff together around the large oak table in my office in the Wisconsin state capitol. Since November, my policy director, Ryan Murray, had been working with Mike Huebsch and his staff at the Department of Administration to crunch numbers and develop a list of options for how to close the budget gap. Now the time had come to make decisions.

Democratic governors in New York, California, and Connecticut were announcing layoffs to balance their budgets, but I was adamant that in Wisconsin there would be no more layoffs and no more furloughs. I was not going to needlessly put people out of work in one of the worst economies in our lifetime.

Mike told me he understood why I was determined to avoid layoffs but didn't understand why I was so adamant that there be no more furloughs. State employees were used to them, and they saved on average about $7 million a day. Over the course of a biennial budget, a dozen furlough days a year added up to a lot of money.

The answer was that furloughs were one-time savings. They were Band-Aid solutions that did not address the underlying condition. I was not interested in gimmicks or temporary fixes. I wanted to solve our budget problems once and for all.

Because we were facing an immediate budget gap of $137 million, we needed to do something to close the gap right away. None of the solutions they put on the table solved the problem. I asked how much we could save if we raised health care and pension contributions right away instead of waiting until the start of the next biennial budget in July.

My staff said that would help solve the problem but asked how on earth we were going to negotiate that with the unions. They had just tried to ram through contracts without the pension and health care contributions. The fight over the contracts in the lame-duck session showed that the unions were not going to let us do it without a fight.

"What if we didn't have to negotiate?" I asked.

There was silence in the room.

"What prohibits us from raising health care and pension contributions?" I continued. "Collective bargaining and union contracts. Well, what if we just pass a budget repair bill that gets rid of the unions and eliminates collective bargaining?"

It took a moment for everyone to realize I was not just asking a hypothetical question. I had already made up my mind.

I walked them through my plan. If I was going to keep my promise not to raise taxes, and avoid massive layoffs or cuts to Medicaid, then the only way to close the deficit was to reduce state aid to schools and local governments by about a billion dollars. The education cuts alone would be the biggest in the history of our state. Having been a local official, I knew what cuts that large would mean. We would devastate education and the legitimate services that local governments provide *unless* we did something dynamic to give them an option to backfill the lost money from the state.

Eliminating collective bargaining would give local leaders the tools to do just that. They could increase health care and pension contributions without having to ask union leaders like Rich Abelson for permission they knew would never come. And if teachers and other public workers did not have to pay union dues, they could use that money to offset much of the costs of those increased contributions.

More important, if we liberated schools and local governments from the grip of the unions, they could save tens of millions more by bidding out their health insurance on the open market, eliminating ridiculous work rules, reining in overtime abuse, and implementing other commonsense reforms that unions vetoed. And they could do it all without cutting jobs or public services.

I asked if there were any better alternatives. Everyone agreed that there were none. Someone had to pay if we were to close a $3.6 billion deficit. We could take the money from the taxpayers through higher taxes. We could take the money from middle-class families by throwing people out of work. We could take the money from schools and local governments and devastate education and services without giving them a way to backfill the lost state assistance. We could take the money from teachers and public workers through higher contributions to their health care and pensions without giving them a way to make up the lost income.

Or we could take the money from the unions.

I decided to take it from the unions.

I asked Ryan and Mike to calculate precisely how much our schools, our local governments, and our technical colleges could potentially save if they no longer had to negotiate with the unions. They found that they could more than make up for the loss in state aid. We would cut about $1.25 billion in state aid, but the school districts and local governments stood to save about $1.5 billion—if they fully used the tools we would give them to control their budgets.

By taking on collective bargaining, we had found a way to make everyone whole—everyone, that is, except the union bosses. They were the only ones who would get hurt in the entire process. Which was fine by me.

I was leaning heavily toward this course of action after my meetings with Mitch Daniels. But even after I became increasingly clear in my own mind on my preferred option, I still spent several months having my staff look at all the other options—everything from implementing the increased health and pension contributions to reforming the arbitration system that regularly awards large pay raises to public workers to eliminating collective bargaining in specific areas, such as health care.

Initially, I did not tip my hand as to where I was leaning because I did not want to prejudice their work. I wanted them to exhaust the alternatives. I wanted to see if they could come up with a better answer. Only after every option had been examined, and it was clear to me that there was none close to being better than what I had in mind, did I tell my staff that this was what we were going to do.

This is generally how I approach major policy decisions. I want my staff to keep pushing the envelope and trying new ideas, even when I'm pretty certain which way I intend to go. Sometimes that process allows me to improve my proposal. Sometimes it helps me think through the different roadblocks we might face. And sometimes it produces an alternative that is better than the one I initially had in mind.

Today, my staff can often figure out where I am leaning by the kinds of questions I ask. But back when we were examining how to close the budget deficit, everyone was so new they still had not figured out my "tells." (I joked with them later that when I stand in front of an open mike at the Milwaukee Press Club and say I'm considering decertifying the unions, that's probably a pretty good tip-off). So they were genuinely surprised when I told them that I intended to eliminate collective bargaining.

When I finally shared my plan, the answer was so obvious that Mike later told me he kicked himself for not thinking of it. But the solution was only obvious to me because I was looking at the problem through the prism not of state government but of local government. As a former local official, I knew firsthand the pure frustration of putting forward innovative solutions only to see them constantly thwarted by the unions.

We knew the union leaders would put up a fight. They would rather have seen us take the money from the poor, lay off middle-class workers, undermine education, and decimate government services—just so long as we did not close the automatic spigot of cash that was filling their union coffers.

Normally, they would have succeeded in thwarting our efforts. But two things suggested to me that we had a unique opportunity to do something that might be impossible at any other time: We had the votes, and we had no choice.

Back when I was Milwaukee County executive, there was a liberal majority on the county board. That meant that while I constantly proposed bold reforms, I often did not have the votes to implement the changes I had proposed. Most of the time it was a struggle to muster the one third necessary to stop the board from overriding my veto.

Now I had been elected governor with Republican majorities in both the assembly and the senate. Not only did we have majorities, we also had a stable of newly elected conservatives in both chambers who were eager to shake things up. Instead of fighting veto overrides, I finally had the chance to do big, bold things. I relished the opportunity not only to make tough decisions but also to actually implement those decisions and see the results—because we finally had the majorities we needed to enact true reform.

Second, we were in a fiscal hole with no way out. I didn't lead our party into this fight when we had a budget surplus. It wasn't like I was Evel Knievel saying "I wonder if I can jump this canyon" just for the sake of jumping over a canyon. I did it because we had a $3.6 billion deficit and no practical way to close it.

Reforming collective bargaining was the right thing to do, with or without a deficit. But even with a Republican majority, there is no way Act 10 could ever have passed if it had not been for the magnitude of the deficit. If I proposed going after collective bargaining today, when Wisconsin enjoys a nearly half-billion-dollar surplus, there would be a mutiny among senate Republicans. I wasn't asking them to be courageous for the sake of courage. The only reason we were able to make the changes we did was the lack of any viable alternatives.

Still, we knew the path ahead would not be easy. The unions would put up every roadblock they could to stop us. We had to be prepared for every possible contingency.

So before we took our plan to the legislature, I called a meeting in the Governor's Conference Room with several key cabinet secretaries and our adjutant general. Among other contingencies, we drew up emergency plans to cover 24/7 operations in prisons and mental health facilities in case workers at these facilities walked off the job. Later, rumors flew around the capitol that I had plans to deploy the National Guard to suppress the protesters. Nothing could be further from the truth. We had a plan to deploy the National Guard to run our prisons if correctional officers went on strike. Our corrections team told us that they could run the prisons for forty-eight hours with nonunion staff, but within two days we would need to call the Guard in. So we put the Guard on standby to cover these essential services.

There was one major issue that still had to be resolved. While we could handle a corrections strike, a strike by police, firefighters, and other law enforcement was another matter. There are over seventeen hundred municipalities in Wisconsin. If police and firefighters walked off the job, there would be no way to fill all the vacant positions in each of those communities. The threat to public safety would be unacceptable. "Fine," I said, "we'll just exempt them."

I made the decision purely for reasons of public safety. At the time, I had no idea how politically fortuitous it would be.

Once we had our legislative and contingency plans ready, we sat down with Scott and Jeff Fitzgerald to brief them on our proposal. Scott had just taken over as senate majority leader, while his brother, Jeff, had become the new assembly speaker.

When we explained what we intended to do, they laughed at first.

"You're not serious?" Scott said in disbelief.

He soon realized we were. Keith Gilkes, my chief of staff, walked them through the details of the draft legislation, the other alternatives we had considered, and why they were inadequate. He explained why we had exempted police and firefighters. And he laid out our plan to deploy the Guard to keep prisons running in the event of a work stoppage.

It did not take long for Scott and Jeff to get over their shock and realize that our plan was not only feasible, it was also the only way to solve the budget deficit without devastating schools and public services.

So Scott took the plan back to Mike Ellis, the president of the senate. Politically, the majority leader is more powerful than the senate president, but Mike Ellis exercised power by virtue of his legend. He is a forty-year senate veteran, and had stared down plenty of governors before me. If he was with us, our plan was certain to prevail; if he opposed us, he would be a powerful adversary.

Scott came back and reported Ellis's reaction, which was more colorful than I can describe here, but his basic message was: "Governor Walker has lost his mind."

So Scott arranged a face-to-face meeting with Senator Ellis. In addition to Ellis, we were joined by Speaker Fitzgerald, as well as by Representative Robin Vos and Senator Alberta Darling, the cochairs of the Joint Finance Committee that would have to mark up the bill.

I walked them through our plan, and when I finished, there was dead silence in the room.

Finally, Robin Vos piped up and asked, "So you mean public workers wouldn't be able to join a union?"

"That's right," I said.

"Wow," said Vos.

Ellis looked at me and said point-blank, "Governor, you can't do this."

He warned that if we went through with our plans, we would unleash holy hell. He even suggested I was trying to curry favor with the editorial page of the *Wall Street Journal*. He insisted that there had to be another way.

Ellis is a longtime budget hawk, and he liked the idea of doing something big to eliminate our budget problems once and for all. But he was worried that if we got rid of collective bargaining, Republicans would be accused of simply going after the unions.

He wanted to close the budget deficit by enacting a 6 percent across-the-board spending cut. We walked him through what a 6 percent cut would mean in terms of education, Medicaid, corrections, and other vital services. We laid out for him the program cuts and thousands of layoffs that would be involved. As we explained the alternatives, it became clear to Ellis and everyone in the room that unless we took on collective bargaining, there truly was no way to solve the budget deficit—at least without putting people out of work and harming public education and services.

We were not doing this to go after the unions, I explained. We were doing it to protect schools.

It was then that Robin Vos said, "Well, this is kind of the 'nuclear option.' What if we talk about 'nuclear lite'?"

Vos suggested that we keep collective bargaining in place, but place strict limits on it. It would be less controversial to reform collective bargaining than to eliminate it. Ellis liked the idea. The legislators asked for some time to work out the details of what such a proposal would entail. So we left.

A few hours later, my staff got called to the senate president's office. When they walked in, they found Ellis, Vos, Darling, and the Fitzgerald brothers hunched over a computer, pecking out a counterproposal.

Keith and Eric looked at the screen. On the top of the page, it read: "Nuclear Lite."

Under their plan, we would institute paycheck protection; take employee contributions to health insurance and pensions off the bargaining table; limit collective bargaining to wages and some other unspecified noneconomic matters; cap any wage increase to something called the Qualified Economic Offer, or QEO (a 3.8 percent maximum annual increase which, if offered, would not be subject to binding arbitration); require a referendum for any larger pay increases; limit union contracts to one year; and freeze school aid for two years.

The plan still needed work, but the good news was that we had moved from "Governor, you can't do this" to discussing *how* we were going to do it.

The legislators printed out their proposal, and my staff took it back to our offices to work on it some more. The next day, we gave Scott and Jeff our counterproposal, which eventually became the basis for Act 10.

They key elements were:

- First, we would limit collective bargaining to base wages capped at the Consumer Price Index, or CPI (which was lower than the Qualified Economic Offer). Any increases above the CPI would have to be approved by the voters in a referendum.

- Second, no other issues would be subject to bargaining, including benefits such as health insurance, which meant school districts and local governments would be free to bid out their insurance on the open market for the first time, saving tens of millions of dollars.

- Third, instead of barring the unions from negotiating with the government, we would require that they first demonstrate they had the support of a majority of all their members by holding an annual recertification vote.

- Fourth, we required teachers and other public employees to contribute at least 5.8 percent of their salaries toward the cost of their pensions, and to pay 12.6 percent of their health insurance premiums—which is about half the average for the private sector.

- Finally, we made union membership optional, and ended the state's practice of automatically collecting union dues (which could be as high as $1,400 a year). By making dues voluntary, we gave teachers and other public workers a free choice of whether they wanted to keep the money to offset some of the increased health and pension contributions, or give it to the unions.

With these changes, we put the unions' fate in the hands of their own members. It would be up to the union members to decide whether the union could negotiate on their behalf. It would be up to the union members to decide whether they paid union dues or kept the money to offset increased pension and health care contributions. Instead of being antiunion, our reforms were pro-choice and pro-worker.

Scott Fitzgerald looked it over and said, "I think we can do this."

He took the plan back to Ellis, who also signed off. That was critical.

With his support, passage of our bill was all but assured. Without him, the bill would never have become law.

Even with Ellis in our corner, we knew passing Act 10 would take a fight.

We had no idea how big it would get.

CHAPTER 7

"Let's Bring Them a Plate of Cookies"

On the Monday night before I introduced the bill, I invited my cabinet to dinner at the Executive Residence. I knew some members of my cabinet were nervous about our plan and needed a "Braveheart" moment before we went into battle.

After dinner, I reminded them of the stand President Ronald Reagan took against the air traffic controllers during his first year in office. His actions were bigger than just a labor dispute. They set the tone for his entire presidency. Reagan's show of courage and strength sent a signal that new leadership had arrived in Washington. It sent a message that Ronald Reagan was serious—that he had backbone, that he was going to fulfill his promises, and that he was not going to be pushed around. And that message had an impact far beyond America's borders. His resolve not only stiffened the spines of members of Congress, it also stiffened the resolve of our allies, it also encouraged democratic reformers behind the Iron Curtain. It helped win the Cold War.

This, I told them, was our chance to take inspiration from Reagan's courage—to show that *we* were serious, that *we* had backbone, and that *we* were not going to be pushed around. The battle ahead would be tough, but we would prevail—and our state would be better because of it for generations to come. And if we succeeded, maybe our display of courage might just have an impact beyond Wisconsin's borders, and encourage fiscal reformers across the country to make tough decisions as well.

Members of my cabinet were not the only ones who needed encouragement. On Thursday, February 10, the day before we introduced the bill, I met with the assembly and the senate Republican caucuses to brief them on our bill. The assembly Republicans were pumped and ready to go into battle. Some of them had been quietly complaining that we were not being bold enough—so when I shared our plans to reform collective bargaining, they were both relieved and excited.

The senate was another matter. When I explained the details of our plan, some of the senators looked like their dog had just died. The newly elected senators were as enthusiastic as their assembly colleagues. But some of the senate veterans had the same initial reaction that Mike Ellis had had.

What ultimately convinced them was the same thing that had convinced Senator Ellis—there simply was no other option. To balance the budget, we had to cut over a billion dollars out of aid to schools and local governments.

"For those who are saying that's going too far, I would say put that in context of what the alternatives are. The alternative is for this year alone fifteen hundred layoffs for state employees. In the next biennium, its fifty-five hundred to six thousand layoffs. That's of state employees. At the local level, you're probably talking about eight to ten thousand teachers being laid off. None of these choices are very attractive," I said.

"It's not a matter of avoiding a tough decision," I explained. "It's a matter of which tough decision you are going to take."

"I don't want to be just like these other governors and these other state legislators where we're looking at cuts without any relief. Our goal is to have the dollar amount reduced equal to the dollar amount in savings, so there is not a gap between the two," I said. "The only way we can look our neighbors in the face and tell them we haven't devastated local governments and local school districts is if we empower those local governments to be able to control their budgets.

"That means you have to tackle collective bargaining."

We laid out our legislative plan, which was mapped out in the minutest detail—from the moment we introduced the bill to the day I was going to sign it. The whole process was supposed to take exactly seven days. The alternative was to include the reforms in our budget, which would require months of debate.

"The only question is do you want to do it now, where you get a week's worth of grief, or do you want to have it in a budget . . . with three and a half months' worth of grief?"

After meeting with the GOP caucuses, I met that evening with two dozen local officials from the League of Municipalities, the Wisconsin Counties Association, and the Wisconsin Association of School Boards. We were not expecting them to lobby for the bill, but we wanted to make sure they understood what we were doing so they would not lobby against it.

As a former local official, I understood how collective bargaining tied their hands. And I explained that the next day we would be introducing legislation to put power back into their hands so they could run their schools, counties, and municipalities.

As I walked them through the key elements of the bill, their reaction was enthusiastic. And once the bill was enacted, they used the tools and reforms we enacted to full advantage. Today, if you were to tell the local officials gathered in that room that Act 10 might be overturned or repealed, even most Democrats would tell you that losing Act 10 would be a disaster. That's because their budgets are built around it.

But when all hell broke loose in the weeks ahead, only a few brave souls would step forward to publicly support us.

As I left the capitol that evening for the short ride to the Executive Residence in Maple Bluff, all was quiet.

That was about to change.

On the morning of February 11, I invited the Democratic leaders of the state assembly and senate, Representative Peter Barca and Senator Mark Miller, to my office. Despite our differences, we had come together and gotten a lot accomplished on a bipartisan basis in the first weeks of my administration.

From the outset, I was determined to keep the lines of communication open across the aisle. When I took office, I started a practice of meeting with the Democratic leaders once a week. Barca, Miller, and I sat down every Wednesday morning when the legislature was in session. In addition to that weekly leadership meeting, I also blocked off time on my schedule every Wednesday morning until noon for twenty-minute meetings with any legislator—Democrat or Republican—who wanted to see me. I still do. My door is open to individual members of either party.

On this particular morning, however, my meeting with the two leading Democrats in the state did not go so well. I invited them into my office and explained that later in the day, I would be announcing our plans to reform collective bargaining.

As I walked through the details of the legislation we would be introducing, to say a look of shock came over their faces would be an understatement. They were almost frozen. After they took it in, they both proceeded to try to talk me out of it.

"There will be no protections for public employees. How will we protect them from being taken advantage of?" they asked.

I pointed to the two staffers they had brought along, who were sitting on chairs behind them, and asked: "Well, what about these two? Do you take advantage of them?"

They looked at me with puzzled expressions. My point went right over their heads.

"They are not in a union," I explained. "They don't have collective bargaining. They're 'at will' employees. Do you take advantage of them? If you don't take advantage of your employees without collective bargaining, why would other state workers be taken advantage of without it?"

I pointed out that Wisconsin has some of the strongest civil service protection laws in the country, a fact that would not change with our reforms. Moreover, most of the more than two million public employees working for the federal government do not collectively bargain—yet no one claims they are being taken advantage of. They are doing quite nicely. Indeed, the average federal worker receives total compensation 16 percent higher than the equivalent private sector worker.[1]

It was not our most pleasant meeting, but I felt I owed it to tell the Democratic leaders face-to-face what I was planning to do. I did not realize it at the time, but it would be the last time I would see Senator Miller for a while.

At ten a.m., with Lieutenant Governor Rebecca Kleefisch and members of my cabinet standing at my side, I announced the provisions of the Budget Repair Bill. I began by saying, "I want to make it abundantly clear as I've said time and time again . . . throughout the campaign, in the transition, and in the just over a month I've had the honor of serving as the governor of the state of Wisconsin: We have good and decent people who work in state and local government. . . . I have great respect for the men and women who work as public servants at the state and local level here in the state of Wisconsin.

"I, for one, don't want to see anybody laid off in the state of Wisconsin. I think the last thing we need are any more people on unemployment." I said that there would be no more furloughs for state employees as well.

The state was broke and it was time to pay the bills. I said that "we can no longer kick the can to the future. That's just unacceptable. We can't expect our children and grandchildren to pay off the debts of the state and we have to get things under control."

It didn't take long for the first protests to begin.

That afternoon, I had a previously scheduled editorial board meeting with the *Appleton Post-Crescent*. The paper had advertised the meeting, which was webcast live, and the news was all over that I was in town.

As my black SUV pulled up to the paper, we were greeted by a group of about twenty to thirty protesters chanting, "Walker's budget is bad for kids!" We went upstairs for the meeting, which lasted about an hour. While I spoke with the editors, my staff watched through the window as more and more protesters gathered. A state trooper from Green Bay heard about the protest on the radio and raced down to help us get out safely. He put my communications director, Chris Schrimpf, in the SUV we had arrived in and sent it out the front entrance as a decoy to confuse the protesters. Meanwhile, he took me out of the back of the building, put me in a Dodge Charger, and took off from a different exit.

Chris told me later that the crowd was infuriated when they saw it was him and not me in the SUV, but the wisdom of our quick exit would later became apparent.

The next night, Saturday, February 12, Tonette and I hosted a dinner at the Executive Residence to celebrate the one hundredth anniversary of Ronald Reagan's birthday. (I had been in Dallas to see the Packers win the Super Bowl on the sixth, his actual birthday, so we postponed the celebration by a week.) Tonette and I host a dinner each year on Reagan's birthday. We serve his favorite foods—macaroni and cheese casserole, and red, white, and blue Jelly Belly jelly beans—and have musicians perform patriotic songs and Irish music. It is a wonderful evening, and serves as a reminder for me each year to be hopeful and optimistic just like Ronald Reagan.

It happens to be a dual celebration because President Reagan's birthday is also our wedding anniversary. Tonette jokes that I never forget our wedding anniversary because it is Reagan's birthday.

Some friends had stayed over with us, and on the next morning the head of my security detail, Dave Erwin, suggested that if our guests wanted to get out conveniently, they might want to leave by eleven a.m.

Why? I asked. Dave explained that they had picked up intelligence that there was going to be a significant protest outside the residence. After our experience in Appleton, he figured once the protesters arrived, it might be hard to get out.

Soon after our guests departed, we watched as hundreds of people gathered outside the house. My youngest son, Alex, turned to me and said, "Dad, why don't we go out and take them a plate of chocolate chip cookies?" Tonette and I must have looked puzzled, because he reminded us of how years before, when I was county executive, there was a lone protester outside our house. It was freezing cold, so Alex and I had walked out and brought the man a cup of hot chocolate. He was upset, but the gesture diffused the situation.

I loved my son's reaction (even if he was half joking), but I said, "Alex, I don't think these people are going to be really pleased with a plate of chocolate chip cookies."

The next Tuesday, February 15, I went to La Crosse for a visit to a manufacturing company. Outside the facility, we were greeted by hundreds of angry protesters, but inside we got an enthusiastic reception from the blue-collar workers. As I recall, they were paying about 25 percent of their health insurance premiums and had to match their employer contributions to their pensions, so they didn't have a whole lot of sympathy for the folks outside complaining about having to pay 5.6 percent for their pensions and 12.6 percent for their health care. It was a great event.

As we prepared to leave, the troopers saw that the protesters had physically blocked the entrance we had used to come onto the property. So they turned the squad car around and headed toward the other exit. We watched in disbelief as the throng of people rushed toward the second exit to block our path. As we tried to pull out, they surrounded the car and began beating on the windows and rocking the vehicle.

Just as we extricated ourselves from their grip, a truck pulled up and blocked our path, playing a game of chicken with the troopers. They turned the lights and sirens on and warned him to get out of way. Eventually he backed up and we sped off.

It was a lesson in how much our circumstance had changed in a matter of a few days. We were dealing with people who were so blinded by their anger that they were not in the least bit afraid to storm and shake a police car. We had never seen anything like it in Wisconsin before.

And that was only the beginning. The protests following us around the state grew bigger and louder—and the protesters got more aggressive with each passing day.

After the La Crosse incident, Dave Erwin took me aside and explained that we needed to increase security—not just for me but for Tonette and the kids. Dave briefed me about the stream of intelligence he was receiving from the Division of Criminal Investigation. Our whole family was being watched, followed, and tracked, he said.

Dave was not prone to exaggeration. He is a former marine who had headed former governor Doyle's security detail. He is the consummate professional.

"Governor, I've been at this awhile, and when the hairs stand up on the back of my neck you have to be concerned," Dave said.

"They know where you go to church, they've been to your church. They're following your children and tracking your children. They know where your children go to school, what time they have class, what time they get out of class. They know when they had football practice. They know where your wife works, they know that she was at the grocery store at this time, they know that she went to visit her father at his residence."

We talked about some of the additional measures he would take to keep the family safe. Dave increased the size of our detail and assigned troopers to keep an eye on the kids at school. (Both of my sons were attending a public high school at the time and the Wauwatosa police officers really looked out for Matt and Alex too.) He also explained that we could no longer do simple tasks like going to the curb to pick up the mail, which would now have to be screened.

We soon began to get a steady stream of death threats. Most of these Dave and his team intercepted, and kept from Tonette and me. They were often graphic (one threatened to "gut her like a deer") but for the most part they amounted to little more than angry venting.

But one afternoon, as I prepared to go out to the conference room for my daily press briefing, Dave came into my office and shut the door. "Sir, I don't show you most of these, but I thought you ought to see this one." He handed me a letter addressed to Tonette that had been picked up by a police officer at the Executive Residence in Maple Bluff. It read:

> *HI TONETTE,*
> *Has Wisconsin ever had a governor assassinated? Scotts heading that way. Or maybe one of your sons getting killed would hurt him more. I want him to feel the pain. I already follow them when they went to school in Wauwatosa, so it won't be too hard to find them in Mad. Town. Big change from that house by [BLANK] Ave. to what you got now. Just let him know that it's not right to [EXPLETIVE] over all those people. Or maybe I could find one of the Tarantinos [Tonette's parents] back here.*
> *Lots of choices for me.*

The letter had a Green Bay postmark, but there were no fingerprints or other indications of who had sent it. Dave explained that it raised red flags because, unlike most of the hate mail and death threats we received, it was very specific. The sender talked about following our kids to school, the street where we lived, and threatened not just me but my children and my in-laws.

I decided not to share the note with Tonette and the kids right away. Security was already tight around the family. Eventually, long after everything was over, I told her, Matt, and Alex about it.

According to my staff, the only time they ever saw me angry during the entire fight over Act 10 was after I read that letter. They were right. I didn't mind threats against me, but I was infuriated that these thugs would try to draw my family into it.

One of the reasons for Dave's increased vigilance was the fact that the protests in Madison came just a month after the shooting of U.S. Representative Gabby Giffords in Tucson, Arizona.

In the wake of that tragedy, I was amazed to see how quickly so many on the left jumped at the opportunity to blame conservative political rhetoric for the shooting. *New York Times* columnist Paul Krugman wrote, "We don't have proof yet that this was political, but the odds are that it was. . . . [V]iolent acts are what happen when you create a climate of hate. And it's long past time for the GOP's leaders to take a stand against the hate-mongers."[2]

Giffords's home-state colleague, U.S. Representative Raúl Grijalva, declared, "[When] you stoke these flames, and you go to public meetings and you scream at the elected officials, you threaten them—you make us expendable you make us part of the cannon fodder. . . . Something's going to happen."[3]

Well, just a few weeks later, when protesters screamed at elected officials, threatened them, and created a "climate of hate" in Madison, their actions were met with silence from these same quarters. Protesters followed us around the state, assaulted police vehicles, harassed Republican legislators, and vandalized their homes. One day, someone scattered dozens of .22 caliber bullets across the capitol grounds.

At the capitol, they carried signs comparing me to Adolf Hitler, Hosni Mubarak, and Osama bin Laden. Those never seemed to make the evening news, so we took pictures to document them. One read "Death to tyrants." Another had a picture of me in crosshairs with the words, "Don't retreat, Reload." Another declared, "The only good Republican is a dead Republican." Another said "Walker = Hitler" and "Repubs = Nazi Party."

It wasn't just the protesters who engaged in such shameful rhetoric.

Democratic Senator Lena Taylor also compared me to Hitler, declaring, "The history of Hitler, in 1933, he abolished unions, and that's what our governor's doing today."[4, 5] Her colleague Senator Spencer Coggs called our plan "legalized slavery."[6] Jesse Jackson came to Madison and compared me to the late segregationist governor of Alabama, George Wallace (who was paralyzed in an assassination attempt), declaring we had "the same position" and that I was practicing the politics of the "Old South."[7]

Later, when the capitol was cleared of protesters, *Time* magazine reported, "The Wisconsin State Capitol had taken on an eerie quiet by late Friday. . . . The chalk outlines around fake dead bodies etched with Wisconsin Governor Scott Walker's name remained in dismembered parts, not yet completely washed away by hoses."[8]

Krugman and his cohorts never got around to taking "a stand against the hate-mongers" in Madison.

In his moving speech after the Giffords shooting, President Obama declared, "at a time when our discourse has become so sharply polarized, at a time when we are far too eager to lay the blame for all that ails the world at the feet of those who happen to think differently than we do, it's important for us to pause for a moment and make sure that we're talking with each other in a way that—that heals, not in a way that wounds."[9]

Those words apparently fell on deaf ears in Madison.

CHAPTER 8

Occupy Madison

O n Tuesday, February 15, the Joint Finance Committee took up our bill in what became the longest budget hearing in the history of the Wisconsin State Legislature. The hearing would soon claim a more ignominious place in history—as the moment that gave birth to the "Occupy" movement.

There is an informal tradition in Wisconsin that when a committee is taking testimony from the public, members stay and listen until the last person has spoken. Opponents of Act 10 abused that tradition to conduct what one of them called a "citizen's filibuster."

Using social media, the unions put out a call for people to come to the capitol and testify. They turned out more people than had ever been seen at a bill hearing. There were lines winding down the stairs. So long as people lined up to testify, the committee could not move the bill. Students and teaching assistants came streaming up State Street from the University of Wisconsin campus into the capitol, where they filled out cards requesting their chance to deliver three minutes of testimony. They were joined by teachers and other public workers who lined up outside the hearing room by the hundreds waiting for the chance to speak.

To accommodate the growing throng, the capitol staff decided to set up several big-screen televisions in the rotunda so the overflow crowds could follow the proceedings.

That was the first mistake.

The second mistake came at three a.m. After hearing seventeen straight hours of testimony, committee cochair Representative Robin Vos decided that was enough. He gaveled the hearing to a close. An uproar ensued. Hundreds of people were still waiting in line to have their say.

The assembly sergeant at arms came over and informed Vos that the Democrats wanted to continue the hearing. Vos threw up his hands and said, "I'm exhausted, they can do whatever they want, but the hearing's not going to be official. They can go sit in a room if they want to and listen to people, but that doesn't matter to me."[1]

The Democrats moved to a new hearing room and continued to hear "testimony" throughout the night and into the morning. Instead of clearing out the crowds camped out in the rotunda (as they normally would once a late hearing had ended), the police let them stay. And once the protesters had spent one night in the capitol, they figured they could do it again the next night . . . and the next . . . and the next. They never left.

The occupation had begun.

Vos said later, "We probably never should have allowed them to continue in there. We should have cleared the capitol and started up the next day." We were not equipped to handle what was coming next.

The following day, February 16, more people showed up and joined the camp that was forming in the rotunda. The ranks of the occupiers grew with each passing day. While protesters chanted "Kill the bill!" outside my office, I remarked to reporters gathered inside, "Everyone has a right to be heard."

When the protests began, the folks in the capitol were teachers and public employees who were scared and concerned about the changes we had proposed. They brought their families out, and behaved civilly. These were decent citizens, respected in their communities.

But as the protests went on, the ranks of those marching against our reform became more and more radical with each passing day. Instead of regular citizens camping out waiting to testify against our bill, people from outside Wisconsin began to take over. Soon, national union organizers were bringing in groups with insignia from Chicago, Washington, New York, and plenty of other locations across the country.

The signs at the capitol became more radical too, comparing us to Nazis, rapists, and terrorists. Some of the protesters wore Che Guevara T-shirts, bearing the visage of the murderous communist revolutionary (an odd choice of clothing when you're chanting "This is what democracy looks like!").

Day after day, the crowds got bigger. A few days before, I had joined more than fifty thousand people at Lambeau Field to celebrate the Green Bay Packers' Super Bowl victory. Soon, nearly twice that number would descend on the capitol building and the square outside. The unions brought homeless people into the capitol to help fill it. The weather was freezing, so living in the rotunda was better than sleeping on a grate outside. The capitol grew so packed with human bodies, the staff who worked there physically could not move around the building. There was no possible way to clean it because the bodies never left. The smell, as soon as you walked into the building, was overpowering.

Protesters urinated on the back door of my office.

Charles Quagliana, a historical architect who participated in the 2004 renovation of the capitol, later surveyed the damage and concluded that "the building experienced three to five years of wear within a two-week period."[2]

The protesters set up a commune inside the capitol. They had a first aid station, information centers, water stations, a yoga studio, and a designated child care area. People could literally drop off their kids and go scream and chant outside my office. They set up makeshift food service areas where they cooked meals for the crowds in Crock-Pots plugged in with extension cords. (It was a fire hazard, so eventually we cut off the power to discourage them.) They organized a sleeping bag exchange, and tent villages were set up in the rotunda and other corners of the building.

The capitol was littered with boxes from a small pizza shop across Capitol Square, Ian's Pizza.[3] People from all fifty states and some twenty-four countries—including Bosnia, China, Egypt, and France—were calling in and sending thousands of dollars' worth of pizzas over to the protesters in the capitol each day. Smart entrepreneurs that they were, the folks at Ian's more than doubled their staff, and even set up an app to take the growing volume of pizza orders online and with mobile devices. Today, that small shop has turned into a virtual Taj Mahal of pizza.[4] With Act 10, it seemed, we were bringing a lot of tourism dollars into the state. The only industry we didn't seem to be helping was the hotel industry—because so many people were sleeping inside the capitol.

The media liked to comment on how "peaceful" the protests were. They must never have tried to get around the capitol in a suit and tie. Since the Democratic legislators were all wearing orange union shirts, anyone in a suit was assumed to be a Republican and accosted.

One day, Ed Wall, the head of the Justice Department's Division of Criminal Investigation, came to my office and shared what had just happened when he walked into the capitol wearing a suit. Protesters started rushing after him yelling "Get him! Get him!" One guy was screaming in his face, yelling "Who are you?" When he barked back at him "I'm a cop!" the guy turned around to the crowd and said, "It's OK, he's a cop!" They thought the police were on their side, so they all backed away. Little did they know, Ed was helping us. From that moment on, Ed said, he was golden. Whenever he walked through the capitol with his badge hanging on his suit pocket, they all said, "How are you, officer?"

Attorney General J. B. Van Hollen was not so lucky. One day, he tried to get to his car parked just outside the capitol building. Protesters swarmed around him, spitting and cursing at him. It took a dozen police officers to finally clear the way for him to depart. He soon began parking across the street at the Risser Justice Center and using the underground tunnels like me.[5]

Republican senator Glenn Grothman was actually chased outside the capitol and cornered by an angry mob of AFSCME, UFCW, and SEIU activists, yelling "Shame! Shame!" and "F——— you!" in unison. He had to be rescued by a Democratic state lawmaker, Representative Brett Hulsey, who prevailed on the mob to let the senator go. The entire incident was caught on video.[6]

Inside the capitol, the protesters tried to physically disrupt legislators from carrying out their constitutional duties by clogging corridors and stairwells and denying them access to the senate and assembly chambers. They used social media to mobilize people in these efforts, sending out tweets with requests like "Calling for people to block stairs to the senate" and "We need to prevent the senate from attaining a quorum."[7]

On February 17, the senate was scheduled to convene at eleven a.m. to take up the bill. But instead of coming to the chamber, minority leader Senator Mark Miller had called a meeting of all his senators at the Democratic Party of Wisconsin headquarters. They had figured out a way to block the bill.

Article VIII, Section 8, of the state constitution reads:

[A]ny law which imposes, continues or renews a tax, or creates a debt or charge, or makes, continues or renews an appropriation of public or trust money . . . three-fifths of all the members elected to such house shall in all such cases be required to constitute a quorum therein.

That meant that twenty senators had to be present to pass the bill. There were only nineteen Republicans. So if all the Democrats left the state, the senate could not move forward.

They decided to leave.

Only thirteen Democrats were at the meeting. The other senator, Tim Cullen, was away from the capitol consoling the family of his good friend former Wisconsin supreme court justice Bill Bablitch, who had just passed away. Cullen then headed to the capitol to brief reporters on Bablitch's passing. When I called Senator Cullen a few days later, he told me that he thought he could have convinced them not to leave if he had been at that meeting.

Around 11:30 a.m., when the senators were called to the chamber, the Democrats were nowhere to be found. Senate Majority Leader Scott Fitzgerald went to the minority leader's office to ask where Senator Miller was, but his staff said they did not know.

Meanwhile, Senator Ellis went through the motions of calling the roll. When the Democrats did not respond, he declared, "The clerk will keep the roll open for Senator Miller and the other senators who are not here yet."

A few moments later assembly Speaker Jeff Fitzgerald got a call from his brother.

"You're not going to believe this," Scott said, "but I think the Democrats have left the state."

"You're kidding me, right?" Jeff replied.

Soon, Scott called again.

"Yeah, they're gone. We don't have a quorum so we can't move the bill."

On her Facebook page, Democratic Senator Lena Taylor posted a message that read "brb" ("be right back").[8] Initially, in our own naïveté, we believed that they would be. And besides, we figured, if the Democrats did not return, all we had to do was send the state troopers out to bring them back. We soon learned that state troopers had no authority to do that. And even if they had had the authority, the sight of state troopers marching senators back to the capitol was one none of us wanted to see.

Very quickly, we figured out how to pass the bill without them. We did not need the Democratic senators to be present if we split the bill—removing the fiscal provisions that required a quorum, and passing the collective bargaining reforms alone. But the senate Republicans were concerned about doing that. They didn't want to send the message that the bill was about breaking the unions instead of balancing the budget. And besides, they were convinced that the senate Democrats would be back in a few days' time.

So they let the standoff go on and the protests build. What should have been a delay of one or two days turned into a multiweek saga. It was an entirely self-inflicted wound. We kept telling senate Republicans they could end this anytime. But they kept thinking that with a few days and a few concessions, their Democratic colleagues would return. It took them more than three weeks of building protests and failed shuttle diplomacy before they finally realized that the Democrats were never coming back.

There was another reason for the lack of urgency on the Republican side. Despite the building protests, we were winning the battle for public opinion.

The senate Democrats had fled to defend the indefensible: the right of most public workers to pay nothing for their pensions and next to nothing for their health insurance premiums.

That was pretty hard to explain to the rest of the state when many workers in Wisconsin had lost their jobs or seen their hours and their benefits pared back in the midst of the weakest economic recovery since the Great Depression. As the *Wall Street Journal* pointed out,[9] in the private sector the average employee paid 20 percent of their health care premium, and contributed about 7.5 percent of their take-home pay for retirement. We were asking public workers to pay just 12.6 percent toward their health care premiums and 5.8 percent toward their retirement—far below the national average.

In other words, the Democrats' position didn't make sense to most people in Wisconsin. My brother, David, was a good example. He works as a hotel banquet manager and a part-time bartender. His wife, my sister-in-law, Maria, sells appliances at a department store. They have two beautiful girls, my nieces, Isabella and Eva. They are a typical middle-class family in Wisconsin.

He reminded me that he pays about $800 a month toward his health insurance premiums and the little bit he can put away for his retirement. He said that workers like him would love to have the type of benefits we were offering to public employees.

David told me that when the protests first started in Madison, a few people at his church who were government workers expressed their displeasure with my reforms. He said that they initially got some sympathy. But then, the more they talked about it, the more people were shocked to learn just how little they paid for their pensions and health care, and the sympathy ran dry. Eventually they stopped talking about it at church.

It was like that all over Wisconsin. The *New York Times* published a story about how private sector workers in Wisconsin were "finding it hard to feel sympathy or offer solidarity, with their own jobs lost and their benefits and pensions cut back or cut off," adding that "away from Madison, many people said that public workers needed to share in the sacrifice that their own families have been forced to make."[10] Even liberal *Washington Post* columnist Eugene Robinson conceded: "Walker is right about one thing: When it comes to pensions and benefits, public workers in Wisconsin have a sweet deal. . . . It's easy to see why the average private-sector worker in Wisconsin—probably paying upward of 25 percent toward health insurance costs and struggling to tuck away something, anything, for retirement—might agree with Walker."

Our internal polls confirmed this. By a margin of 77 to 21, Wisconsin voters agreed that "when it comes to pensions and benefits, state employees have a pretty sweet deal . . . it is time the average government worker paid a little more."

It didn't help the unions' cause that while people were learning about what cushy benefits teachers and government employees enjoyed, classrooms across the state were empty because tens of thousands of teachers were at the capitol protesting. In Madison, 40 percent of all teachers called in sick[11]—which meant either that Madison schools had been hit by one of the largest epidemics in Wisconsin history, or teachers were abusing sick leave to protest.

It is illegal under Wisconsin law for teachers and government workers to go on strike, but many teachers effectively went on strike anyway. So many called in sick that schools from Milwaukee and Madison to Racine and Beaver Dam had to close for days at a time.

That meant not only kids were missing school, it also meant that many hardworking parents had to take unpaid days off from their jobs to watch their kids—all thanks to the protests.

And to make matters worse, while the parents were losing pay because school was closed, physicians had set up stations at the capitol to write doctors' notes for the teachers so that they would not lose *their* pay. The MacIver Institute filmed some of the doctors roaming the crowds handing out sick notes, and posted the video on YouTube.[12] In the video, an interviewer asks a woman in a white medical coat what she and her colleagues are doing:

"We are writing sick notes for anybody who needs them," she says.

"Who's sick?" the interviewer asks.

"Everybody is sick of Scott Walker," she replies.

The doctors and teachers were lying to their employers and defrauding the taxpayers. Later, when the protests were over, the *Wisconsin State Journal* reported that "UW School of Medicine and Public Health disciplined 20 doctors for writing questionable sick notes for protesters last year . . . with three doctors getting the harshest penalty: fines of up to $4,000 and loss of leadership positions for four months."[13] Meanwhile, the paper reported that the state Medical Examining Board reprimanded thirteen doctors and gave seven others administrative warnings.[14]

So each day, thousands of kids missed school and thousands of parents missed work so that the teachers could cut class and fight to preserve benefits that the parents could only dream of.

For the unions, that was a public relations disaster.

Our argument, by contrast, was simple and compelling: It was not fair that public workers enjoyed better benefits and better job security than their employers (the people of Wisconsin), who were losing their jobs and benefits in the worst economy in modern times.

Most people in Wisconsin agreed. We were winning the "fairness" debate.

But that was about to change.

CHAPTER 9

A Racket, Not a Right

On Friday, February 18, I traveled to Volk Field to welcome home Task Force Badger, the 724th Engineer Battalion of the Wisconsin National Guard. Nearly one thousand friends and family braved freezing cold temperatures to greet three hundred of Wisconsin's bravest citizens on their return from their second tour of combat duty in Iraq. They had been responsible for clearing some two hundred thousand kilometers of routes across the country—including the dangerous task of searching for and removing roadside bombs.[1]

It was so uplifting to be with those returning soldiers. But what blew me away was how many of the troops and their families came up and said, "Hey governor, you've got guts" (along with some other more colorful descriptions of my fortitude).

It was also one of the first moments I realized that, outside of Madison, there were people who really appreciated what we were doing. It taught me an important lesson: When you come under attack, one of the best things you can do is get out of the capital. There may have been tens of thousands of people protesting in Madison, but for every protester, there were thousands who stood with us, and their support sustained Tonette and our family in the most difficult moments.

I recall on one trip when an airport worker at the town we flew into came up to me and handed me a piece of paper. I looked at it when I got into the plane. It read: "Isaiah 54:17." I pulled out my phone and looked up the passage: "No weapon forged against you will prevail, and you will refute every tongue that accuses you."

On another occasion, as I sat in a chair on the set of a morning television show in Green Bay, the floor manager, kneeling down next to me to put on my microphone, whispered to me that she and her kids got down on their knees each night and prayed for me and my family.

Those kinds of moments inspired me throughout the fight over Act 10. The more I got out of the capital, the better it was, for both me and for my family. I was so moved by all the people I met who told me that their families were praying for us. It meant the world to us. I resolved to spend less time listening to the drums and horns outside my window and more time listening to the folks in factories and farms and small businesses across the state whose voices were being drowned out by the agitators in Madison.

While I was visiting with our returning troops, back in Madison the unions were beating a tactical retreat.

Wisconsin voters overwhelmingly agreed it was unfair that public sector workers should receive lavish benefits that private sector workers could only dream about—especially in an economy where many were losing their benefits, if not losing their jobs. Increasingly, the unions realized they were getting clobbered on equity and fairness, and that holding out for their current benefits was a losing scenario.

So on February 18, the leaders of the Wisconsin chapter of AFSCME and the Wisconsin teachers union announced that they would accept the 5.8 percent increase in health care premiums and 12.6 percent toward their pensions, so long as we promised not to take away their collective bargaining "rights."

It was a smart move. Our internal polls showed that 73 percent of

Wisconsinites backed requiring public employees to pay more for health insurance and 80 percent supported requiring them to contribute to their pensions. By contrast, they opposed ending collective bargaining by a margin of 51 to 46 percent.

By conceding the point on benefits, the unions reclaimed the high ground in the fairness debate. Instead of defending their lavish benefits, they were now defending their collective bargaining "rights." No one wants to see "rights" taken away from anyone. And they began to hammer that message home. If there had been any doubt who had directed the move, the national AFL-CIO quickly put up a powerful TV ad featuring a Wisconsin fireman who declared, "Governor Walker, public employees have agreed to the cuts you asked for, and now they're simply asking that you not take away their rights."[2]

Of course, the union offer was not serious. Having been a local official for eight years, I knew that just because two statewide union bosses said they would accept the increased pension and health care contributions, it did not mean those increases would be implemented by unions at the local level. Contracts are not negotiated statewide but by local collective bargaining units in Wisconsin's 424 school districts, more than 1,700 municipalities, and 72 counties.

Indeed, we saw local union after local union go to their school boards and city councils and try to "Walker-proof" their benefits—rushing through contracts that had no contributions to the pension and no increased contribution to health care.

On February 16, for example, the *Janesville Gazette* ran a story titled "Cities rush to settle contracts before Legislature approves bill." It reported:

> Some area municipalities are hurrying to settle union contracts before a vote is taken on Governor Scott Walker's proposal to curtail collective bargaining rights.
>
> In Janesville, the city Tuesday reached tentative agreements with three of its unions and will meet with

representatives of a fourth today or Thursday. The contracts for Janesville's four unions expired in December.

In Evansville, city officials contacted the union representing the majority of city staff other than police and library and offered to strike a deal before the state forced its hand.

In Milton, city administrator Jerry Schuetz said the city's been working on labor contracts with its police and public works employees as part of "business as normal" and planned to consider final approval of both contracts this week.

If the agreements are ratified before the legislation is passed, the municipalities would not be able to take advantage of any cost savings the legislation is expected to yield. . . .

In Evansville, the city on Tuesday called Teamsters Local No. 695, which represents the majority of city clerical staff, public works and water and light employees, and "offered that if we can strike a bargain locally rather than have our hands forced, we're open to it," city administrator Dan Wietecha said.

"(That) means someone needs to nail down a lot of stuff in the next day (or two)," he said. . . .

The city wrote this year's budget expecting no increases in salaries and no increases or savings in retirement and health insurance, Wietecha said.

"We don't need to suddenly change just because there's a new variable," he said.[3]

The *Wisconsin Radio Network* similarly reported that "the rush is on to get local contracts approved ahead of the governor's budget repair bill taking effect, including in Racine."[4] Contracts without increased health care and pension contributions were approved not only in Racine but also in

La Crosse County, Sheboygan County, Madison, and at the Milwaukee Area Technical College. (When an official at the college was asked if the school was "rushing" through the contract to beat the legislative clock, she replied, "Rush is such a subjective word.")[5]

In Janesville, the unions were actually pushing through a pay *increase*.

"Actions do speak louder than words," I said, explaining why we rejected the union "offer."

While local unions tried to push through last-minute deals to protect their benefits, the national and state union officials had a bigger concern—protecting the system of political cronyism that allowed them to perpetuate their political power.

The unions liked to paint collective bargaining as a civil "right," like free speech. But collective bargaining isn't a right, it's a racket. Here is how the scam works in the public sector:

1. The government automatically collects compulsory union dues from the paychecks of public workers.

2. The government then gives the money to the union bosses.

3. The union bosses then give that money to pro-union politicians in the form of campaign contributions.

4. The union-backed politicians use that money to get elected.

5. Once elected, the union-backed politicians then sit across the table from the union bosses to "negotiate"—purportedly on behalf of the taxpayers.

6. But instead of representing the taxpayers, they do the bidding of the unions by providing excessive wages, benefits, and pensions.

7. They line the pockets of union bosses through sweetheart deals, such as contracts requiring school districts to buy insurance from union-affiliated insurers, like the Wisconsin Education

Association (WEA) Trust, when they could have gotten much cheaper insurance on the open market.

8. Taxpayers lose tens of millions every year in higher health insurance costs—money that could have gone into classrooms but instead goes to the union bosses.

9. The union bosses then line the campaign coffers of the politicians with whom they just negotiated all over again, so they can elect more pro-union politicians who will continue this racket.

10. The cycle starts all over again.

This is why, as George Will so eloquently put it, public sector unions are nothing more than "government organized as a special interest to lobby itself to expand itself."[6]

Collective bargaining gives the union bosses the keys to the statehouse, city hall, and school. It allows them to effectively sit on both sides of the bargaining table when contracts are negotiated, while no one represents the interests of the taxpayers (whose money is at stake) or the children (whose education hangs in the balance). It is cronyism, plain and simple.

Case in point: When I was Milwaukee County executive, the chair of the board of supervisors' personnel committee, Pat Jursik, recalled how some of her colleagues actually wanted to bring the unions in to talk about the contracts *before* they started the negotiations.

Why on earth would they want to do that, she asked them? They explained to Supervisor Jursik that they needed to listen to the unions and take their interests into account as they formulated their negotiating positions. She was incredulous. "We're management, they are labor," she told them. Why would they want to bring in the unions to discuss what the position should be in negotiations with the *unions*? Why would we meet with them like a group of constituents?

The answer is that this is precisely how they saw the unions—as their constituents. They thought their job was to represent the unions' interests in negotiations. They were negotiating *with* the unions and on *behalf* of the unions at the same time. Supervisor Jursik had to explain to them the basic premise that they were supposed to negotiate on behalf of Milwaukee County *taxpayers*, not the unions. Their job was not to meet with the unions and find out what the unions needed. It was to sit down with the department heads and other constitutional officers and find out what *they* needed in a contract. And then they were supposed to get the best possible deal they could for them and for the taxpayers.

Supervisor Jursik's story illustrates one of the fundamental problems with collective bargaining: It creates a kind of "Stockholm syndrome" among local officials. They are held hostage by the unions but end up sympathizing with, and advocating for, their captors.

My friend New Jersey governor Chris Christie recalls how his predecessor, Jon Corzine, once stood on the front steps of the state capitol in Trenton at a public sector union rally and yelled, "We will fight for a fair contract!"[7] Chris wondered: Who exactly was he going to fight? Himself? Corzine was running to represent the people of New Jersey, but he was promising to represent the unions at the negotiating table.

This is why what we did in Wisconsin so enraged the union bosses and sparked their unprecedented campaign to stop us. They could live with it if we were to lay off tens of thousands of workers. They could live with it if we cut aid to schools and local governments. They could live with it if we raised workers' contributions to their pensions and health care premiums.

What they could *not* live with is if we broke up the system of cronyism and corruption that allowed them to preserve their power and perpetuate their prerogatives.

So long as they succeeded in protecting that system, they could wait us out and then go back and restore spending or change the health and pension deal after we left office. But if we succeeded in dismantling the corrupt system itself, not only would our changes stay in place in the short term, but the entire apparatus they had created for sucking up taxpayer dollars would be upended—permanently.

Without the automatic collection of dues, the union bosses could no longer force public workers to involuntarily fill the union offers. Without the power to negotiate anything but wages (capped at the CPI), there was little incentive for public workers to send their dues voluntarily or vote to recertify the union. Without the monopoly they had enjoyed on health insurance, the unions could no longer force schools to buy gold-plated health plans at inflated prices. And with the spigot of free money turned off, the unions could no longer control who sat across from them at the negotiating table.

They quickly realized that what we were doing was qualitatively different from what had been done in other states: We didn't just go after the money. We decided to fix the entire *system*.

So it came as no surprise when the unions gave up the fight against increasing health and pension contributions, and focused their efforts on defending their protection racket. In the end, for the unions, it was all about the money. The only thing they ultimately cared about was keeping the automatic withholding of union dues from the paychecks of Wisconsin's approximately three hundred thousand public workers.

The unions were willing to give up anything to keep their hands on that cash. They were worried that given a free choice, their members would choose to keep the money for themselves.

As we would later learn, they were right to be worried. But for now, their retreat on benefits had succeeded in shifting the terms of the debate in their favor. They were starting to sway folks outside of Madison (including many who supported me) that what we were doing was fundamentally unfair—that we were trying to take away people's "rights."

We would have to reclaim the moral high ground.

CHAPTER 10

"Scott, Why Are You Doing This?"

The union offer on pensions and health care was nothing more than a political ploy to buy time, but it was an effective one.

Not long after the unions made their announcement, my chief political strategist, R. J. Johnson, took me aside and said, "Governor, you're in trouble."

Polls showed that people agreed with our demand that public workers contribute to their pensions and health benefits to put them more in line with private sector workers, he explained. That seemed only fair. But now that the unions had "conceded," people did not understand why we were still insisting on changing collective bargaining itself. Even Republicans were telling pollsters, "I voted for the governor, but I don't understand why he is doing this." The unions were effectively reframing the debate, and I was sliding precipitously in the polls. R.J. told me we needed to get the bill passed as soon as possible.

I took note of his concerns, but I was not terribly worried. I was confident that once we got the bill enacted, the reforms would eventually sell themselves. I was absolutely certain from my experience in

Milwaukee County that they would save money, strengthen education, and improve public services. And once people saw that that was the case, they would come around. We just had to put our shoulders to the grindstone, not give in to union pressure, and pass the reforms.

As the intensity of the protests grew, Tonette became increasingly worried about me, our family, and our safety. The vitriol that was being directed at us, the people picketing outside our home, distressed her to no end.

One night we were standing in our bedroom and she turned to me, visibly upset, and said: "Scott, why are you doing this?"

The question took me aback. At first, I thought she was blaming me for the protests. But it was more than that.

"Why are these people so upset with you?" Tonette demanded to know. "You got what you wanted. Why are you pushing this?"

I had just assumed that Tonette understood why our reforms were necessary. The fact that she didn't was a wake-up call to me. If my own wife didn't see why we needed to change collective bargaining, how could I expect the voters of Wisconsin to see it? I was obviously doing a lousy job of explaining our reforms.

Before we had introduced Act 10, we had methodically gone through every aspect of our plan of action with my cabinet. We had the legislative plan mapped out to the smallest detail. We had prepared for every contingency—even down to having the National Guard at the ready to take over state prisons if corrections officers went on strike. But the one thing we had not done was prepare the people of Wisconsin for the changes we were about to enact.

Usually in government, politicians talk about problems but never fix them. My mistake was, in my eagerness to get busy fixing the problems of our state, I didn't spend enough time laying out what they were to the people of the state. We did not do enough to help people understand why we had chosen this path, how collective bargaining was hurting schools and local governments, and why reforming it was the only way to get our fiscal house in order. I figured the people of Wisconsin had just elected me to make bold changes, and had sent me to Madison backed by strong Republican majorities in both houses—so they expected us to go ahead take bold action.

I was elected based on a core set of ideas. I promised to balance the budget. I promised to do it without tricks and gimmicks. I promised to do it without raising taxes. I promised to do it in a way that improved the economy and fostered job creation. If I was to keep all those promises, what other choice was there?

I did what I had to do to keep my promises and balance our budget. I remembered how in 2009, when I was Milwaukee County executive, Governor Doyle announced that he was cutting funding for education and local government by 5 percent.[1] The governor didn't give us any tools we could use to make up for the lost aid through efficiencies. I was already struggling to close a $90 million budget shortfall, and trying any reforms I could to save jobs and avoid layoffs. But under collective bargaining, the unions were able to block us from doing so. The result was that other local officials and I had to lay off thousands of teachers and public workers in order to close the budget gap and make up for the lost aid from the state.

When I became governor, and had to make even deeper cuts in aid to schools and local governments, I knew what the effects of these cuts would be on local officials if we did not give them tools to make up for the lost funding. I was determined not to put them in the same position Governor Doyle had put me in a few years before.

If the protests over collective bargaining reform were bad, just imagine the blowback I would have gotten if I had cut a billion dollars from education and local government and had *not* reformed collective bargaining. If I had cut all that money from schools and local governments without giving them the tools to replace those lost funds, education and local services across our state would have been devastated—and the public would have been outraged. I would have been recalled from office—and rightly so.

I knew I was doing the right thing, but I had not taken the time to explain why it was the right thing to do. I wish that on my first day in office I'd told the taxpayers how, under collective bargaining, school districts were forced to buy health insurance from just one company that happened to be affiliated with the teachers union—and that it cost them tens of millions of dollars more than it had to because there was no competition. The citizens would have told me to go ahead and fix the problem. I wish I had pointed out that because of overtime rules in a collective bargaining agreement, there were bus drivers in the City of Madison who made more than the mayor. If I had explained these things, the people would have said to me: "Fix it."

But I had not done that. Now the Democrats and union activists were charging that I wanted to take away workers "rights" and my fellow citizens (including my own wife) were asking, "Why has he got these folks all upset?" I had to start making the case for our reforms, or I would lose the citizens of our state.

I started with the citizen closest to me. Tonette is an excellent political barometer for me because she is like a lot of Wisconsin voters—smart and well read but focused on things other than politics. Despite being married to me, her life is centered not on events in Madison but on raising our two sons, her work at the American Lung Association, and her volunteer work with teens and young adults recovering from substance abuse addictions. She is your typical informed voter.

Now here she was, demanding to know: "Why are these protesters in front of our house? Why is this so important that it is worth all this grief to our family?" We talked it over and prayed about it together. Eventually, I convinced her that our reforms were a necessary course of action and worth the pain and grief they were causing our family. That gave me hope. If I could convince Tonette, I could probably convince most of our citizens as well.

Little did Tonette know at the time how much worse things were about to get.

The protests frayed her nerves. One night, Tonette went downstairs to get something. While she was in the kitchen, I opened the door to our bedroom and saw a bat flying around in the air. I yelled to warn her not to come into the room and to ask security to bring up a broom. She did not hear me mention the bat. She was certain that a protester had broken into the house and was trying to kill me. She told me afterward that she was thinking, "Oh my God, they got him. It's over." Tonette actually thought that a protestor had attacked me in our own house. That's how intense it was during these days.

At Christmastime in 2011, our staff put together a book with pictures of the most awful signs the protesters had carried comparing me to Hitler and Hosni Mubarak, and calling for me to be recalled, impeached, and much worse. I smiled as I flipped through the volume, but the pictures brought tears to Tonette's eyes.

"Now when we're old and sitting in our rockers, we can look back and remember how one hundred thousand people hated you," she said.

The experience taught me an important lesson: It is always so much harder to see a loved one attacked than to be the one under attack.

Like most spouses, Tonette is generally more hurt by things said against me than I am. But don't think for a moment they got the best of her. I'm tough, but Tonette is even tougher.

In the 1980s, her first husband died of kidney failure, and her brother (and only sibling) died of bone marrow cancer. Both had been terminally ill for some time.

Years later her mother, Geri, was diagnosed with a level 4 brain tumor. She left her job to help take care of her mother. Geri made it another two years, but the cancer finally won. Tonette's aunt Annette died about the same time. They were close because Annette was much younger than Tonette's father. We were at the hospital when she passed away.

Then Tonette's father got COPD, a lung disease that causes the airways to narrow over time. Tony lasted about a dozen years. He had to use oxygen and had many visits to the hospital. We took him into the hospital yet again on New Year's Eve in 2012. He spent a month in the ICU and another month in rehab. Eventually, we moved him into an assisted living apartment near our home in Wauwatosa. Unfortunately, he went back into the hospital on the eve of Easter, and died that Sunday.

The protests and recalls were tough on Tonette, but none of that was as tough as the losses she has experienced throughout her life. She is strong. Her strength, and her wisdom, strengthened me.

Tonette was my rock throughout the fight over Act 10. It was Tonette who showed me I was losing the argument over collective bargaining. And it was Tonette who showed me that if I got out there and explained myself, we could prevail.

But I would have to start making the effort.

CHAPTER 11

"The Power of Humility, the Burden of Pride"

On Tuesday, February 22, I decided to go over the heads of the press and take my case directly to the citizens of our state. We scheduled a televised fireside address from the capitol. It was a chance to counter the passions of the protesters and personally explain why collective bargaining reform was necessary.

I began by making clear my respect for public workers. "In 1985, when I was a high school junior in the small town of Delavan, I was inspired to pursue public service after I attended the American Legion's Badger Boys State program," I said. "Tonight, I thank the three hundred thousand–plus state and local government employees who showed up for work today and did their jobs well. We appreciate it. If you take only one message away tonight, it's that we all respect the work that you do."

I then went on to explain why our reforms were necessary:

> Now, some have questioned why we have to reform collective bargaining to balance the budget. The answer is simple: the system is broken. It costs taxpayers serious

money—particularly at the local level. As a former county official, I know that firsthand.

For years, I tried to use modest changes in pension and health insurance contributions as a means of balancing our budget without massive layoffs or furloughs. On nearly every occasion, the local unions (empowered by collective bargaining agreements) told me to go ahead and lay off workers. That's not acceptable to me.

Here's another example: In Wisconsin, many local school districts are required to buy their health insurance through the WEA Trust (which is the state teachers union's company). When our bill passes, these school districts can opt to switch into the state plan and save $68 million per year. Those savings could be used to pay for more teachers and put more money into the classroom to help our kids.

I also urged the Democratic senators to come home: "Do the job you were elected to do. You don't have to like the outcome, or even vote yes, but as part of the world's greatest democracy, you should be here, in Madison, at the capitol."

It was a good evening, and I felt we had made progress. The speech was broadcast live across the state and made front-page news the next morning. The *Milwaukee Journal Sentinel* had a big photo of me delivering the address with a banner headline that read "WALKER STATES HIS CASE."

But unbeknownst to me, I had done something stupid that wiped out any positive effect.

The morning of the fireside speech, after a week or more of insistent pleas, my staff had arranged for me to take a call from David Koch, the billionaire industrialist who with his brother Charles had founded the conservative grassroots organization Americans for Prosperity. For some reason, I had hesitated taking the call. We were so busy trying to pass the bill, I did not want any distractions from that effort. But my staff finally convinced me by pointing out that Mr. Koch's company owns Georgia Pacific in Green Bay, which, with more than two thousand workers, was one of Wisconsin's largest employers. I was told that he was concerned about the impact of the protests on the business climate in the state. Against my better instincts, I took the call.

I had never spoken with Mr. Koch before so I didn't know what to expect. The call started out seeming fairly normal, but eventually it got odd. At some point it got uncomfortable (like when he made a lewd comment about *Morning Joe* cohost Mika Brzezinski), and I looked for a way to get off the call. After I hung up, I thought nothing more about it.

The next morning, my staff came in and told me that the caller had not been David Koch at all, but a prankster named Ian Murphy. The call had been taped and posted online and now the national media was all over it.

Murphy was immediately celebrated by union activists for supposedly "exposing" my ties to the Koch brothers and proving that I was doing their bidding. If anything, his call proved the opposite. It showed that I had never spoken to David Koch before in my life. I couldn't even recognize the guy's voice. If I had really been doing Koch's bidding, I would have recognized immediately that it was not Koch on the other end of the line. Instead, I spoke to the fake Koch at length.

Moreover, we were getting killed in the "air war" with the unions vastly outspending us for paid advertising. The situation was so bad that my chief political adviser, R. J. Johnson, called the Wisconsin airwaves a "no fly zone" for us, such was the union saturation. If we had been in league with the Koch brothers, that would not have been the case. The call made Murphy something of a celebrity, and Democrats later enlisted him to campaign against me and build support for my recall. He was later photographed hobnobbing with some of the Democratic senators who had fled the state,[1] and Democratic officials appeared with him at union rallies.[2] They should have chosen their company more carefully. It emerged that in 2008, Murphy had written a disgusting essay for an alternative paper in Buffalo titled "[EXPLETIVE] the troops,"[3] in which he declared: "So 4,000 rubes are dead. Cry me the Tigris. Another 30,000 have been seriously wounded. Boo-[EXPLETIVE]-hoo. They got what they asked for—and cool robotic limbs, too. . . . As a society, we need to discard our blind deference to military service. There's nothing admirable about volunteering to murder people."[4] Pretty much tells you everything you need to know about the guy.

Still, I was not as mad at him as I was at myself. Listening to my voice on the recording of the call, my heart sank. I came across as pompous and full of myself. I bragged about my television appearances: "We've had all the national shows," I told the fake Koch. "We were on *Hannity* last night, I did *Good Morning America* and the *Today Show* and all that sort of stuff, was on *Morning Joe* this morning. We've done Greta [Van Susteren]. We're going to keep getting our message out; Mark Levin last night. And I gotta tell you, the response around the country has been phenomenal." But the worst moment came when the prankster asked about whether we'd considered putting agitators in the crowd. "What we were thinking about the crowd was, uh, was planting some troublemakers," he said. I did not want to insult Mr. Koch by saying that we would never do something so stupid. So instead, I stammered:

> You know, well, the only problem with that—because we thought about that. The problem with—my only gut reaction to that would be, right now the lawmakers I've talked to have just completely had it with them. The public is not really fond of this. The teacher's union did some polling and focus groups I think and found out that the public turned on them the minute they closed school down on them for a couple of days. The guys we've got left are largely from out of state and I keep dismissing it in all my press comments, saying ehh, they're mostly from out of state. My only fear would be if there's a ruckus caused is that

would scare the public into thinking maybe the governor has to settle to avoid all these problems. You know, whereas I've said, hey, we can handle this, people can protest, this is Madison, you know, full of the sixties liberals. Let 'em protest. It's not going to affect us. And as long as we go back to our homes and the majority of people are telling us we're doing the right thing, let 'em protest all they want. So that's my gut reaction. I think it's actually good if they're constant, they're noisy, but they're quiet, nothing happens. Sooner or later the media stops finding them interesting.[5]

It was a really dumb thing to say. The fact is we never—never—considered putting "troublemakers" in the crowd to discredit the protesters. The unions were doing a good enough job of that on their own with the agitators they were bringing in from outside the state. But I had made it seem like we had. Now the press was all over the "we thought about that" line. Who had suggested it? How seriously did I consider it?

My staff wanted to know what I was going to do in response. My answer was simple: Schedule a press conference and take it on directly.

So I stepped out into the Governor's Conference Room, where I held daily press conferences, and faced a room full of state and national reporters. I took a deep breath and stepped up to the podium. When the inevitable question came, I acknowledged that it was me on the call, and that it was stupid, but that what I had said wasn't inconsistent with anything I said at the podium every day. Then I opened it to questions, and took my beating.

I got through it, but that press conference was one of my toughest days. I felt like an idiot. Sure, I was upset that my staff had let the call get through to my office, making me look so silly. But ultimately, I was responsible for what I said and how I came across.

Only later did I realize that God had a plan for me with that episode.

In my office is a devotional book on leadership by John Maxwell that I read for its daily message. The day we learned the call had been a prank, we had been so busy that I never had a chance to pick it up. After my press conference, when I had a moment to catch my breath, I opened up the book.

The title for that day was: "The power of humility, the burden of pride."

I looked up and said, "I hear you, Lord."

Up to that point the national media had been all over our story. Conservative circles were writing and saying some pretty nice things about my political future. We were getting all sorts of abuse from the protesters and the mainstream media, so the accolades we were getting nationally were certainly encouraging. But it got to the point where I was reading many of the columns each night and getting pretty caught up in it all. Slowly, it was becoming too much about me.

My parents had taught me that the only time you get into trouble in life is when you lose your perspective and stop doing things for the right reasons. That's why that devotion for February 23 was so important. God was sending me a clear message to not do things for personal glory or fame. It was a turning point that helped me in future challenges, helped me stay focused on the people I was elected to serve, and reminded me of God's abundant grace and the paramount need to stay humble.

CHAPTER 12

Meet Ms. Sampson

The prank call was a setback, but by taking it head-on and admitting our mistakes we were able to move past it.

Now I had to correct another mistake: my failure to explain to the people of Wisconsin why we needed to reform collective bargaining.

When we first announced our legislation, I had been overly cautious in explaining just how bad some of the collective bargaining rules were. Funny as it sounds now, I did not want to tar all the good government employees in our state by pointing out how some of them were abusing collective bargaining rules to game the system, at a cost of millions of dollars to the Wisconsin taxpayers.

My reticence had prevented me from explaining why collective bargaining had to be changed. It also prevented me from showing how our reforms were truly pro-worker and pro-teacher.

The people most hurt by collective bargaining abuses were dedicated public workers. They were the ones who lost their jobs because the unions would not make concessions. They were the ones laid off first, while workers with seniority saw their jobs protected regardless of performance. They were the ones who had to pick up the slack when less productive workers failed to do their jobs. They were the ones who had union dues collected from their paychecks without their say.

There was another problem. We had expected a seven-day fight, not a monthlong standoff. We quickly ran out of messaging ammunition. We began scrambling to find stories that illustrated the abuses and perverse incentives created by collective bargaining, and sharing them with the people of Wisconsin. Fortunately, the examples were as numerous as they were shocking.

Collective bargaining rules facilitated overtime abuse—allowing some state workers to bilk taxpayers for hundreds of thousands of dollars. For example, in February 2010, the *Wisconsin State Journal* reported that "Madison's highest paid city government employee last year wasn't the mayor. It wasn't the police chief. It wasn't even the head of Metro Transit. It was [a] bus driver."[1] According to the paper, the driver in question earned $159,258 in 2009—a base salary of $49,366 plus $109,892 in overtime that was guaranteed by a collective bargaining agreement. This individual, and another driver who earned $125,598, were among the city's top twenty earners, according to the paper. In total, seven City of Madison bus drivers made more than $100,000 per year in 2009.

How did they do it? They were able to double or triple their salary, the paper explained, "thanks to a union contract that lets the most senior drivers who have the highest base salaries get first crack at overtime." In all, the Madison bus system had spent $1.94 million on overtime in 2009—$467,200 more than the city budgeted and the most ever for the system. But that was not all. The overtime rules in the collective bargaining agreement not only allowed drivers to boost their annual income, they also allowed them to artificially boost their retirement income—because retirement payouts were based on an average of the drivers' three highest earning years.[2] So the costs of the excess overtime would continue for years to come.

Incredibly, Madison Metro general manager Chuck Kamp (who

earned $118,690—or $40,568 less than the bus driver working for him)
defended the employees' actions, saying that they were simply following
"the rules that have been negotiated with the Teamsters."

That was precisely the problem. Our reforms, we pointed out, would
ensure unions could no longer negotiate those kinds of sweetheart deals
into public-worker contracts.

It wasn't just bus drivers who were taking advantage of the system.
As the American Enterprise Institute's Mark Perry points out, "Correctional officer collective bargaining agreements allow officers a practice
known as 'sick leave stacking.' Officers can call in sick for a shift, receiving 8 hours of sick pay, and then are allowed to work the very next shift,
earning time-and-a-half for overtime. This results in the officer receiving
2.5 times his or her rate of pay, while still only working 8 hours." In part
because of these practices, Perry points out, thirteen correctional officers
made more than $100,000 in 2009—despite earning base wages of less
than $60,000 per year. The officers received an average of $66,000 in
overtime pay for an average annual salary of more than $123,000—with
the highest paid officer receiving $151,181.

Later, when our reforms went into effect, unions could no longer use
collective bargaining to impose such schemes on Wisconsin taxpayers.
According to the *Appleton Post-Crescent*, Act 10 cut overtime in the
state's Department of Corrections by $10 million in 2012[3]—a 25 per-
cent drop for an agency responsible for more than half of all state employee overtime.[4] The paper reported that the "policy changes—which
took effect throughout state government in January 2012 as a result of
the state law that eliminated most collective bargaining powers for most
public workers—allow time-and-a-half overtime only after 40 working
hours in a week. Previously, sick time and vacation counted toward the
40 hours."

Collective bargaining also facilitated overtime abuse in more subtle
ways. For example, my friend Waukesha County Executive Dan Vrakas
told me that because of collective bargaining, his parks workers had to
be paid between 7:30 a.m. and 3:30 p.m. Monday through Friday. If

they worked after 3:30 p.m. they had to be paid overtime. Well, when do most people use parks? The answer is simple: after school and on weekends. The union had rigged the system for parks workers to get overtime to work when they were most needed.

Collective bargaining not only allowed public workers to abuse overtime—it also permitted some to collect salaries for not working *at all*. In Milwaukee County, under collective bargaining rules that mandated paid time off, fourteen employees received salary and benefits for doing union business. Of the fourteen, three were on full-time release for union business—at a cost of over $170,000 in salary alone for these employees to participate only in union activities such as collective bargaining.

Think about that: Milwaukee County taxpayers were paying workers to help unions negotiate the very collective bargaining agreements that perpetuated these kinds of abuses.

They were paying for the privilege of being fleeced!

Collective bargaining also prevented other commonsense reforms to improve services and save taxpayers money. For example, in Racine County, when the state cut back on the amount it would pay to mow along state highways during the summer months in the past, officials had begun using inmates to cut the grass in medians. The inmates volunteered to do the work at no cost to the taxpayers.[5] The program not only saved money for the county, it also helped the prisoners by giving them skills and work experience they could carry with them once they returned to the community, which would ultimately help reduce recidivism.

Seems like a commonsense solution?

Not to the union bosses. The county employee union filed a grievance declaring it was the right of government workers to cut the grass—even though there was no money available to pay for the work. The union argued that the reduced sentences the inmates received were "compensation" and thus violated collective bargaining rules. A mediator agreed and the program was shut down.

Later, thanks to Act 10, Racine officials were able not only to reinstate the inmate mowing program, they also expanded it to other areas. On the day our reforms finally kicked in, the *Racine Journal Times* reported that "with Governor Scott Walker's collective bargaining changes going into effect today, County Executive Jim Ladwig said inmates will be able to perform more tasks such as landscaping, painting, and shoveling sidewalks in the winter." Ladwig told the paper, "We have a win-win when we use the inmates. It gives them a sense of value they are helping the community." At the same time, he told the paper, the county was able maintain property that would otherwise have been neglected.[6]

None of this would have been possible when the unions still had the power to veto such reforms.

One of the most appalling examples of how collective bargaining defied common sense came when the unions filed a grievance against an eighty-six-year-old retired man in the Wausau school district. His crime? Volunteering as a school crossing guard.[7]

Warren Eschenbach lived just two doors down from Riverview Elementary School, and he enjoyed helping the kids get safely to and from school. Eschenbach told Riverview principal Steve Miller, "This gives me a reason to get up in the morning to come and help these kids in the neighborhood." But the local union that represents crossing guards said he should be banned and replaced by a paid crossing guard hired by the city.

"For a half-an-hour job, do you really need to pay somebody?" Eschenbach asked during an interview with a local TV station.

The answer, according to the union, was yes.

We also found that the Milwaukee Teachers' Education Association (MTEA) had used a policy established by collective bargaining to obtain health insurance coverage that specifically paid for Viagra. Cost to the taxpayers? $786,000 a year. According to ABC News, when the school district cut the Viagra coverage as a cost-saving measure, the teachers' union actually sued to reinstate it.[8]

In the Green Bay School District, we found that 140 teachers and

15 administrators (about 1 in 12 teachers in the district) had joined in the district's "Emeritus Program," under which teachers can retire and then receive a full year's salary for working just ten days a year over a three-year period.[9] That is *in addition* to their already guaranteed pension and health care payouts.

Where did the idea for such a boondoggle come from? According to a WLUK-TV Fox 11 news report, "The emeritus program is something that has been negotiated into the teachers' contract through collective bargaining."

As we found stories like these, we began pointing out the ways that collective bargaining rules stopped managers from scheduling workers based on operational needs without the advance notice and approval by the union. We explained that collective bargaining prevented managers from adjusting work hours to meet budgets, or reducing hours to prevent layoffs. We showed how they prevented managers from exploring privatization of public services to save taxpayers money. They made government expensive, inefficient, and open to abuse.

But perhaps the most compelling example of how collective bargaining hurt schools and students was the story of a Milwaukee high school teacher named Megan Sampson.

In June 2010, Ms. Sampson was named the outstanding first-year teacher by the Wisconsin Council of Teachers of English. A week later, she received another certificate—a layoff notice from the Milwaukee Public Schools system. My predecessor, Governor Doyle, had cut aid to schools without giving them any tools to offset reductions in state aid—which meant they had no choice but to lay off teachers.

But why on earth would they get rid of a great new teacher like Ms. Sampson—especially in Milwaukee, which is one of the most troubled urban school districts in the nation? Well, under the collective bargaining rules, when there were layoffs the last teachers hired were the first to be fired. It didn't matter that she was one of the best new teachers in the state. She did not have seniority, so she was out. Our reforms eliminated these absurd rules. Now schools can choose whom to keep and whom to retain based on merit, not seniority.

But the story got worse. The reason Ms. Sampson and hundreds of other educators received layoff notices in the first place was that, under collective bargaining, the school district was required to offer teachers a "Cadillac" health care plan and cover 100 percent of the costs—and the teachers' union would not allow the district to switch to a lower-cost health insurance plan and save the teachers' jobs. Milwaukee School Board president Michael Bonds told the *Milwaukee Journal Sentinel* that if the district switched plans, they could have saved about $48 million— enough to pay for about 480 educators.

"We could literally save hundreds of jobs with the stroke of a pen if teachers switched to the lower-cost health-care plan," he said, adding "I'm not aware of any place in the nation that pays 100% of teachers' health-care benefits and doesn't require a contribution from those who choose to take a more expensive plan."[10]

For her part, Ms. Sampson said switching plans should be a no-brainer. "Given the opportunity, of course I would switch to a different plan to save my job, or the jobs of ten other teachers," she told the paper.

We wanted to give Ms. Sampson and teachers across Wisconsin that opportunity with Act 10.

Her story underscored a critical point: Reforming collective bargaining was necessary not just to close our deficit and balance our budget; it was also needed to restore fundamental fairness to the system.

It was not fair that corrections officers used collective bargaining agreements to more than double their pay by gaming sick leave rules.

It was not fair that bus drivers used collective bargaining to collect so much overtime that they made more money than the mayor—and far more than the taxpayers they drove around town each day.

It was not fair that collective bargaining agreements prevented Racine County from using inmates to mow the grass at no cost to taxpayers.

And it was certainly not fair that an award-winning young teacher like Ms. Sampson had to be thrown out of the classroom because the unions would not permit the school district to switch to a lower-cost health plan and because collective bargaining rules would not allow school officials to take merit into account when determining whom to lay off.

At the start of the debate, when we argued for bringing public-worker benefits closer in line with people in the productive sector of the economy, we had the fairness argument on our side. Then, when the unions conceded on benefits and made it a fight about collective bargaining "rights," they took the initiative in the fight over fairness. Now, by telling stories like these, we slowly started to reclaim the moral high ground in the fairness debate.

The experience taught me an important lesson: Fairness is one of the strongest arguments we have in politics. Never, ever, cede it to the other side. People won't care about the effectiveness of your policies if they are not first convinced that your policies are also morally right. To win any public policy fight, you have to be able to first win the "fairness" debate.

Going forward, I was determined to do just that—to make not just the economic but also the moral case for our reforms. So I made sure that everyone in Wisconsin got to know Ms. Sampson. I shared her story in speeches, television and radio interviews, and even columns written in national publications.

Later, I would meet Ms. Sampson myself—in circumstances that neither of us could have possibly foreseen.

CHAPTER 13

Enter the Thunderdome

Mr. Speaker, I can't guarantee your safety.

It was Friday, February 18, and with the Democratic senators still on the run, the state assembly was preparing to take up the bill. The crowds inside the capitol had surged to unprecedented proportions and were growing increasingly agitated. Capitol police chief Charles Tubbs came to Speaker Jeff Fitzgerald's office and told him it was no longer safe for the legislators to be in the building. If the protesters decided to rush the assembly floor, he did not have enough manpower to stop them.[1]

Fitzgerald had the votes to pass the bill, but now the police were warning him that there could be a riot if he proceeded with a vote. He had no choice but to suspend debate and recess for the weekend.

That was a big risk. He had seen bills with much stronger support unravel and fall apart. The lawmakers had not been back to their districts since the fight over Act 10 began, and Jeff worried what Republicans were going to hear from their constituents. Were people elsewhere in the state as upset as the folks in Madison? Was it perceived that

Republicans had gone too far? If what the legislators heard back home echoed what they were hearing in the capitol, the debate over Act 10 would be finished.

That weekend, as the legislators fanned out across the state, Representative Robin Vos decided to get some errands done back home.[2] He stopped by Catrine's, a little three-chair barbershop in downtown Racine, to get a haircut. As he sat down for a trim, everyone in the shop was talking about the protests in Madison. The fellow in the chair next to Robin explained how his daughter had just been laid off and had to move back in with them because she couldn't afford to pay her rent. "So when I hear these folks say they don't need to pay towards their pension and health insurance," the man said, "I can't believe how out of touch they are."

The fellow in the other chair told Robin that he was an architect, and had just had his pay reduced by 25 percent with one week's notice. "I'm not complaining," he says, "because I'm just happy to have a job. But when I hear these people telling me they want a guaranteed job and they don't want any reduction in their pay when times are tough, I say [EXPLETIVE] them."

And the first guy says, "You know, you're doing the right thing, Robin, that's why we sent you guys there; you've got to fix this."

It was the same all across the state. As the legislators came back to Madison the next week, they all had similar stories about walking into their local diner and getting a round of applause, or people coming up to them and saying, "Hang in there." Far from weakening his caucus, the involuntary recess had actually strengthened their resolve.

While the legislators were out of town, we used mutual-aid agreements to bring hundreds of additional police officers from counties across the state to Madison. With security at the capitol strengthened, on Tuesday, February 22, the assembly met again to begin debate.

In the morning, I went over to meet with the GOP caucus. That day, I got a taste of what it is like to be a University of Wisconsin running back as the state troopers formed a "flying wedge" to get me through the masses in the capitol. We learned it is impossible to program the antique elevators in the capitol to skip floors, so the elevator doors opened on each floor as we went up to the fourth-floor meeting room. Fortunately, none of the protesters recognized me behind the phalanx of troopers. If they had, a real riot might have started.

When I arrived, the room erupted. It was an emotional meeting. I explained to the members of our caucus that "every one of us who's ever sought public office wonders, in the back of our minds: Will our term in office really make a difference? Will we have a lasting impact for the good of the people of your state? In the totality of our careers, whether we've been here one term or twenty terms, what will our impact be?

"This is one of those moments where you can do something that will fundamentally change the course of history and the State of Wisconsin for the better of the taxpayers," I continued. "For those of you who are new, you're fortunate to be having this opportunity right off the bat. For those of you who have been here for many years, this might be the high point of your legislative accomplishments. . . . But," I said, "we have a chance to do something that will change the course of history in our state." I knew how hard this vote was and the pressures they were all feeling. "If there was ever a moment you could pull deep within your reservoir of courage, this is that time. This is that moment."

There was long, sustained applause. After I left, several legislators got up to speak. A first-term lawmaker from a heavy union town, Representative Joe Knilans, told his colleagues, "I just want to say that taking this vote today will probably cost me my job. But that's why I came to Madison—to take votes like this. I never wanted to be a career politician—it's about doing the right thing."[3]

Then, the longest serving Republican in the assembly, Representative Al Ott, asked everyone to pray. For about fifteen minutes, everyone held hands and asked God to give them guidance and to protect their families. Later, Robin Vos said that after that experience, "there was nothing that the other side could do that would make this group of people not pass the bill."

After the caucus meeting, the Republicans proceeded into the assembly chamber, with the crowds of protesters chanting and stomping their feet outside. It was like entering the Thunderdome. The debate lasted more than sixty-one hours. By the time it ended, the legislators had become virtually incoherent from exhaustion. The Democrats had offered 128 amendments but were demanding time to debate and vote on 40 more. After two and a half days of nonstop debate, Speaker Fitzgerald took the floor and said, "This is the longest in the history of the state assembly that a bill has ever been debated. In the end, you know we're going to have to take this vote." After allowing the debate to go on a few more hours, Republicans finally offered a motion to send the bill to the senate and adjourn. It was Friday at 1:06 a.m. when the assembly finally voted. The bill was approved by a voice vote.

As the vote was called, the assembly Democrats exploded—yelling, screaming, throwing water, cups, and paper at their Republican colleagues. Robin Vos said the fracas on the assembly floor got so bad "it was impossible to tell a protester apart from a legislator." At one point, Democratic representative Gordon Hintz turned to his Republican colleague Representative Michelle Litjens on the assembly floor and said: "You're F———ing dead!"[4] He later apologized for the comment,[5] but it illustrated how heated and uncivil the debate had become.

All the critics who charged that we rammed collective bargaining reform through without notice or debate seem to forget about the time two years earlier when Governor Doyle rammed a budget repair bill that raised taxes by more than a billion dollars through both houses in *twenty-four hours—without a public hearing*. By contrast, Republicans held a record sixty-one hours and fifteen minutes of debate on our bill *in the assembly alone*. (Not to mention a record seventeen-hour committee hearing before that.)

After the vote, I praised the Republican leadership for its action, adding that "assembly Democrats should also be commended for coming to work every day and giving their constituents a voice at the state capitol." Now, I said, "all attention is on the senate. The fourteen senate

Democrats need to come home and do their jobs, just like the assembly Democrats did."

That was not happening anytime soon. With the Democrats hiding out in Illinois, we could not move forward. The senate Republicans were paralyzed because they did not want to split the bill. Meanwhile, the unions had shifted the debate, and public opinion, in their favor. If the senate had just acted, it would have been over and saved us weeks of grief.

Instead, we were stuck.

CHAPTER 14

"1 Walker Beats 14 Runners"

The Saturday after the assembly passed the bill, we saw the largest crowds yet gather at the capitol—an estimated seventy thousand people. Those calling in "sick" from work during the week had been joined by others who had a legitimate day off on Saturday.

Tea Party groups organized a counterprotest that day. I was grateful for their support, but having seen how some of the union protesters accosted Republican legislators and officials, I worried how they might respond to a sizable contingent of conservatives. I spent much of that day praying for the safety of folks on both sides, and asking my staff for regular updates. Thankfully, while there was some yelling back and forth, nothing happened.

The following weekend, I was supposed to attend the National Governors Association meeting at the White House, but with fourteen Democratic senators hiding out in Illinois, I didn't think I should travel to Washington, D.C. So Tonette went in my place, and instead I flew into the legislative districts of some of the more vulnerable

Democratic senators to deliver a message: "These senators need to come home and do their jobs."

We traveled to Kenosha, Green Bay, Rhinelander, La Crosse, Eau Claire, and Superior, and were greeted by hundreds, sometimes thousands, of protesters at every stop.

As the public fight over Act 10 heated up, behind the scenes we had begun discussions with the senate Democrats in an effort to end the impasse and bring them home.

Our intermediary with the fourteen Democrats was Senator Tim Cullen. Cullen had been senate majority leader in the 1980s until he left the senate and crossed the aisle to join Governor Tommy Thompson's cabinet. He was highly regarded by both Republicans and Democrats, and prided himself on the fact that the last time a bipartisan budget had passed the senate was under his leadership. He saw himself as someone who could bring people together and get things done. Cullen had made his fortune in business before returning to public service in 2011. He didn't need the job. He had nothing to prove.

When the Democrats left, Cullen was not in Madison because his dear friend, former Wisconsin supreme court justice Bill Bablitch, had just passed away. Cullen had gone to console the family. I reached him on his cell phone to offer my condolences. He had joined his fellow Democrats in the Land of Lincoln but told me that if he had been there, he thought he could have persuaded them not to leave because it was a stupid idea. He said, "Give me a little time, we'll work this out."

Another Democrat who wanted to return was Senator Bob Jauch. Jauch is no centrist, but he loves the senate and saw the standoff as a taint on the institution. Together, Cullen and Jauch led a quiet effort to bring the Democrats back to Madison.

The problem was that the rest of the Democratic caucus had no interest in coming back. Most of the senators were from liberal enclaves, so their constituents didn't want them to return. Moreover, for many of them this was the biggest thing they had done in their lives. They had become folk heroes on the left—hailed by the protesters and interviewed on

MSNBC almost every night. They kept hearing reports from the unions about how big the capitol protests were growing, and became increasingly convinced that, sooner or later, our side would have no choice but to fold.

What they did not realize was that the protests were having the opposite effect on their Republican colleagues back in Madison. It was next to impossible to get into and out of the capitol. Every day that the senators came to work, they were yelled at and cussed at and spit on and subjected to barbs and invective. The protesters followed them everywhere, picketing their homes and harassing their families. The longer the protests went on, and the nastier they became, the more the Republican senators' patience ran thin and their resolve stiffened. They became less concerned about losing their seats and more concerned about not giving in to organized intimidation. Instead of breaking them apart, the protests brought them closer together. The more the protesters tried to intimidate them, the more the senate Republicans locked arms and decided they would not be bullied.

It quickly became clear to us that the unions were calling the shots, and that their only interest in talking to us was to buy time. One day Keith Gilkes got a phone call from Mick Foti, the former majority leader of the state assembly. Mick told Keith that AFSCME had approached him and wanted to put him on retainer to negotiate with us. Mick said he told the union leaders he didn't think it was likely he could cut a deal.

But the union leaders told Mick they didn't need them to cut a deal; they just wanted him to buy them two more weeks of time.

The episode underscored for us two facts: First, the unions were directing this from the beginning, and were not interested in compromise; and second, they were simply looking to buy time to build pressure on us so that we would cave.

At one point, Senator Cullen got so frustrated he told me that he was coming back to Madison on his own. I urged him to make sure he let us know when he was coming so we could provide security. He was shocked. "Why would I need security?" he asked. Because, I explained, they would tar and feather him if he tried to enter the capitol to be the lone Democrat who gave us the quorum to pass the bill.

He clearly had no idea what was going on back in Madison.

A former adviser to Governor Thompson named Jerry Whitburn, who had served in the governor's cabinet with Cullen, was working behind the scenes to get both sides to the negotiating table. He arranged a phone call between Senate Majority Leader Scott Fitzgerald and Minority Leader Mark Miller that had not gone well. But he did not give up. At his urging, on Sunday, February 27, Fitzgerald called Cullen and they agreed to meet the next day at a McDonald's off the interstate, just inside the Wisconsin border in Kenosha.

On Monday, Fitzgerald went down to Kenosha to meet with Cullen and Jauch to see if a deal was possible. He asked them point-blank if the labor unions were not going to allow them to come back to the state. They insisted that they could come back anytime. He told them he would not amend the bill now that it had passed the assembly, but that he would convey their negotiating positions to us. When Scott returned, he briefed us on their discussions and told us it was up to us to decide whether to continue them.

So on Thursday, March 2, I sent Keith and the deputy chief of staff Eric Schutt to sit down with Cullen and Jauch. They met at the same McDonald's near the border. They were joined this time by Senator Mark Miller, who in the coming week would do everything in his power to undermine our talks.

Eric told them, "We're here to negotiate in good faith. Where are you guys at?" Cullen and Jauch presented a list of proposed changes to the bill. After listening to the four of them go back and forth for some time, Miller finally spoke up.

"You guys have misplayed your hand," Miller said. "The governor is in real trouble. He's got real problems out there. The people of the state have turned against him."

Miller had not come to negotiate. He had come to accept our

surrender. His message was: Anytime you are ready to cry "uncle" we'll just forget the whole thing and come home.

Miller wasn't entirely wrong about our situation. A poll that week from the Wisconsin Policy Research Institute showed that by a margin of 65 to 33 percent, voters wanted us to compromise with Democrats and opposed stripping public employees of collective bargaining "rights" by a margin of 58 to 32.[1]

Miller believed the protests were working and saw the fact that we had come to negotiate as a sign that we were feeling the pressure. In fact, the opposite was true. I knew in the long run that our standing with the people would rise after Act 10 passed and our reforms began to work. I had sent Keith and Eric to Kenosha with instructions not to find a face-saving way out but to try to give *the Democrats* a face-saving way to come home. We were willing to make some changes to the bill, but we would not gut the key provisions.

Over the course of two hours, they talked about a host of issues, but the discussion kept coming back to one topic: the automatic collection of union dues. The unions would have given up anything else in the bill to keep the dues. The involuntary dues were their lifeblood, the source of their power. They knew that if government workers had a free choice, most would decide to keep their dues and the union coffers would run dry. They could not allow that to happen. They could not care less if we were to lay off fifteen hundred workers or fifteen thousand workers, so long as they could keep their precious dues.

Keith and Eric made clear that restoring the dues was a nonstarter. But they made progress on other issues and agreed to keep talking. Keith and Eric were encouraged enough that they drew straws to see who would call and wake me up at 11:45 p.m. to say they thought a deal was possible. Later, Eric sent an e-mail to the senators offering concessions on several issues they had raised. A substantive discussion was underway.

But while we were exchanging e-mails with Cullen and Jauch, Senator Miller had returned to Illinois and held a meeting of his caucus, where he told the other senators that we were not serious. When we learned about it, we considered pulling the plug on the talks. But Cullen and Jauch prevailed on us to keep talking. There's no doubt in my mind that they were sincere in their efforts to bring the Democrats back. And there is no doubt in my mind that Mark Miller did not share their interest in finding a compromise.

Cullen kept saying, "Give me a little more time. I'm close. I won't get them all, but I'll get a few to come back." But every time we got close to a deal, it seemed, Miller would step in like Lucy in the *Peanuts* comic strip and pull out the football.

While Keith and Eric kept the lines of communication open with Cullen and Jauch, on March 2 I went to the funeral of Army 1st Lieutenant Daren Hildago, a West Point graduate from Waukesha who had been killed in Afghanistan. His father was a veteran, and all of his brothers wore the uniform. They were so strong. They told me they were praying for me. I was just amazed that here in their moment of grief, they were talking about praying for me. It was yet another sign that no matter how difficult the coming days would be, they were nothing compared to the sacrifice of our men and women in uniform—and of their families.

That night, former governor Tommy Thompson came to the capitol for a celebration of the one hundredth anniversary of the Joint Committee on Finance. He had been planning to just walk into the capitol building, but we had a former adviser of his escort him through the tunnels instead. When I greeted him up in his old office, he lit up. But I could see he was worried about me. He told me, "You're doing the right thing, but you've got to figure out a way to not let this go on much longer."

As the talks continued behind the scenes, we tried to ratchet up the pressure on the senators to return. While I barnstormed their districts, senate Republicans had begun using the senate rules to make life difficult for the missing Democrats. Senators in Wisconsin routinely participate in committee meetings by phone, and are allowed to offer amendments and vote on measures. This is not a right under the senate rules. It is a courtesy offered in a spirit of comity. When Democrats violated that spirit by fleeing to Illinois, senate Republicans refused to continue extending the courtesy. So the senate took up bills important to the Democrats and refused to let them vote by phone.

The senate also voted to hold the missing senators in contempt. They voted to fine them $100 for every day they missed a session. They voted to change the senate rules so the missing senators could no longer have their paychecks automatically deposited into their bank accounts but would have to come to the senate floor to pick them up. (One Democrat, Jon Erpenbach, got around it by giving his chief of staff power of attorney.) After a while, it was clear none of these tactics were having much of an effect. It became a bit like Wile E. Coyote setting an "Acme Senator Trap."

We knew the standoff with the senate Democrats had become a truly national story that week when late-night talk show host Jimmy Fallon featured it on a segment he called "Slow Jam the News." With the help of his house band, The Roots, and NBC News anchor Brian Williams, Fallon performed a "slow jam" about the Madison protests and the departed senate Democrats.

"Looks like those Democrats left in the middle of the night without even saying goodbye," Fallon crooned. "Now they're creepin' with the lights off and curtains down at a hotel out of town."

I wasn't up late enough to catch Fallon's show that night, but Matt and Alex showed it to me on the computer. They were pretty excited. I think it was the first time it crossed their minds that maybe, just maybe, dad was kind of cool (just kind of).

The lighter mood soon dissipated, however, when police discovered forty-one live .22 caliber rifle shells near doorways around the capitol, leading to a heightened security at all entrances. That same day, a judge had ordered that protesters who had been spending the night in the building after normal operating hours had to leave. As police attempted to enforce the judge's order, the capitol suffered a major breach when two people rushed past law enforcement and opened locked doors, allowing about seven hundred protesters to overrun the police and enter the building. The mood at the capitol was tense.

That evening, as we exited the capitol through the underground tunnel to the Risser Justice Center, we saw that the bags of riot gear that always lined the hallways were open and the floor was covered with small circular sheets of plastic. I asked my security detail what they were. They were covers from the gas mask filters. The Wisconsin State Patrol had been placed on "Ready Status" in their full civil disturbance gear—including gas masks.

I sensed my staff was nervous, so to lighten the mood I pulled out my phone and asked if they had seen the *Daily Caller*'s new list of "top ten ways to tell if you might be a member of a public-sector union." It read (with apologies to David Letterman):

10. You take a week off to protest in Wisconsin and your office runs better.

9. On a snow day when they say "nonessential" people should stay home you know who they mean.

8. You get paid twice as much as a private sector person doing the same job but make up the difference by doing half as much work.

7. It takes longer to fire you than the average killer spends on death row.

6. The worse you do your job, the more your boss avoids you.

5. You think the French are working themselves to death.

4. You know by having a copy of the Holy Koran on your desk your job is 100% safe.

3. You spend more time at protest marches than at church.

2. You have a Democratic congressman's lips permanently attached to your butt.

1. You pay more in union dues than you do for your healthcare insurance.[2]

It did the trick, putting them at ease again.

As the security situation at the capitol worsened, time was running out to close the budget deficit. I had warned that if the senators did not return and let us pass our bill, we would have no choice but to send layoff notices to fifteen hundred state workers. The unions dismissed this as a scare tactic. It wasn't. There were only a few months left in the fiscal year. We faced an immediate $137 million budget deficit (left over from the remaining Doyle budget that ran through June 30). Absent legislation that authorized other cost savings, there was no other way to close it. On Friday, March 4, I announced the layoff notices were going out.

Then, on Saturday, March 5, something happened that changed the course of the debate. For weeks, Senator Fitzgerald had had protesters parked outside his home who screamed at him and his family as his wife tried to go to work and his kids tried to go to school. For the most part, they stayed outside by the gate. At 6:45 a.m. that Saturday morning, a group of protesters came onto his property and began pounding on the door and windows of his rural house.

For Scott, that was the last straw.

That night, I attended a Lincoln Day dinner in Columbia County, where I was greeted by hundreds of protesters chanting and hurling epithets. On the car ride home, I called Scott and told him about it, and he told me about the protesters who had come onto his property that morning.

I said, "You know, Scott, if you just broke apart the bill and passed it, it would all be over."

He told me, "Okay, I'll take it back to the other senators."

He was tired of the abuse and delays and was ready to act.

We agreed to make one last try with Cullen and Jauch. On Sunday morning, March 6, I sent Keith and Eric to South Beloit, just over the Illinois state line, for one more meeting with the two Democrats. If they made progress, we would keep talking. If not, we were pulling the plug.

They met in the dining room of a hotel right next to a Beefaroo. Cullen had figured out that state troopers were not going to haul him back to Madison, so he was actually living at home in Beloit, just inside the Wisconsin border. Ironically, Keith and Eric actually passed his exit in Wisconsin on the way to negotiate with him in Illinois.

After a three-hour meeting with the senators, they called me on the way home and suggested we get together with Scott and Jeff Fitzgerald at the Executive Residence to formulate our best and final offer. Later that day, Eric sent an e-mail to Cullen and Jauch that laid out a number of concessions and proposed changes to the bill:

- We agreed to their request to remove the Consumer Price Index cap on any wage increases in negotiations.
- We agreed to remove the requirement that any wage increases above inflation be approved in referendum.
- We agreed that unions could collectively bargain on certain economic issues beyond base wages, including mandatory overtime, performance bonuses, hazardous duty pay, and classroom size.
- We agreed that unions could collectively bargain on issues relating to workplace safety and physical health.
- We agreed that collective bargaining agreements would be good for two years instead of one.
- We agreed that the unions would have to hold recertification votes every three years instead of every year.
- We agreed to allow the University of Wisconsin Hospital and Clinics Authority to continue collective bargaining.

It was a good faith offer that substantially altered the bill. Cullen and Jauch were encouraged and agreed to take it back to their caucus. We waited to hear back.

Then, on Monday, March 7, Senator Miller sent me a public letter that seemed intended to blow up the discussions.[3] Despite the fact that my aides had met with him just a few days before, and had been meeting with and negotiating with Senators Cullen and Jauch, he accused us of keeping "lines of communication closed." He declared that Democrats would not come back unless we agreed to "modifications that restore collective bargaining rights for Wisconsin workers." He even attached a memorandum signed by the missing Democrats that declared that "Wisconsin is not 'broke,' as you claim."[4]

The missive came from across the border in Illinois, but it might as well have come from another planet. When Scott Fitzgerald saw the letter, he said, "Screw this. I'm not doing this anymore. They're never coming back."

We had kept the details of our talks quiet, but now that Miller had publicly accused us of bad faith we held a press conference to tell the people of Wisconsin about the past week's negotiations. Miller called Keith just before the press conference. Keith told him, "Mark, it's over. You had your chance and you blew it. We're done negotiating."

Standing with Scott and Jeff, I informed voters about the three negotiating sessions, the exchanges of e-mails, and the progress we had made with Cullen and Jauch toward a compromise. I held up Miller's letter and said, "For the last several weeks, both Senator Fitzgerald and my administration have been reaching out to reasonable senators— many of whom are very interested and willing to come back to the state of Wisconsin. And time and time again, the person standing in the way of making that possible is Senator Mark Miller."

Cullen and Jauch would have kept talking, but it was clear that the rest of their caucus wasn't interested in compromise. We kept getting hoodwinked into believing that they could convince at least some of the other Democrats to return.

During the press conference, I had intentionally mentioned the exchange of e-mails, and afterward we encouraged reporters to file an open records request, which we quickly accommodated. The documents showed that we were in fact negotiating and had been willing to compromise.

Now the negotiations were over; it was time to split the bill. Scott called me and said he needed my help selling his caucus. So on Wednesday, March 9, I came over at 11:20 a.m. and explained our plan of action. The meeting was a little testy. Some of the senators were gung ho (Alberta Darling, who would soon face a recall, said, "Governor, we're with you. We're ready to go"), but others were still hesitant. I explained that if they didn't want to do this, then they had only two choices: raise taxes or gut schools.

No one wanted to pick either of those two options.

"You can't live like this forever," I said. "We have to end this. And once we do, every day that goes forward we will be better off because people will see the positive results."

We laid out a carefully planned strategy, a choreographed process where we would announce the hearing, make our case, and explain to voters what we were doing, then a day later take a vote in the conference committee and then take the bill to the floor. I left to do a hangar tour across the state. But after listening to the exchange in that caucus meeting, Scott decided he might not have these votes for very long. He turned to his brother, Jeff, and senate president Mike Ellis, and said, "I think we should do this today." There were a lot of senators who were just scared and wanted to get it done and over with.

Scott asked the chief clerk, Rob Marchant, how much notice was required for a conference committee meeting. Marchant told him there was no requirement other than posting notification on the bulletin board. He asked how long it would take to get the bill ready. Marchant told him a couple of hours. So Scott posted a notice that the committee would meet at 6:00 p.m.

At the appointed hour, the committee met for precisely four

minutes, split the bill, and passed it amid fierce objections from Democrats that the meeting violated the state's open meetings law. The senate then passed it by a vote of 18-1 (Senator Dale Schultz was the only "no" vote), as thousands of protesters flooded the capitol.

When we learned about what they had done, we were incredibly upset with the senate leaders. Their quick push gave opponents the pretext to file lawsuits charging the senate had violated the state's open meetings law—though they were very careful to do everything by the book, and the lawsuits ultimately failed.

But in retrospect, senate leaders were probably smart to get the vote out of the way. If they had waited a day after announcing the committee meeting, it would have given the unions more time to rally people and the protests could have been even worse. As for complaints about the process, the senators had been through three weeks of delay and disruption as Democrats used arcane rules to obstruct the bill. Now Republicans were using those same rules to legitimately overcome that obstruction.

The next morning, when the assembly gathered to take up the revised bill, tactical SWAT teams from the attorney general's office were guarding members of the assembly and my staff. It showed how bad things had gotten that we had to call in tactical units to protect the state legislature. I ordered my staff to stay home. I flew around the state, holding rallies to make the case for our reforms while the assembly passed the bill 53-42.

Representative Cory Mason stood on the assembly floor and compared his Republican colleagues to white supremacists, declaring, "Martin Luther King was assassinated while fighting for the rights you're trying to take away."[5]

On Friday, March 11, I signed Act 10 into law, and the following Saturday the Democratic senators returned to Madison. At a rally outside the capitol, they were greeted like astronauts returning from outer space—which is actually a pretty apt comparison. Senator Fred Risser promised the crowd "the war is not over."[6]

While the unions and protesters hailed the fourteen senators and talked of war, I traveled to northern Wisconsin for a Lincoln Day dinner at the Steak Pit, a supper club in Washburn. We were greeted by thousands of protesters outside. We came around the back, where we saw a sea of cars parked for the protest. I was amazed at how many of them had Minnesota and Illinois license plates.

The crowd outside was large and agitated, but the crowd inside was even bigger and they were fired up. Folks were thrilled to be with us to celebrate the occasion.

I was introduced by Congressman Sean Duffy. He presented me with a gift that neatly summarized our battles—a bumper sticker designed just for the occasion.

It read: "1 Walker Beats 14 Runners."

The fight to pass Act 10 was over. But the battle over Act 10 had just begun.

CHAPTER 15

The Proxy Fight Begins

Supreme court races in Wisconsin are rarely controversial affairs, and it had been pretty much assumed that Justice David Prosser would coast to reelection. In February, before the fight over Act 10 heated up, Prosser won a multicandidate primary with 58 percent of the vote. His closest rival, former assistant attorney general JoAnne Kloppenburg, came in a distant second with just 25 percent. He would face her in the general election in April, but it seemed to everyone that the race would be a nonevent.

Then, between February and April, all hell broke loose in Madison, and suddenly an obscure state supreme court election became a multimillion-dollar battle royale—and the future of our reforms hung in the balance.

The normal practice after the governor signs a law is for the secretary of state to publish it the next day in the *Wisconsin State Journal*. Separately, the nonpartisan Legislative Reference Bureau also publishes the law, thus putting it into effect. But Secretary of State Doug La Follette, a Democrat, technically had ten days to publish it. He withheld publication for the full ten days, and told the Legislative Reference Bureau to do the same, giving Democrats time to seek a judicial restraining order to stop the bill.

On March 16, the Democratic Dane County district attorney—acting on the complaint filed by the assembly Democrats—filed a court challenge to Act 10. His complaint alleged that the law was invalid because the senate had not given forty-eight hours' notice for the conference committee under the state's open meetings law. Dane County circuit court judge Maryann Sumi heard the complaint, and two days later found that the DA was likely to prevail in court. She issued a temporary restraining order blocking La Follette from publishing the law.

We were confident that her order would be overturned. There was supreme court precedent that Judge Sumi had no authority to enjoin publication of the law. Moreover, while she had enjoined the secretary of state from publishing the law in the *Wisconsin State Journal*, her order did not mention the Legislative Reference Bureau.

So Senate Majority Leader Scott Fitzgerald told the Reference Bureau that they had a legal responsibility to go ahead and publish Act 10 within the ten-day period required by law. After examining the statutes, they agreed, and published the law on March 25. Once they did so, Secretary of Administration Mike Huebsch announced that the law was in effect and ordered all state agencies to start collecting higher health insurance premiums and pension contributions. Judge Sumi followed up with another ruling declaring the law "not in effect."

The case would go to the state supreme court, where conservatives had a 4-3 majority. That meant that suddenly the fate of Act 10 hung on the result of the Prosser race. If Prosser lost, it would flip the majority on the court and give Democrats and their union allies the votes to uphold Judge Sumi's order and invalidate the law.

The Democrats and the unions were transparent in their objectives. Having failed to stop our reforms in the legislature, they were determined to undo them by judicial fiat. The American Federation of Teachers sent a letter to its members declaring "a Kloppenburg victory would swing the balance [of the Court] to our side. A vote for Prosser is a vote for Walker."[1] For her part, Kloppenburg hinted broadly that she would vote on the bench to strike down Act 10, declaring that "the events of the last few weeks have put into sharp relief how important the Supreme Court is as a check on overreach in the other branches of government."[2]

The union-backed Greater Wisconsin Committee spent almost $1.36 million[3] to defeat Justice Prosser—an unprecedented amount for a state supreme court election. And seven days out, our internal polls showed Prosser was losing by five to six points.

What was killing Prosser was not opposition to Act 10 but an ad aired by Kloppenburg's allies that had nothing to do with the fight over collective bargaining. They alleged that as a district attorney many years earlier, Prosser had protected a pedophile priest. The ad declared:

> A priest sexually abuses children for thirty years across Wisconsin. A mother tells DA David Prosser her two young sons were sexually assaulted. What does Prosser do? Prosser refuses to prosecute. Doesn't even ask the police to investigate. Instead, Prosser meets with the bishop. To avoid scandal, they send the priest to another community and the assaults continue. Tell David Prosser judges should protect our children, not sex offenders.

It was an explosive allegation, but there was one problem: One of the victims, Troy Merryfield, said the charges in the ad were "offensive, inaccurate, and out of context."

Merryfield was living in Virginia, and when he found out about the ad, he was outraged that the unions were using his story to tear down Prosser. He issued a statement explaining that Prosser had decided not to file charges back in 1979, when the abuses were first discovered, in order to protect him from "the emotional toll that a jury trial would have on my brother and me due to our young age at the time." Merryfield said that later, in 2002, when he and his brother were adults and "more comfortable being able to publicly testify about some very sensitive information," and "were able to remember more detailed information about the abuse that was not made known to the police and prosecutor back in 1979," the priest was tried and convicted. By then, Prosser had left the DA's office, but Merryfield said that he was consulted and had "encouraged the prosecution."[4]

Merryfield asked Kloppenburg to tell her supporters to take down the ad and to "stop portraying this case inaccurately and out of context." Amazingly, she refused. During her debate with Prosser, Kloppenburg refused even to condemn the ad, declaring, "Like it or not, third parties have a First Amendment right to run ads of their own choosing."[5] By refusing to criticize the ad or demand it be taken off the air, she took ownership of it in the eyes of voters.

With days to go before the election, Merryfield cut an ad for Prosser. In it, Merryfield looked into the camera and said:

> In 1978, my brother and I were abused by someone our family trusted. With the help of David Prosser and law enforcement, we brought our abuser to justice. Now, we're being victimized again. This time, Joanne Kloppenburg's allies want to use our pain for their own gain. I asked Joanne Kloppenburg to try and stop these false ads. Joanne Kloppenburg refused. It's just wrong.

After the Merryfield ad, Kloppenburg was finished—though we did not know it at first.

When the results came in on April 6, the *Associated Press* reported that Kloppenburg had received 740,090 votes to 739,886 votes for Prosser—giving her a narrow 204-vote lead. Kloppenburg declared victory. "Wisconsin voters have spoken and I am grateful for, and humbled by, their confidence and trust," she said.[6]

Despite the razor-thin margin, the opponents of Act 10 could not wait to gloat. Senate Minority Leader Mark Miller sent out a boastful e-mail declaring, "Walker's good friend Supreme Court Justice David

Prosser was defeated in his re-election bid—despite leading in initial polls by 30 percent! Clearly the people of Wisconsin are standing up and rejecting Scott Walker's agenda." Moveon.org sent out an e-mail declaring: "We just had a HUGE win!! I'm literally breathless. I'm witnessing history. Incumbent candidates for the Wisconsin Supreme Court generally get re-elected in a landslide. But in the general election yesterday, progressive JoAnne Kloppenburg closed the gap and, with 100% of precincts reporting, has beating [sic] conservative justice David Prosser!" The *Huffington Post* headline read: "Scott Walker Struggles to Downplay Wisconsin Election That His Allies Built Up as a Referendum."[7]

But the next day, April 7, the Waukesha County clerk announced that she had accidentally omitted an estimated 14,000 votes from conservative-leaning Brookfield from the unofficial results she had shared with the press. According to the *Milwaukee Journal Sentinel,* "The new totals give 10,859 more votes to Prosser and 3,456 more to Kloppenburg"—putting Prosser over the top by more than 7,500 votes.[8]

A recount confirmed Prosser's victory, and on May 31, Kloppenburg finally conceded.

The irony is, if Kloppenburg and her union allies had made the race about Act 10, Prosser might very well have lost. Voters still had not seen the results that Act 10 would soon produce. And if Kloppenburg had won, and Act 10 had been invalidated, they might *never* have seen the results. Without the results, I probably would not have survived my recall election a year later.

So while I was not on the ballot that day, my political fate—and the fate of our reforms—certainly were and we won.

In the end, the unions lost because they overreached. Their ugly tactics alienated voters. It was a story that would play itself out over and over again in the months to come.

The first proxy battle over Act 10 was over. Prosser won, and the law survived. With Justice Prosser back on the bench, the supreme court overruled Judge Sumi's decision that Act 10 was invalid under the open meetings law. In a 4-3 ruling, the court found that Judge Sumi had "exceeded [her] jurisdiction, invaded the Legislature's constitutional

powers . . . and erred in enjoining the publication and further implementation of the Act." In his concurring opinion, Justice Prosser declared, "This is not a close question."

Act 10 was formally reinstated.

This was just the first of many legal challenges to Act 10. Having
failed to defeat Justice Prosser and flip the state supreme court, the unions
turned to the federal courts. They filed a lawsuit arguing that Act 10 was
unconstitutional because, among other reasons, our "paycheck protection" provision barring forced collection of union dues violated the First
Amendment and the Equal Protection Clause because they exempted
police and firefighters—creating two classes of public employees.

For unions, this was the core of their opposition. Paycheck protection gave government workers the right to choose whether or not to join
a union and pay union dues. The unions didn't want them to have that
choice. They knew that in Indiana, after Governor Mitch Daniels enacted paycheck protection, only 5 percent of state employees continued
paying union dues[9]—dropping from 16,408 in 2005 to just 1,490 in
2011.[10] Now, they worried, the same could happen in Wisconsin.

They were right. Once the Wisconsin supreme court upheld Act 10,
and the paycheck protection provision went into effect, many public
workers did in fact decide to keep the money, using it to offset their increased pension and health care contributions. Without the ability to
coerce workers into paying involuntary dues, the *Wisconsin State Journal*
reported in August 2011 that "the statewide teachers union issued layoff
notices to 42 employees Monday, about 40 percent of its staff. . . . The
shrinking size of WEAC's office staff could be a bellwether for the future of other public sector unions in the state."[11]

Indeed it was. The following year, in June 2012, the *Wall Street
Journal* reported that "public-employee unions in Wisconsin have experienced a dramatic drop in membership—by more than half for the
second-biggest union—since a law championed by Republican Governor Scott Walker sharply curtailed their ability to bargain over wages
and working conditions." The paper reported that in March 2011, when

we passed our reforms, membership in AFSCME stood 62,818. A year later, membership had fallen by more than half to 28,745.[12] "Much of that decline came from AFSCME Council 24, which represents Wisconsin state workers, whose membership plunged by two-thirds to 7,100 from 22,300 last year," the *Journal* wrote.

The paper also reported similar declines for the Wisconsin chapter of the American Federation of Teachers. "In the nearly 15 months since Mr. Walker signed the law, 6,000 of the AFT's Wisconsin 17,000 members quit, the union said. It blamed the drop on the law," the *Journal* wrote.

It was exactly as Mitch Daniels had predicted.

The fact is, when union membership was no longer compulsory and workers were given a free choice of whether to pay dues, well over half chose to quit the union.

The declines have apparently continued apace.

In July 2013, the *Wisconsin Reporter* found that "AFSCME Council 24's dues-paying membership fell from about 5,900 security and safety employee members pre-Act 10 to 690 in the early months of this year—an 88 percent drop."[13]

The *Washington Examiner* reported in April 2013 that "more than two years after Scott Walker's showdown with organized labor in Wisconsin, the official numbers for the state's public sector union membership are in—and they are down. Way down." Membership for Wisconsin's AFSCME Council 40 dropped precipitously, from 31,730 in 2011 to just 20,488 in 2013. "That's a drop of more than 11,000—about a third—in just two years," the *Examiner* declared.[14] Another union, Wisconsin AFSCME Council 48, saw its membership plummet 61 percent following passage of Act 10.[15] That was the AFSCME local headed by Rich Abelson, the union leader who told me to "go ahead" and lay off hundreds of public workers when I was Milwaukee County executive. According to the *Examiner*, his AFSCME chapter's membership dropped from 9,043 members in 2011 to just 3,498 today. The declines, the paper said, "show why the state worker unions and their liberal allies fought such a protracted, bitter battle in 2011 over Republican Governor Scott Walker's changes to the state's labor laws."

AFSCME Council 48 lost not only most of its members, it lost its official status by failing to win a recertification vote—which meant public officials could no longer recognize the union or negotiate with it. Having lost official recognition and much of his membership, Abelson came up with a new strategy to justify his union's continued existence: He adopted the tactics of ambulance-chasing trial lawyers and filed a series of frivolous lawsuits. After he sued Milwaukee County over pensions, insurance, and other benefits, he then pitched the benefits of his litigation to try to lure back thousands of public workers who had quit his union.

In a desperate letter to former AFSCME Council 48 members, Abelson warned, "All of these lawsuits are filed on behalf of AFSCME members only—nonmembers will not benefit. So, if you are not now a member, become one today and ensure that you are included in any successful lawsuit settlements and that your Union remains a powerful voice to protect your rights and interests."[16]

He might as well have ended the letter by urging his members to call 1-800-LAW-SUIT.

Even Milwaukee County executive Chris Abele—a Democrat who was endorsed by Abelson's union—told the *Milwaukee Journal Sentinel* that Abelson's claim was false. "If the courts ruled against these reforms, the impact would extend beyond union members," Abele said. "Any claim made that only represented employees would receive money or benefits is false."[17]

The episode demonstrated that the unions were out of touch with many of their own members. Given the freedom to choose whether to join the union and pay dues, many decided it wasn't worth it. In other words, the tens of thousands of protesters banging drums and blasting horns at the state capitol, outraged over our reforms, not only did not represent the majority of Wisconsinites—they did not even represent *the majority of Wisconsin union members.*

The unions' lawsuit against the "paycheck protection" provision failed as well. In January 2013, a three-judge panel of the Seventh Circuit Court of Appeals upheld Act 10 and rejected the union's claims. Our decision to exempt police and firefighters out of a concern that a strike would endanger public safety, the court found, protected a legitimate state interest. And the court found that the automatic payroll deductions were not a "right" to which the unions were constitutionally entitled.

As Judge Joel Flaum wrote, "The Bill of Rights enshrines negative liberties. It directs what government may not do to its citizens, rather than what it must do for them." If the unions can't convince public employees to pay their dues, they have no constitutional right to demand that the government compel them to do so.

The unions chose not to appeal the case to the United States Supreme Court. I suspect they knew they would lose, and did not want to have the supreme court affirm Judge Flaum's finding that *collective bargaining is not a constitutional right.*

But they have not ceased waging "lawfare" against Act 10. More lawsuits are winding their way through the courts. But as of this writing—despite the many novel and often frivolous legal roadblocks that have been thrown in its path—Act 10 still stands.

I am confident it will ultimately survive all the legal challenges.

CHAPTER 16

"This Is War!"

Justice Prosser and Act 10 had survived, and now the unions were eager to target me—using an obscure provision in the Wisconsin constitution which allowed for the recall of elected state officials.

The recall amendment had been passed in 1926 as a progressive, good-government measure designed to reduce the influence of special interests in Wisconsin politics by allowing voters to remove corrupt officials from office.[1] Until 2011, it had rarely been used. Only two state officials had been successfully recalled in the eighty-five years since the amendment passed, and no governor had ever faced a recall in Wisconsin history.

Ironically, our opponents were now using a tool intended to reduce the power of special interests to punish us for challenging the power of a special interest—the union bosses.

As much as they wanted to launch a recall against me, the unions could not do so yet because under Wisconsin law you can't recall an elected official until he or she has been in office for a year. They had to wait until November to begin collecting signatures to remove me from office.

So they did the next best thing—and went after members of the state senate who had been in office long enough to face a recall, and who had voted for our reforms.

One of their first targets was Senator Dan Kapanke.

You've probably never heard of Dan, but I wish there were more like him in our nation's capital. When I think of courage, I think of Dan Kapanke.

I didn't know where Dan would come out when we first put forward our plan to reform collective bargaining. He had worked with the unions in the past and had been endorsed by the correctional officers union in his last election. Moreover, President Obama had carried his district with 61 percent of the vote in 2008, so voting for collective bargaining reform could be a politically fatal move for him.

Dan had more than his senate seat at risk. He and his family own the La Crosse Loggers, a semipro summer baseball team that brings together top college players from across the country and gives them a taste of life in the pros. The Loggers have sent players on to almost a dozen major-league teams, including the Milwaukee Brewers.

The Loggers are Dan's family's business and livelihood. He mortgaged his home and everything he owned to start the team, and put his heart and soul into making it a success. When he wasn't in Madison during the summer, Dan was at home running the stadium and even selling popcorn and Cracker Jack in the stands.

Opponents of Act 10 had threatened to boycott businesses that supported us. Dan realized that his vote could affect not just his political career but also his business, his retirement, and his ability to support his family as well.

On the morning of March 5, Dan called a family meeting to talk the decision through. He told them that in his six years in Madison, he had watched our state descend into debt due to fiscal irresponsibility by members of both parties. This, he said, was his chance to finally do something about it. But he also laid out the possible ramifications for all of them. A boycott could put the Loggers out of business. They could lose everything. It was an emotional meeting, and he didn't ask them to take a vote. He just asked them to pray.

Driving into Madison that day, Dan made his decision about thirty miles out. He was going to support our bill. I had gotten word from Majority Leader Scott Fitzgerald about Dan's family meeting that morning, and had asked to see him when he got to the capitol. I was ready to talk him through what I knew was an enormously difficult decision. But when he came into my office, before I could even say a word, he gave me a big bear hug.

"I'm with you, Guv," Dan said. "I'm with you all the way."

I was blown away. The price Dan was willing to pay, personally and politically, to help rescue his state was enormous. I reached for my daily devotional, and we turned to a reading called "The Heart of Leadership." It recounted the Gospel passage where Jesus washes his disciples' feet, and then it read:

> You can just as easily detect whether a leader has a servant's heart. The truth is the best leaders desire to serve others, not themselves. . . . In the end, the extent of your influence depends on the depth of your concern for others.[2]

We prayed together over those words.

Dan Kapanke has a servant's heart. He put his concern for others, and his concern for his state, over his own interests. Without him, Act 10 would never have become law.

Once Dan made his decision to support us, he never wavered, no matter what the other side threw at him. And they threw a lot his way. Dan's wife, Ruth, is a nurse who often comes home late after a long shift in the hospital. One night she pulled up to their home and found that someone had carefully placed roofing nails, pointy-side up, all over the driveway. It happened to them both several times.

Dan was harassed almost daily at the capitol by the protesters. And his was the first name listed on a death threat sent to GOP senators that warned:

> Please put your things in order because you will be killed and your familes [sic] . . . due to your actions in the last 8 weeks . . . I hope you have a good time in hell. Read below for more information on possible scenarios in which you will die. . . . We have all planned to assult [sic] you by arriving at your house and putting a nice little bullet in your head. . . . We Will 'get rid of' (in which I mean kill) you."[3]

Dan was unintimidated—and when the moment came, he voted for our reforms.

Dan stood with me. Now, as the senate recall elections geared up, it was my turn to stand with him.

The truth is, Dan had no chance of winning. Even before the vote on Act 10, his poll numbers were upside down. His district was becoming increasingly liberal, and he had been badly damaged when he ran unsuccessfully for Congress in 2010 against U.S. Representative Ron Kind, who decimated him with negative ads. Still, I believe if Dan's race had come a year later, after the results of Act 10 were in, he might have survived. But as it was, he had to run before the people of his district had a chance to see the positive results.

At one point, as I was preparing to do an event for Dan, one of my advisers asked me why I was spending time and energy on Dan's race, when there were other tough fights where I could make a difference. My answer was simple: because Dan had done something courageous. I owed it to him as a matter of personal loyalty. And I wanted others to know that when they stuck their necks out on tough votes, they could count on me to be in the trenches fighting beside them.

We raised an impressive $12.5 million to fight the senate recalls, but the unions poured in an unprecedented $25 million—outspending us two to one. The unions took over an entire floor of the Madison Concourse Hotel to run their campaigns. When we put up our first ad buy in Dan's district, they came back with a buy double our size.

The message was unmistakable: Don't even think about it. This one is ours.

As expected, Dan lost his seat in the recall. Yet to this day, he has no regrets. "I was doing my job," he said after it was all over. "People elected me to make tough decisions."[4]

Protesters did show up at his ballpark, and some season ticket holders did cancel their subscriptions. But his team has not only survived, it has also thrived. In 2012, the La Crosse Loggers won their first Northwoods League championship. And today, Dan Kapanke walks with his head held high. He is the epitome of a leader who cares more about the next generation than the next election. We need more leaders like him.

Dan's race was not the only one where we were in trouble. We also were certain to lose Senator Randy Hopper's seat—which he had barely won in 2010. Randy's troubles also had little to do with Act 10. He had a very public split with his wife because of his relationship with a twenty-five-year-old former capitol staffer, which did not go over well in his conservative, Christian district.

So from the very beginning, we started the senate recall elections down by two seats. With those two races out of reach, the Democrats needed to pick up only one more seat to take control of the senate. In other words, we had to sweep all four of the remaining races—Sheila Harsdorf, Rob Cowles, Luther Olsen, and Alberta Darling—to keep our majority.

Sheila Harsdorf looked like she was in trouble when she drew a schoolteacher named Shelly Moore as her opponent. Moore was an unknown, and portrayed herself as a uniter who would bring Wisconsin together. "We can solve any problem if we sit down and talk to each other," she declared. She came across as soothing and appealing—until we found video of her screaming and pumping her fist at union rallies. "We are WEAC and they WILL respect us!" she yelled in one clip. "This is war!" she declared in another.[5] Those were immediately turned into campaign ads. Her own words undermined the premise of her campaign. In the end, Harsdorf trounced her 58-42.

We shored up Rob Cowles early. A columnist tried to insinuate that I had threatened him to vote for the reform bill (a charge denied by both of us). But instead of focusing on Act 10, the unions ran ads accusing him of corruption—voting to sell Wisconsin power plants to political donors through no-bid contracts. The charge got a "pants on fire" rating from independent fact checkers, who called the accusation "ridiculous."[6] Cowles easily defeated his opponent, Nancy Nusbaum, 57-42.

Initially, Luther Olsen was trailing in his race, but he was aided by the fact that his opponent, Representative Fred Clark, had a penchant for reckless driving. Clark had received six speeding tickets, been caught driving with a suspended license,[7] and had been ticketed twice in one week for rear-ending other drivers.[8] Then, in 2009 Clark ran a red light and broadsided a bicyclist with his SUV, sending the rider flying through the air.[9] Unfortunately for him, the event was caught on video by a street camera and replayed across the district.

To make matters worse, during the fight over Act 10, Clark took a call from a female constituent who was angry with his vote against our reforms. After he thought she had hung up, he said to an aide, "I feel like calling her back and smacking her around."[10] He did not realize she was still on the line . . . and recording the call. That became the centerpiece of a campaign ad.

In the final weeks, the Democrats ran ads linking Luther to me— declaring "Scott Walker's cuts have gone too far and Luther Olsen supported him every step of the way."[11] We could not have run better ads if we had paid for them ourselves. The conservative base had been lukewarm on Luther because they saw him as lukewarm on Act 10. By linking him to me, the Democrats energized our base behind him and helped put Luther over the top. He ended up winning by four points, 52-48.

That left Alberta Darling's District 10 race as the one that would decide control of the senate. Democratic Party of Wisconsin chairman

Mike Tate had called the race the "crown jewel of our recall efforts."[12] Three years earlier, when President Obama carried her district, she had won on the same ballot by a narrow thousand-vote margin. The Democrats and their union allies believed she was vulnerable and spent more than $8 million (more than a typical congressional race in Wisconsin) to oust her. They ran negative ads accusing her of gutting education and voting to keep fired cops accused of crimes on the payroll. We ran positive ads with teachers talking about how she had stood up for them. Early returns showed a close race, but in the end she defeated her challenger Sandy Pasch by a comfortable 54-46 margin.

The night of the senate recalls, Tonette was in northern Wisconsin with one of her best friends, Candee Arndt, staying at a lodge in a remote area. She wanted to see the recall results, but the only channel that she could get up there with news of the recalls was MSNBC. So she ended up watching Ed Schultz, who had come to Madison to broadcast the Democrats' victory live. At first, when it looked like the Democrats were prevailing, Schultz looked triumphant. But Tonette said she got a kick out of watching as the night went on and it became clear that Republicans were prevailing. She said Schultz grew more despondent. When Alberta Darling was declared the winner, he nearly lost his mind.

The unions had now failed to flip the supreme court, failed to flip the state senate, and they had secured not one victory at the polls on the merits of their arguments against collective bargaining reform. But the biggest fight was still to come.

Now they were coming after me.

CHAPTER 17

You're Welcome, Madison!

I was confident that we would win the recall election, but truth be told
I was extremely vulnerable. Our internal polls showed that 54 percent
of voters viewed me unfavorably, and that my likely opponent, Milwaukee mayor Tom Barrett, would defeat me decisively in a head-to-head
matchup.

But then, suddenly, my political fortunes changed. I can tell you
precisely the moment it happened:

The first day of school.

During the August senate recalls, the unions had run ads charging
that I had "cut $800 million from the state's schools."[1] But as kids in
Wisconsin prepared for the start of a new school year, stories started
appearing in newspapers across the state reporting that, thanks to our
reforms, dozens of school districts were able to balance their budgets for
the first time—and do so *without* laying off teachers. Indeed, many were
able to hire *more* teachers, reduce class sizes, and make long-delayed
improvements.

News report after news report showed school districts saving millions thanks to our decision to break the union's near monopoly over the provision of health insurance to local school districts.

Thanks to Act 10, health insurance was no longer subject to collective bargaining. For the first time, school districts could shop for health insurance on the open market. Suddenly, instead of being stuck with the WEA Trust, many districts had three or four insurers competing for their business. Some switched carriers and got deep discounts. Others stayed with the WEA Trust but saw the union insurer drastically drop its prices because it finally had to compete for their business.

This one reform saved school districts tens of millions of dollars— money they were able to put into classrooms instead of union coffers.

One of the best examples of how this worked was in the Port Washington–Saukville school district. The *Ozaukee Press* reported that the "WEA Trust, the longtime provider of insurance to the district, initially told school officials to expect an *8 percent increase* in premiums this year. But when the company was informed the district was shopping for insurance it revised its proposal to show a 3.3 percent decrease in the premium."[2]

In other words, the union insurer had been preparing to bilk the school district. But once our reforms gave Port Washington other options, suddenly the WEA Trust was ready to offer the exact same health plan at a steep discount.

But the story gets even better. Two other insurers submitted bids offering *7 percent* decreases in health care premiums without plan changes. In other words, because we broke the union's monopoly over health insurance, the Port Washington-Saukville school district went from facing an 8 percent *increase* in health insurance costs to enjoying a 7 percent *decrease*—saving a cool $1 million.

Sara Hames, an employee benefits adviser hired by the Port Washington-Saukville district to handle the competing bids, said the "decrease was due to competition alone with no changes to the plan." According to the *Ozaukee Press*, thanks to our reforms, the school district was able to erase "a $1.9 million deficit without compromising educational programs or raising taxes."[3]

Similar stories started appearing in newspapers in other school districts across the state.

For example, the *Appleton Post-Crescent* reported that "the [Appleton] school district bid out its health insurance for the first time in six years, as part of contract extensions with its employee unions. The result? It's getting the same coverage it had been, from the same insurance carrier it had been, for $3.1 million less." The district kept the WEA Trust as its insurer. But with other insurers bidding for Appleton's business, the WEA Trust had to cut its prices dramatically.

The Appleton school district was also able to "recover more than $7 million by having its employees pay their share toward their pensions, plus an increased share of their health care premiums,"[4] the *Post Crescent* reported. Our combined reforms resulted in a total of more than $10 million in savings. One school board official told the paper, "[W]e've pretty much made up most of the [reduced state aid] through the tools, if you will, that Governor Walker is giving us."[5]

In the Muskego-Norway school district, superintendent Joe Schroeder told the Associated Press that, after twenty-eight years with the WEA Trust, "the district discovered it could now cut its $8.5 million bill for health insurance by about $2 million by switching to United Healthcare." He added, "For whatever reason there's a much more competitive environment now."[6]

The reason is Act 10.

The same thing happened in Hudson, Oshkosh, Germantown, Superior, Hartford, Brown Deer, Milwaukee County, and dozens of other school districts across the state.

In all, according to the Wisconsin Taxpayers Alliance, the overall cost of employee health insurance for K–12 schools decreased by about $91 million, or 24 percent, in the 2011–2012 school year, the first school year under Act 10.[7] That figure is the result of insurance changes *alone*.

In addition to savings from insurance changes, school districts were also able to save millions more by requiring employees to increase their contributions to health care premiums and contribute to their retirement plans—just like private sector workers.

In Fond du Lac, "School Board President Eric Everson recently announced an expected balanced budget due to Governor Scott Walker's initiatives," according to the *Fond du Lac Reporter*. "Our balanced budget is definitely because of [Act 10]."[8]

In Green Bay, assistant superintendent for finance and business Alan Wagner told the *Green Bay Press-Gazette* that the district saved about $12 million by using Act 10, adding, "There have been no reductions in programs."[9]

And most satisfying of all, in Madison—the epicenter of the protests against Act 10—the *Wisconsin State Journal* reported that thanks to our reforms the school district had "avoided teacher layoffs, launched a four-year-old kindergarten program, opened a new middle school and gave teachers raises." Not only that, the *Journal* noted that "thanks to Walker's budget, homeowners are finally getting some property tax relief."[10]

You're welcome, Madison.

I saw the effects of Act 10 up close in my sons' school district of Wauwatosa. There, school board officials were facing a $6.5 million shortfall and had planned to eliminate one hundred jobs. But they used the tools in Act 10 to save them all.[11]

I recall going to parents' day with my oldest son, Matt, and visiting one of his classrooms. Matt had a very nice teacher who got up and explained to all the parents what was going on in his class. He shared some good news with us: In previous years, the school had been forced to limit the number of classes it offered and they were packed with kids. But this year, he said, they were able to offer more classes, and they would not have as many kids in each class because they were able to add another teacher. Parents across Wisconsin were hearing the same thing when they visited their children's schools.

Oh, and remember that Milwaukee teacher, Megan Sampson, whom I told you about earlier—the one who had been named one of the best new teachers of the year in Wisconsin, only to receive a layoff notice soon after from the Milwaukee school district under the "last hired, first fired" rule? Well, as Paul Harvey would say, now you know the rest of the story: The *Milwaukee Journal Sentinel* reported that the Milwaukee school district attempted to rehire her, but she turned them down. She had already found a new job . . . in my sons' school in Wauwatosa.[12]

Last semester, Ms. Sampson taught my son Alex. He told me that she was indeed an awesome teacher. I sat down with her for a parent-teacher conference, and could not agree more. It was the first time I had ever met her.

Act 10 never came up.

The opponents of Act 10 had warned that the law would mean fewer teachers, larger class sizes, devastating program cuts, and worse. The opposite was true. According to a survey by the Wisconsin Association of School District Administrators, new teacher hires across the state outnumbered layoffs and nonrenewals by 1,213 positions in the year following enactment of Act 10. They found little change in course offerings, sports programs, or the ratios of students to teachers, librarians, and counselors.

While most school districts benefitted from Act 10, in the interest of full disclosure, there were some prominent exceptions to the rule. Three of the largest school districts in the state—Milwaukee, Kenosha, and Janesville—were forced to lay off more than eight hundred teachers.[13] Despite having 12.8 percent of Wisconsin students, those three districts together accounted for a whopping 68 percent of all teacher layoffs for the entire state.

They had something else in common as well: During the debate over collective bargaining, all three districts had rushed to lock themselves into long-term union contracts—and thus were unable to take advantage of the tools we made available in Act 10.

The Education Action Network did an analysis of the Milwaukee teachers' contract and found that the school district could have saved as much as $61 million if they had been able to take advantage of the tools in Act 10.[14] Instead, Milwaukee schools were forced to lay off more than 500 employees, including 345 teachers. Many of those layoffs could have been avoided if the school board had not locked itself into a contract and had allowed us to free them from the grip of collective bargaining.

If you want a picture of the state of education in Wisconsin without Act 10, look no further than the Milwaukee, Kenosha, and Janesville school districts.

The effects of Act 10 were delayed for these districts, but eventually even they began to benefit. For example, on June 30, 2013, the teachers contract that Milwaukee Public Schools (MPS) rushed into before passage of Act 10 finally expired. Result? The *Milwaukee Journal Sentinel* reported that, according to an analysis by the Thomas B. Fordham Institute, "the Walker administration's landmark union bargaining law helped MPS shave more than $1 billion from its long-term benefit obligations to retirees."[15]

It was not just the school districts that benefitted from the changes in Act 10. Suddenly, newspapers were reporting that local governments were using Act 10 to improve services and put their towns and cities on a firmer financial footing.

In Marathon County, county administrator Brad Karger told the *Wausau Daily Herald* that our reforms allowed the county "to close a $1.1 million budget deficit without increasing property taxes, laying off employees, or significantly reducing services." In Portage, County Supervisor John Tramburg told the *Portage Daily Register* that changing health care coverage for employees was saving the county more than $1.7 million.[16] In Marquette County, our reforms allowed officials to balance their budget without having to cut personnel or programs. In Juneau County, board chairman Al Peterson told the *Juneau County Star-Times* that "with Governor Walker's budget bill, we didn't have to lay off anybody, which would have had to happen without it."[17]

The tools in Act 10 did not just save money—they also helped make local government more efficient and allowed officials to deliver improved services at a lower cost. In Jefferson County, for example, administrator Gary Petre told the *Wisconsin State Journal* that thanks to our bill, "he no longer uses seniority to dictate who fills openings," giving him "the ability to hire the very best workers."[18]

But perhaps the best evidence that the tools worked is this: My opponent in both the 2010 election and the 2012 recall, Milwaukee mayor Tom Barrett, used our reforms to save his city millions of dollars.

Barrett had warned that Act 10 would make Milwaukee's "structural deficit explode."[19] But six months after I signed the Act 10 into law, the *Milwaukee Journal Sentinel* reported that "despite early criticism from city officials, new figures show Milwaukee will gain more than it will lose next year from the state's controversial budget and budget repair legislation. The city projects it will save at least $25 million a year—and potentially as much as $36 million in 2012—from health care benefit changes it didn't have to negotiate with the unions, as a result of provisions in the . . . budget repair measure that ended most collective bargaining for most public employees."

The paper reported that the city would come out with a net gain of at least $11 million for its 2012 budget, "reducing the spending cuts that Mayor Tom Barrett and the Common Council must impose."[20]

Somehow he failed to mention this during the recall campaign.

Far from devastating public schools and local governments, our reforms were providing new ways to direct money to students in the classrooms, and improve public services, without asking for more money from taxpayers.

As they read stories like these, people began to think: Maybe there might be something to this collective bargaining reform after all.

CHAPTER 18

Ending the "Lemon Dance"

It was now clear to the people of Wisconsin that the dire predictions that Act 10 would decimate education had not come true. But failing to decimate education is not, on its own, a compelling case for reelection. To win the recall, I had to do more than prove that our reforms had helped balance budgets without hurting schools—I had to show our reforms had in fact allowed school districts to offer students a *better education.*

That is precisely what they did.

Around the time I was elected governor in the fall of 2010, a remarkable documentary hit theaters called *Waiting for Superman.* The film, by liberal director Davis Guggenheim (the man behind Al Gore's global warming documentary, *An Inconvenient Truth*), was a searing indictment of our nation's failing public schools—including those in Milwaukee.

Waiting for Superman told the stories of parents who were desperately trying to get their kids into high-performing charter schools. To make it in, they had to win a lottery, with dozens of families competing for each spot. The children's fates were left, literally, to random chance. Some got in, others did not. It was heartbreaking to watch the ones who didn't make it.

In Wisconsin, we came up with a solution to the problems outlined in *Waiting for Superman*: We gave every public school in Wisconsin the same freedom to innovate and function like a high-performing charter school.

For years, officials in traditional public schools had complained that if they were just given the same kind of flexibility as charter schools, they could deliver the same quality education in a traditional school setting. Well, in Wisconsin we gave it to them.

Collective bargaining agreements had tied the hands of school administrators—restricting their decisions on everything from the length of the school year to the length of the school day. Union contracts determined everything from whether teachers could be assigned to lunch duty, to how many field trips could be taken in a given year, to how teachers were assigned and transferred, how promotions were decided, how raises were determined, how professional development dollars were spent, how changes to the curriculum were to be made, and how many faculty meetings could be held with a principal—and even how long those meetings could be.

In Milwaukee, the first agreement between teachers and the school district in 1965 was just 18 pages long.[1] By 2007–2009, it had grown into a 246-page monstrosity. To put this in context, the teacher contract at Messmer Preparatory School, a Catholic school in Milwaukee, is just 3 pages long, plus a fourth page explaining teachers' compensation and the benefits package.[2, 3] By contrast, the Milwaukee teacher contract has 75 pages covering salaries and benefits and another 64 pages covering teaching conditions, teacher assignments and reassignments, and grievance procedures.

For example, the teacher contract in Milwaukee limited faculty meetings to just two hours per month (down from two and a half hours), and stipulated that "the administration shall notify the teachers . . . at least one calendar week prior to the inservice or faculty meeting date if it is to last longer than one hour." As for teacher supervision, MTEA once advised its members that while a school principal "may occasionally check the lesson plans of all teachers," he or she "cannot require a faculty to submit lesson plans weekly nor on any other periodic basis."[4]

In other words, public school principals and administrators had no power to run their schools. All power was in the hands of the union stewards.

Worst of all, collective bargaining made it nearly impossible to fire bad teachers.

Why? Because the teachers had "tenure," which effectively guaranteed them jobs for life, regardless of poor performance. Under collective bargaining, teachers got tenure after just a few years on the job—and once they got tenure it was almost impossible to get rid of them, no matter how bad they were.

In *Waiting for Superman*, former Milwaukee schools superintendent Dr. Howard Fuller recounts how, when he would visit schools, good teachers would come up to him and quietly pass him notes saying things like, "go to Room 222." They wanted him to see where the worst teachers were. But before he walked into the classroom, the principal showing him around would pull him aside and say, "OK, Howard, I want to tell you, this is one of my, what they call, Two-80-Ts." That, Fuller explains, "is a provision in the contract that provided what we call the 'dance of the lemons.'"

"Lemons" are chronically bad teachers. Every school had them, but thanks to tenure rules, principals could not get rid of them. So at the end of the school year, the "lemon dance" occurs as many of the failing teachers transfer out of their schools and use seniority to claim a slot at another school.

With the passage of Act 10, we ended the "lemon dance" in Wisconsin. We limited collective bargaining to wages only, and got rid of seniority and teacher tenure. Now, Wisconsin principals no longer have to subject students to the "Two-80-Ts" or transfer them to other schools. Today, they can get rid of them.

We gave principals and superintendents in traditional schools the freedom to make decisions about hiring and firing, and without consulting the union stewards. With the passage of Act 10, we empowered principals to hire based on merit, pay based on performance, and spend professional development dollars on teachers who deserve it rather than on the basis of seniority.

Today, school officials in Wisconsin can assign teachers as they see fit, extend school days, lengthen the school year, make the curriculum more rigorous, change classrooms and scheduling, supervise the development and implementation of lesson plans, and hold as many faculty meetings as they want—all without consulting the teachers' union.

No more "last in, first out" rules like the one that forced the Milwaukee school district to lay off a great new teacher like Megan Sampson. No more tenure rules that protect chronically negligent teachers like the ones Howard Fuller tried to fire.

A school superintendent in northern Wisconsin I spoke with explained that Act 10 had allowed him to save money, hire more teachers, reduce class sizes, and improve performance. "But the best part," he told me, "is I get to go back to my office and work on the curriculum instead of worrying about union grievances."

Our reforms made Wisconsin's public schools better places to learn. That is important to me not just as a governor but as a father. Both my sons, Matt and Alex, attended traditional public schools—as do my nieces today. So for me, Act 10 was not simply about saving money; it was also about improving education for my kids, my nieces, and all of the other children across Wisconsin.

I am a strong supporter of expanding options at charter schools and choice schools—and we have done both. But even with those changes, between 80 and 85 percent of students in our state will still be educated in the traditional public schools for the foreseeable future. The reforms in Act 10 gave us a chance to make those traditional public schools better.

For some, it's difficult to change. As the American Enterprise

Institute's Rick Hess points out, "It's really hard for Pan Am or TWA to just turn into JetBlue. The way that usually works is that old, established ventures fail and the baton gets passed to somebody who gets to start on a fresh sheet of paper." That's why charter schools are still important. They give innovators a chance to start the educational equivalents of Jet-Blue. But today, every Wisconsin school has the freedom to function like a high-performing charter, if it wants to do so. Ultimately, it's up to principals and school officials to use the flexibility we gave them, but it is available now thanks to Act 10.

It's amazing how some portrayed our reforms as attacks on teachers and public education, when all we did was give school districts the flexibility they had been requesting for years. Our reforms were not antiunion; they were pro-student, pro-teacher, and pro-education. Our goal was to put the kids ahead of the bureaucracy, and to put resources into the classroom instead of the union coffers. That is precisely what we did.

I am proud that we were able to take a $3.6 billion deficit and turn it into a surplus. Balancing a budget is great, and improving the economy is awesome. But in the long term, the most important thing we did with Act 10 is improve education. That will have an impact not only on my kids but also on kids all across Wisconsin for generations to come.

During the recall election, my opponent, Mayor Tom Barrett, was asked by *Weekly Standard* reporters Stephen Hayes and John McCormack if he could name a single school hurt by our reforms. "After two attempts to dodge the question, he finally gave up. 'We can do an analysis and get back to you on that,' Barrett told the *Weekly Standard*."[5]

He never did.

On the day that I signed Act 10 into law, many had predicted it would be my political undoing. If anything, the opposite was true. If I had balanced the budget by simply cutting aid to schools and local governments by nearly $1 billion without reforming collective bargaining—*that* would have led to my political demise. We would have decimated education, law enforcement, fire protection, sanitation, and services for the poor. We needed to reform collective bargaining not simply to balance budgets but also to empower local government to better serve the people.

From the beginning, I knew that we would be all right once the reforms were implemented and started to work. There would be a lag between the time when Act 10 went into effect and the moment it became clear that our reforms were working. But given the time to work, I had been confident that the people of our state would see that we had done the right thing.

Now, my faith in our reforms had been validated. Every morning, citizens across our state were picking up their newspapers and reading stories like these about how our reforms had saved jobs, strengthened education, and improved services.

Our reforms were working. And people could feel it.

CHAPTER 19

"Does Anyone Remember
What This Recall Was All About?"

In late November, as the unions began gathering signatures for my recall, I was raking leaves one Sunday with one of my son's friends, Gavin, in front of my home in Wauwatosa, which is on a busy street. A car came by and honked the horn. I looked up and as the window rolled down the driver proceeded to flip me off.

Gavin turned around and asked how I put up with stuff like that. I said that it was good to ignore these things, to stay positive, and if you did, then good things would eventually happen. I went back to raking leaves.

A few minutes later, I heard more honking, this time from *two* cars.

"Lord," I thought, "maybe I should have waited until dark to rake."

I turned to look. Sure enough, two drivers had their windows down, arms out. But this time, both of them gave me a thumbs up.

Gavin yelled over, "Mr. Walker, did you know that was going to happen?!"

No, I had not, but God had heard my prayer. It was one of many signs that cheered me up and gave me comfort.

I could feel things were turning around. Yet despite the good news, our polls were still in the basement. But I was confident we could win back the people of our state because I had seen it done before—here and in other places.

Back in 1991, when Governor John Engler took office in Michigan and began working to tackle a billion-dollar deficit and controversial welfare reform legislation, his approval rating dropped to 18 percent.[1] By 1994, Engler was reelected to his second term by an overwhelming 61-38 margin—and again in 1998 by an almost identical 62-38 margin.

It was a similar story in Indiana. A March 2006 *Indianapolis Star* poll found that "Governor Mitch Daniels' approval rating has dropped to 37 percent as many Indiana residents object to the pace of change in state government during his first 14 months in office."[2] By 2008, he was easily reelected to second term by a margin of nearly 58 to 40—receiving more votes than anyone who had ever run for office in the history of Indiana.

The reason both Engler and Daniels won is simple: Their reforms worked. I knew our reforms would work as well. That is why, when my approval rating dropped to 37 percent, I was not the least bit worried. I knew that every day, every week, every month that went by, things would get better. The reforms just needed time.

Of course, Engler and Daniels both had one advantage we did not enjoy—a full four years to implement changes before they had to face the voters again. That was plenty of time to demonstrate that their reforms had been effective. I did not have the luxury of four years to prove my case. I had to face a recall election just seventeen months after my inauguration. Engler and Daniels were reelected to second terms. I had to get elected again just to finish my *first* term.

I was fortunate that Wisconsin law required that an official had to be in office for at least one full year before a recall. That gave us at least some breathing room. If the law had allowed me to be recalled in 2011 instead of 2012, I would almost certainly have lost.

In Ohio, Governor John Kasich was not so lucky. He had also passed collective bargaining reform legislation that outlawed strikes for public employees, banned arbitration, implemented merit pay for teachers, and gave cities and school boards greater flexibility. Thousands of union activists stormed the Ohio state capitol to protest the changes about the same time as the protests in Wisconsin.

One big difference between our bill and the bill in Ohio was that we exempted firefighters and police officers from our collective bargaining reforms. Kasich had not. This allowed the unions to cast Kasich as an enemy of public safety. As Robert Costa reported in *National Review*, "In one commercial, an elderly woman whose daughter was saved from a burning house warns—after a montage of flames—that 'fewer firefighters could mean the difference between life and death.'"[3]

After Ohio, it looked like genius on our part to exempt police and firefighters. I wish I could take credit for having that kind of foresight, but the truth is our decision was not political—it was policy driven. We had contingency plans in place to have the National Guard take over state prisons if corrections workers went on strike, but if police and firefighters walked off the job, the risk to our citizens would have been unacceptable.

Another advantage we had over Ohio was time. Kasich never got a chance to implement his reforms. Under Ohio law, Kasich's opponents simply needed to gather 230,000 signatures to trigger a referendum on his law. By July 2011, they had gathered 1.3 million. That meant his reform law was immediately suspended and put on the ballot in November, where it was repealed before the changes could take effect. Ohio voters never got an opportunity to see whether or not the reforms had worked as Kasich promised (which is too bad, because I believe that they would have worked there too).

In Wisconsin, by contrast, voters would not cast their ballots until after they saw that our reforms were working. And now they were finally seeing stories appear about how our reforms had saved schools and local governments millions of dollars. They were hearing school superintendents, principals, and mayors explain how Act 10 had allowed them to save money, improve services, and avoid layoffs. They were hearing their kids come home and tell them that school was the same or better than it was before.

The *Milwaukee Journal Sentinel* summed up the mood in an editorial on August 9, 2011:

> So it turns out that the sky isn't going to fall on all local governments in Wisconsin. The numbers now starting to come in show that Governor Scott Walker's "tools" for local governments apparently will help at least some of them deal with cuts in state aid imposed by the state budget. That's contrary to the expectation and the rhetoric of critics in the spring, and it's to Walker's credit. It bears out the governor's assessment of his budget-repair bill.[4]

In November, after the results started coming in, our campaign began running ads with stories from real people testifying to how our reforms were working.

In one ad, a high school teacher in the Kenosha School District named Kristi LaCroix looked into the camera and declared:

> I'm not big on recalls and I think that at this point, in my opinion, and I'm only speaking from the "I," it feels a little like sour grapes. It's, you know, "we didn't get our way and so we want to change the outcome." The person I'm going to stand behind and that is going to get my vote is the man or woman who says what they mean and mean what they say and it's not about being popular, you know, it's not about getting the votes—it's "this is what's right." Scott Walker said from the beginning, "I'm going to do what's right for Wisconsin" and he did. He did.[5]

I was grateful for her words, and her ad was *very* powerful. She came across not only as a teacher, but as someone you could trust, someone who could easily be your friend.

The union reaction, however, was not so friendly. The reprisals began almost immediately. Activists formed a "Fire Kristi" page on Facebook where people posted vicious messages. Teachers in her own school called her a "Judas" and a "scab"—engaging in the very kind of name-calling that would be punished with a visit to the principal's office if one of their students had done it.

According to WISN 12 News, Kristi was "blistered by negative and vicious emails and phone messages at school and on Facebook, including one suggesting she get protection. 'You are alone in the wilderness,' one person wrote to her in an email. 'Your best bet is to start a job search soon. Better hope the unemployment gets extended. Enjoy your isolation.'"[6]

Someone even posted her home address and phone number, and the names of her children, online.[7]

Kristi was unintimidated. "There are other teachers that are like-minded," she said. "They just need the courage to come forward and stand up to the union."

I've always believed that courage begets courage. So I was not surprised when, after word got out about the attacks against Kristi, we started getting e-mails and calls from other teachers who offered to be in ads themselves.

More and more, teachers and retired teachers began coming up to me to thank me for what we did. Initially, I could tell when a teacher was going to mention their support for our efforts. He or she would come close to me, look around to see if anyone was near, and then quietly tell me, "Governor, you're doing the right thing." Often the teacher was married to someone who ran his own business. As much as anyone, he understood the real costs of employee benefits and was not put off by our reforms.

Many of our friends who are teachers expressed their support for

Act 10 and told stories of being blackballed at school. Several mentioned that other teachers would actually turn their backs on them when they entered the faculty lounge. It was certainly odd behavior for the very people who are supposed to discourage bullies on the playground.

Teachers like Kristi weren't the only ones confronted with union intimidation. The Greater Wisconsin Political Fund, a 527 group backed by union allies, sent intimidating letters to Wisconsin voters, listing their neighbors and whether they had voted in recent elections. The letter declared: "The chart shows the names of some of your neighbors, showing which have voted in the past. . . . After the June 5th election, public records will tell everyone who voted and who didn't."[8]

Businesses got threatening letters as well. After Act 10 passed, the *Wall Street Journal* reported on one letter from AFL-CIO Council 24 field representative Jim Parrett[9] addressed "DEAR UNION GROVE AREA OWNER/MANAGER."[10] It read:

It is unfortunate that you have chosen "not" to support public workers' rights in Wisconsin. In recent weeks you have been offered a sign(s) by a public employee(s) who works in one of the state facilities in the Union Grove area. These signs simply said "This Business Supports Workers Rights," a simple, subtle and we believe non-controversial statement giving the facts at this time. . . . [W]e'd ask that you reconsider taking a sign and stance in support of public employees in this community. Failure to do so will leave us no choice but do [sic] a public boycott of your business. And sorry, neutral means 'no' to those who work for the largest employer in the area and are union members.[11]

The threat was not "subtle" at all. Neutrality was not an option. Tow the union line, or we'll ruin your business.

Another threatening letter was uncovered and posted online by conservative radio host Charlie Sykes. It came from Jim Palmer, head of the

Wisconsin Professional Police Association, and was signed by representatives of the Professional Fire Fighters, the International Association of Fire Fighters Local 311, the Dane County Deputy Sheriffs Association, and the Madison Professional Police Officers Association, among other organizations. It read:

> The undersigned groups would like your company to publicly oppose Governor Walker's efforts to virtually eliminate collective bargaining for public employees in Wisconsin. While we appreciate that you may need some time to consider this request, we ask for your response by March 17. In the event that you do not respond to this request by that date, we will assume that you stand with Governor Walker and against the teachers, nurses, police officers, fire fighters, and other dedicated public employees who serve our communities. In the event that you cannot support this effort to save collective bargaining, please be advised that the undersigned will publicly and formally boycott the goods and services provided by your company.[12]

The message was clear: Take your time and think it over—but not too much time. If you do not agree to support us by a certain date, we will do everything in our power to destroy your business and take away your livelihood.

Worst of all, the threat was coming from representatives of the police and firefighters responsible for *protecting* the business receiving the letter. Recipients would be excused if they wondered whether they would get a quick response to calls for help from police and firefighters if they failed to respond or put anti-Walker signs in their windows. As Sykes put it, the message seemed to be: "That's a nice business you got there. Pity if anything were to happen to it if, say, you didn't toe the line and denounce Governor Walker like we're asking nice-like."[13]

It was sad that the unions had stooped to threatening hardworking Wisconsinites to support them. "Having lost their fight in the legislature," the *Wall Street Journal* declared, "Wisconsin unions are now getting out the steel pipes for those who don't step lively to their cause."[14]

As word of the success of our education reforms spread, property tax bills started arriving in mailboxes throughout Wisconsin in early December. Since 1998, property tax increases in Wisconsin had become as dependable as winter snow—rising by 43 percent.

But this year, the tax bills contained an early Christmas present: Property taxes went down for the first time in over a decade.[15]

Without our reforms, property taxes would have risen by an average of $700 over the course of the biennium for the average taxpayer. Instead, thanks to Act 10, they declined on a median-valued home.

Suddenly, voters saw that not only were their kids' schools the same or better and that local services had not been decimated, but now they also had more money in their pockets. As the *Wall Street Journal* put it, "The unions said such policies would lead to the decline and fall of civilization, but the only things that are falling are tax collections."[16]

The first day of school, and now the arrival of property tax bills, had changed the political dynamic in Wisconsin.

Yet despite the good news and the ads we ran, my standing in the polls did not rise. The fight over Act 10 had bitterly divided our state in ways no previous political debate ever had. To this day, there are people who no longer speak to each other because of it. Wisconsinites were happy with the results of our reforms, but many were still angry about how we got there.

Some of my advisers argued that I should apologize to the state. I could not do that. We had done the right thing. Apologizing would have been dishonest. Moreover, it would have dispirited those who were standing with us because we stood on principle. I was not going to do it.

Still, I became convinced voters needed to hear directly from me. They needed to hear me explain why we did what we did, how our reforms had helped our state turn a corner, and that Wisconsin was better off despite all the rancor—that this divisive fight had not been for nothing.

So I decided to speak directly to the people of our state. We cut a series of ads in which I looked straight into the camera and explained the changes we made and how they were working.

On January 3, we ran the first ad called "Results." I said:

Hi, I'm Scott Walker. When I ran for governor, I promised to rein in spending, eliminate the deficit and hold the line on taxes. And you know what? That's exactly what we did. We had to make some tough decisions, but thankfully, we wiped out a $3.6 billion dollar deficit without raising taxes. And because government workers are now contributing to their health and pension benefits, like most people do, we saved the taxpayers hundreds of millions of dollars and kept thousands of teachers, firefighters, and police officers on the job. In the three years before I took office, Wisconsin lost 150,000 jobs, but now, well, employer confidence is up, and since the start of the year, Wisconsin has added thousands of new jobs. Instead of going back to the days of billion-dollar budget deficits, double-digit tax increases, and record job loss, let's keep moving Wisconsin forward.

The effect was nearly instantaneous. On December 19, 2011, our internal polls had showed me losing the recall by an eleven-point margin, 54-43 percent.

By January 23, 2012, after three weeks on the air with the new ad, we pulled ahead for the first time, 47–46.

It was not because I was so eloquent or persuasive. Had I put up the exact same ads three months earlier, they would have bombed. Only after people in Wisconsin had seen with their own eyes, and felt with their own wallets, that our reforms were working—only then were they ready to listen to me explain why we had done what we had done.

After that, the debate over collective bargaining was essentially over. As the campaign progressed, collective bargaining faded as the driving issue—even for Democrats. In 2010, the Obama administration recruited Milwaukee mayor Tom Barrett to run against me, and now he was running again for the Democratic nomination in the recall election. But the unions now opposed him. Why? Because while Mayor Barrett promised to do everything in his power to restore collective bargaining, he would not promise to veto any budget that failed to repeal Act 10. The unions' handpicked candidate, former Dane County executive Kathleen Falk, did promise such a veto. Since the GOP would likely still control at least one legislative chamber after the recall, her veto threat promised another bruising showdown over collective bargaining that no one in Wisconsin wanted.

Barrett also said he would keep public employee contributions to health care and pensions at the new, higher levels we had set, while Falk promised to open the issue up again in restored union negotiations.[17] There was very little support in Wisconsin to restore public workers' benefits to their generous, pre–Act 10 levels.

So the unions burned millions of dollars on the Falk-Barrett primary—money they could have instead held in reserve to use against us. In the end, Barrett defeated Falk by a whopping 58-34 percent. The twenty-four-point margin showed that even Democrats were not relishing another legislative showdown over Act 10.

Another remarkable thing happened on primary day. I faced no real opponent in the GOP primary (save for a fake Republican the protesters ran against me to make sure GOP voters did not cross over to vote in their primary). Yet when the votes were tallied, I still received more votes than Barrett and Falk *combined*. The *Milwaukee Journal Sentinel* called it "an unexpected turnout bomb."[18]

What made it all the more amazing was that we had done almost nothing to turn out our voters. Our supporters came to the polls because, after enduring the protests and occupations, it was their first chance to have their say on the matter. Republicans did not come down to Capitol

Square to demonstrate their support for our reforms with drums and bullhorns; they demonstrated their support at the polls instead.

The turnout showed that our base was not just excited, they were champing at the bit for the chance to make their voices heard.

Our reforms had energized GOP primary voters, while Democratic primary voters rejected the union's handpicked candidate who promised to make the campaign a referendum on Act 10.

But the best evidence our reforms had worked was this: Once Mayor Barrett had secured his party's nomination, he essentially stopped talking about Act 10 altogether. As the *Wall Street Journal* put it, "Milwaukee Mayor Tom Barrett has made his campaign chiefly about jobs, women's rights, the environment, community safety, and especially an investigation into the conduct of aides who worked for Mr. Walker when he was Milwaukee County executive. Mr. Barrett is running on everything except the collective bargaining reforms."[19]

There was a reason for that: The polls had shifted in our favor. Back in March 2011, a Rasmussen poll showed that voters opposed attempts to "weaken the collective bargaining rights of state employees" by a margin of 52 of 39 percent.[20] Now, in May 2012, the numbers had flipped. A Marquette University Law School poll[21] found that Wisconsin voters favored "limiting collective bargaining for most public employees" by a margin of 55 to 41 percent. A Reason-Rupe poll found that more than 70 percent supported our changes requiring public workers to contribute to their pensions and pay more for their health care premiums.[22]

Indeed, 57 percent said we should not have exempted police and firefighters.

Even among those who opposed me, collective bargaining was not the driving issue. As Stephen Hayes of the *Weekly Standard* reported, "A recent poll of Wisconsin Democrats found that just 12 percent of those surveyed said 'restoring collective bargaining rights of public employees' was the most important reason to remove Walker, behind three other choices."[23]

A May 13, 2012, strategy memo from Democratic Party chairman Mike Tate titled "Strategic Plan to Defeat Scott Walker" did not so much as mention collective bargaining. Indeed, a Democratic Party spokesman told the left-wing journal *Mother Jones* that the "Democrats' anti-Walker strategy will center on two key issues: the secret 'John Doe' investigation targeting Walker aides and what Democrats calls [sic] Walker's 'war on women.'"[24]

In other words, we had won the collective bargaining debate and turned public opinion around.

During the last few months of the recall campaign, I would get up in front of crowds at rallies and ask, "Does anyone remember what this recall was all about?"

Collective bargaining had been the reason for the recall. But now our reforms were so popular that my opponent did not even dare to mention them.

Mayor Barrett may not have wanted to talk about our reforms, but I relished the chance to do so. I welcomed the chance to talk about how Act 10 was helping us balance the state budget while improving education and local government. I welcomed the chance to talk about how our reforms were lowering property taxes and leaving more money in the pockets of our citizens. I welcomed the chance to talk about how, when given a free choice, tens of thousands of our citizens had chosen to leave the unions and keep their dues. I welcomed the chance to talk about the layoffs we had avoided because of our reforms and the jobs we created by improving the business climate in our state.

I welcomed the recall. I was ready to make our case.

CHAPTER 20

P.O.T.U.S. Is M.I.A.

When the protests began, it seemed like every Democratic politician, union activist, and B-list celebrity had made an appearance in Wisconsin. But now, with recall day fast approaching, there was one politician whose absence was becoming more glaring by the day—someone who had promised to stand with the unions but now was nowhere to be found:

President Obama was missing in action.

In December 2010, soon after my election, I traveled to Washington for a meeting with the other new governors. At Blair House, I met President Obama for the first time and we went right to the heart of the issue that divided us: the Packers and the Bears. Eventually, we found an issue on which we could agree: wanting to defeat the Vikings.

Not long after that meeting, the Packers won the NFC championship against—you guessed it—*da Bears*. When President Obama came to Wisconsin for a stop at Orion Energy Systems on January 25, I was waiting for him at the bottom of the steps with a gift—a Packers jersey that read "Obama 1."

As he bounded down from Air Force One and spotted the jersey, the president grinned and said, "I knew you would rub it in, Walker."

It was the last time we would see him in Wisconsin for a while.

The following month, I turned down a chance to attend a meeting of the National Governors Association and a dinner at the White House. With fourteen senators hiding outside the state and holding up the people's business, I didn't think it was the right time for me to travel to Washington. But that did not stop the president from taking a shot at me during a lunch with the assembled governors. My friend New Jersey governor Chris Christie called to tell me about it. "It does no one any good when public employees are denigrated or vilified or their rights are infringed upon," Obama declared.[1]

The president also took a shot at me during an interview with a Milwaukee television station calling our reforms "an assault on unions."

> Some of what I've heard coming out of Wisconsin, where you're just making it harder for public employees to collectively bargain generally seems like more of an assault on unions. And I think it's very important for us to understand that public employees, they're our neighbors, they're our friends. These are folks who are teachers and they're firefighters and they're social workers and they're police officers. They make a lot of sacrifices and make a big contribution. And I think it's important not to vilify them or to suggest that somehow all these budget problems are due to public employees.[2]

Of course, we had not "vilified" anyone. If anything, I had bent over backward to avoid criticizing public workers. Moreover, we were giving our public workers in Wisconsin a much better deal than President Obama gives most federal workers in Washington, D.C.

President Franklin Delano Roosevelt had once said that "the process of collective bargaining, as usually understood, cannot be transplanted in the public service."[3] And ever since 1978, when President Jimmy

Carter signed into law the Civil Service Reform Act, collective bargaining for federal employees has been severely limited. Today, federal workers cannot bargain for benefits or wages, and cannot be compelled to
join a union or pay union dues. I don't recall President Obama suggesting that they were being abused in any way, or lifting a finger to right
this supposed injustice. To the contrary, Obama unilaterally froze their
pay[4]—and he didn't have to get permission from a union steward to do
it. If limiting collective bargaining in Wisconsin constituted an "attack
on unions," then why didn't the president champion giving collective
bargaining powers to workers at the federal level?

I responded with a written statement:

> I'm sure the President knows that most federal employ-
> ees do not have collective bargaining for wages and
> benefits while our plan allows it for base pay. And I'm
> sure the President knows that the average federal worker
> pays twice as much for health insurance as what we are
> asking for in Wisconsin. At least I would hope he knows
> these facts.
>
> Furthermore, I'm sure the President knows that we
> have repeatedly praised the more than 300,000 gov-
> ernment workers who come to work every day in
> Wisconsin.
>
> I'm sure that President Obama simply misunder-
> stands the issues in Wisconsin, and isn't acting like the
> union bosses in saying one thing and doing another.

After that, we did not hear a thing from the White House or the
president until the eve of my recall election the following year.

But the president had been doing more than just weighing in. PO-
LITICO reported on February 17, 2011—the same day President
Obama made his comments to that Milwaukee TV station—that the
president's campaign group, Organizing for America, was

playing an active role in organizing protests against Wisconsin Governor Scott Walker's attempt to strip most public employees of collective bargaining rights. . . . OfA Wisconsin's field efforts include filling buses and building turnout for the rallies this week in Madison, organizing 15 rapid response phone banks urging supporters to call their state legislators, and working on planning and producing rallies, a Democratic Party official in Washington said.[5]

On the OfA blog, regional field director Jessie Lidbury wrote, "We have one thing to say right now: to our allies in the labor movement, to our brothers and sisters in public work, we stand with you, and we stand strong."[6]

They would not stand strong very long. By May 2012, *Washington Post* blogger Greg Sargent reported that "top Wisconsin Democrats are furious with the national party—and the Democratic National Committee in particular—for refusing their request for a major investment in the battle to recall Scott Walker."[7] He quoted a top Wisconsin Democrat as saying, "We are frustrated by the lack of support from the Democratic National Committee and the Democratic Governors Association. Scott Walker has the full support and backing of the Republican Party and all its tentacles. We are not getting similar support."

Wisconsin Democrats had apparently asked the DNC for $500,000 to help with their massive field operation, but the money never came.

Finally, with a month to go before the vote, President Obama broke his silence sending out an e-mail to his supporters that read:

The next election here in Wisconsin is coming up on June 5th—and it's important to make sure your voice is heard. For the last year and a half, Governor Walker has divided Wisconsin—siding with big corporations and the super-rich at the expense of working, middle-class families. He's broken our trust in state government: Too many Wisconsin families are out of work, students face crowded classrooms, and working men and women will be hurt by cuts to health care funding.[8]

Like Mayor Barrett, he failed to mention Act 10 or collective bargaining. And the fact is, the president never set foot in Wisconsin to deliver that message in person. After his January 2011 visit, the month of my inauguration, President Obama made only one other pre-recall visit to Wisconsin—an official visit to Master Lock in Milwaukee in February 2012. He didn't return again to the state until Labor Day—three months after the recall election.

Making the snub hard to miss, on June 3, 2012, the president attended three fund-raisers in Minnesota and then traveled to nearby Chicago to attend three more fund-raisers in his home state. He was a short helicopter ride away from Wisconsin but could not find the time to visit us. In fact, he actually flew *over* Wisconsin not once, but twice—on his way from Washington to Minnesota, and then on his way from Minnesota back to Chicago—but didn't bother to stop.

Before President Obama arrived in the region, my opponent, Tom Barrett, almost pleaded for the president to make a pit stop. "We'd love to have him zip over to western Wisconsin. I'm happy to meet him for a fish fry," Barrett said hopefully.[9]

But when the president came and went without stopping in Wisconsin, Barrett was left to say that he wasn't concerned. "We understand that he's got a lot going on."[10]

For her part, Obama deputy campaign manager Stephanie Cutter explained the president's failure to campaign for Barrett this way: "This is a gubernatorial race with a guy who was recalled and a, you know, a challenger trying to get him out of office. It has nothing to do with President Obama."[11]

Translation: You're on your own.

According to a Marquette University Law School poll, the president enjoyed a 52 percent approval rating in Wisconsin, and led Mitt Romney 51-43 among likely voters at the time of the recall—a comfortable eight-point margin.[12] Yet he was unwilling to spend any of that political capital to help defeat me.

When he ran for office in 2008, Senator Obama had promised to stand with the unions in no uncertain terms. "If American workers are being denied their right to organize when I'm in the White House," candidate Obama declared, "I will put on a comfortable pair of shoes and I will walk on that picket line with you as president of the United States."[13] So if he truly believed that we were engaged in an "attack on unions," why didn't he put on some comfortable shoes and show up in Wisconsin?

It was the ultimate validation that our reforms had worked, that we had turned the debate around. The president of the United States was unwilling to campaign against us.

I believe the reason that President Obama failed to campaign against us in Wisconsin is simple: He knew a significant number of his support-ers were also backing me in the recall, and he did not want to alienate them before the presidential election. It was a smart decision. If he stayed out of it, these Obama-Walker voters were free to support both of us. But if he came to Wisconsin to campaign against me, he would be effec-tively asking them to choose. And if they chose me, it could have been a major blow to his aspirations for a second term.

After the recall, exit polls showed that roughly one in six of those who voted for me on June 5 also planned to vote for President Obama on November 6.[14] These Obama-Walker voters constituted about 9 percent of the overall electorate. Since then, their ranks have expanded. In May 2013, the *Milwaukee Journal Sentinel* wrote: "Remember those confounding Obama-Walker voters of 2012? They're still with us. In Marquette [Law School's] two 2013 polls, 11% approve of both politzians."[15]

The Marquette poll found that President Obama and I enjoyed almost identical approval ratings: 51 percent approval and 45 percent disapproval. The *Journal Sentinel* explained the phenomenon this way: "Walker and Obama occupy a similar niche in Wisconsin. They are loved in their own party, loathed in the other party and performing just well enough with independents to come out even or slightly ahead in the overall court of public opinion."

In the recall, we had done more than simply mobilize the conservative base. We had persuaded at least some of President Obama's supporters to support us. We took our message to the persuadable segment of the electorate, and persuaded them.

If Mitt Romney had done the same thing, he might well be sitting in the Oval Office today.

CHAPTER 21

What Wisconsin Looks Like if We Lose

With just six weeks to go before the recall election, on April 17, 2012, I campaigned in a place where no one could vote for me: Springfield, Illinois.

It might have seemed like an odd decision at the time. Polls showed that the race in Wisconsin was neck and neck, too close to call. So why was I wasting precious time traveling out of state a few weeks before voters went to the polls?

The answer was simple: Illinois was central to our plan for winning the recall.

Our strategy was to frame the recall election as a choice between going forward and going backward. We could go backward to the days of billion-dollar budget deficits, double-digit tax increases, and record job losses. Or we could keep moving Wisconsin forward—balancing our budget without raising taxes or massive layoffs while creating tens of thousands of new jobs for the people of our state.

Well, just across the border in Illinois was a real-time example of what moving backward looked like. By highlighting the failures of the politicians in Springfield, we would show voters in Wisconsin what would become of our state if I lost the recall election.

That's why, when I was invited by the Illinois Chamber of Commerce, I jumped at the opportunity to highlight our record in Wisconsin and compare it with the dismal record of the politicians in a state the *Wall Street Journal* had dubbed "The Greece Next Door."[1] Like everywhere else I went, union bosses sent protesters to greet me in Springfield.[2] Several thousand people showed up to picket my speech. They brought the same giant rat that had graced the Capitol Square in Madison, and signs with my picture on them that read, "Don't Badger us!"

Inside, the reception from business leaders was much warmer. "Members of my fan club are outside, many of whom were bused into Wisconsin last year," I told the crowd. "If voters in our state want to know the difference between going forward or backward, they need only look at the mess that you have in state government here in Springfield to know what it would be like if the recall ultimately prevails."[3]

The contrast between our states was stark indeed: In 2010, the citizens of Illinois already paid the ninth-highest state and local taxes in the nation according to the nonpartisan Tax Foundation.[4] Then, in 2011, Governor Pat Quinn announced the largest state income tax increase in Illinois history, raising taxes on individuals by 67 percent and taxes on businesses by 46 percent.

Quinn had explicitly declared that he was not going to do what Wisconsin was doing. A year later, it was clear that he had not. In Madison we made the tough choices that allowed us to avoid massive layoffs, tax increases, and cuts to programs like Medicaid. In Springfield, by contrast, Governor Quinn had proposed shutting down fourteen state facilities, raising taxes more, cutting Medicaid by $2.7 billion, and laying off thousands of public employees.

According to the *New York Times*,[5] Illinois's pension system is the worst-funded in the country, underfunded by an estimated $96 billion. In January 2012, Moody's downgraded Illinois's bond rating to the lowest in the nation (even worse than California's), declaring that "the state took no steps to implement lasting solutions to its severe pension underfunding or its chronic bill payment delays."[6] Worse still, in March 2013, the Securities and Exchange Commission (SEC) charged Illinois with securities fraud for shortchanging the state pension system. In contrast Wisconsin's is the only pension system in the country that is essentially fully funded. At this writing, Wisconsin is running a budget surplus, while Illinois' debt is $9 billion and growing.

To put the Illinois fiscal disaster in context, Fox News reported earlier this year that Illinois owed $165,462 to a company called Seville Staffing for "third-party debt collection."[7] As correspondent Steve Brown explained, that meant that "Illinois owes money to a company it hired to collect money owed to the state of Illinois."

That is how bad it is in the Land of Lincoln: Illinois is so broke, it can't even afford to pay its own debt collectors.

One Illinois official who desperately needs the tools in Act 10 is Chicago mayor Rahm Emanuel. In 2011, thanks to rising salaries, pensions, and health care costs, the Chicago public school system was facing an immediate $700 million deficit. According to the *Wall Street Journal*,[8] the average Chicago teacher was making $71,000 a year in salary, plus pensions and benefits worth $15,000 or more a year.[9] By contrast, the median household income for a Chicago worker in the private economy was $47,000—and that private worker contributed much more to his or her pension and health care (if he or she had them at all).

No matter, the teachers were about to get a 4 percent annual pay raise that would have added another $100 million to the Chicago school district's $700 million deficit.

The situation was unfair and unsustainable. So Mayor Emanuel canceled the teachers' pay raise. "I can't, in good conscience, continue an implicit understanding between parties that left our children on the side of the road," Emanuel declared. "I will not accept our children continuing to get the shaft."[10]

Not only did Emanuel cancel the pay raise, he also demanded a series of reforms, such as lengthening the school day (at five hours and forty-five minutes, Chicago's elementary schools had the shortest day of any urban district in the country), modest changes in health care, an expansion of charter schools, merit pay, and a principal assessment system in which student test scores make up half of an educator's evaluation.

Local reporters dubbed Emanuel "The Democrats' Scott Walker."[11] For President Obama's former chief of staff, that was not a compliment. But the fact is, Emanuel's proposed reforms were much more modest than those we had enacted in Madison. During his campaign for mayor he had even assured Chicagoans that he would "totally . . . reject the approach the Governor of Wisconsin has taken."[12]

But that did not prevent union leaders from responding as if he had taken on collective bargaining itself.

They called a strike that kept 350,000 students out of school for seven days. When the dust settled Emanuel ended up with a few concessions, such as extending the school day. But according to local press accounts, the union came out ahead on most other issues. Teachers got a raise of 17.6 percent over four years—an increase that the *Chicago Sun-Times* reports "drained every last penny of reserves" from the school district's budget, thus requiring "four years of up-to-the-limit property tax increases."[13]

The results were unfortunate, but entirely predictable. On March 22, 2013, Emanuel announced he was shuttering sixty-one school buildings—closings that would affect some thirty thousand students, almost all in African-American neighborhoods on the South and West Sides.

Chicago schools were closing to pay for the new teachers' contract. Thanks to collective bargaining, Chicago's kids are "continuing to get the shaft."

The school closings did not solve the mayor's fiscal problems. Soon after the closures were announced, the *Wall Street Journal* reported that the mayor was about to face "a showdown with labor unions" over the city's municipal pension shortfalls.[14] Chicago's retirement system for teachers and city workers is underfunded by almost $24 billion, the *Journal* reported. Within three years, annual pension costs for city workers will more than double, from less than $500 million today to $1.1 billion. Covering these costs would require a 150 percent increase in property taxes to cover the costs—which Emanuel has ruled out.

So what are his options? "Mr. Emanuel could try to reach agreements on benefits cuts with individual unions, though such efforts so far have fallen flat," the *Journal* wrote. "Or he could bypass unions by persuading the Illinois legislature to trim pension benefits for city employees and current retirees or give the city the power to do it."[15]

In other words, if the unions' intransigence continues, Emanuel will have no choice but to seek authority from the Illinois legislature to impose the changes on the unions.

Maybe he will be the "Democrats' Scott Walker" after all.

In Wisconsin, we don't have any of these problems. We made the structural changes and the tough decisions necessary, to balance our budget without mass layoffs, school closures, or protracted negotiations with public sector union bosses who put their interests ahead of students and their state.

This wisdom of our approach became even clearer when, in March 2013, the state of Illinois struck a new collective bargaining agreement with its public employees union, AFSCME 31. Behind the scenes, Governor Quinn apparently decided to follow Wisconsin's lead after all by demanding significantly higher health care contributions from state workers. But because he did not reform collective bargaining, as we had, the unions were able to resist his entreaties.

In a secret memo to his members, AFSCME executive director Henry Bayer boasted that while the governor had "cited the state's dire fiscal straits, high health care costs, and soaring deficits in pressing for lower compensation for state workers," the union "resisted a barrage of attacks on the rights and benefits of union members" and made clear "we would not be made scapegoats for fiscal problems we didn't cause."[16]

In the end, AFSCME agreed to a modest 1 percent increase in employee contributions to health care premiums. But, the union declared, that increase will be "more than offset" by a 4 percent general pay increase during the contract period. As the union boasted to its members, "The Bargaining Committee fought for more than a year against these excessive increases—and beat them back!"

When people ask why I insisted on ending collective bargaining for everything but wages, the answer is simple: because this is precisely the kind of inflexibility we would have seen from public sector unions in Wisconsin. It is the same inflexibility I saw from the union bosses when I was Milwaukee County executive. Now, because of our actions, they cannot stand in the way of commonsense reforms in Wisconsin the way they still do in Illinois.

The results are there for all to see. In 2009, before I took office, a survey by the statewide chamber of commerce found that just 4 percent of the employers in Wisconsin thought the state was headed in the right direction. Today, 94 percent of those employers said Wisconsin is heading in the right direction. (I'm a competitive guy, so I won't be satisfied till we win over that last 6 percent.)

In the *Chief Executive Magazine* annual survey on the best and worst states for business, Wisconsin made the biggest jump of any state following our reforms, and one of the largest in the history of the survey, rising seventeen points in one year—from forty-first in the nation in 2010 to twenty-fourth in 2011.[17] (By 2013, we had risen even further, to seventeenth—a twenty-four-point upswing since we took office.[18]) By contrast, that same ranking saw Illinois drop forty spots in five years. The Land of Lincoln, *Chief Executive Magazine* declared, "is now in a death spiral."[19] That's because politicians in Springfield failed to make the same kinds of tough decisions we made in Madison.

In my speech to the Illinois Chamber of Commerce, I noted that there was an old Wisconsin tourism slogan we once used to lure visitors across the border from Illinois: "Escape to Wisconsin." It still works, I told them, only now we use it to lure Illinois businesses.

The message was received loud and clear back home in Wisconsin. As the recall approached, I told folks every chance I got that if they wanted to see what going backward looked like, all they had to do was take a look across the border at the fiscal disaster in Illinois.

That was what was at stake in the recall election.

In Milwaukee County it was a struggle to muster the votes to stop the board from overriding my veto. Now I had been elected governor with Republican majorities in both the assembly and the senate. Instead of fighting veto overrides, I finally had the chance to do big, bold things.

Election night 2010. In the last four years Republicans have picked up governorships from Democrats in Iowa, Michigan, Ohio, Pennsylvania, Kansas, New Mexico, Oklahoma, Tennessee, Wyoming, North Carolina, New Jersey, Virginia, Maine, and here in Wisconsin. Not exactly the record of a party that is out of touch with the priorities of the American people.

After we introduced Act 10 an army of thousands marched toward the capitol.

Inside, the capitol was packed wall-to-wall with protesters. They banged drums and blasted horns day and night, harassed and spat on lawmakers as they made their way through the capitol, and turned our historic rotunda into a theater of the absurd.

Protesters carried signs comparing me to Hosni Mubarak . . .

. . . and Osama bin Laden. Others read "Death to tyrants," "Don't retreat, reload," and "The only good Republican is a dead Republican."

Not everyone at the capitol opposed Act 10. Tea Party groups organized counterprotests to support us. I was grateful for their support.

Physicians set up stations at the capitol to write doctor's notes for the teachers so that they could protest without losing pay. So many called in sick that schools had to close for days at a time. The teachers and doctors were lying to their employers and defrauding the taxpayers. Many of the doctors were later disciplined for their actions.

The capitol grew so packed with sleeping bags and human bodies, there was no possible way to clean it. The smell, as soon as you walked into the building, was overpowering. Protesters urinated on the back door of my office.

A historical architect who participated in the 2004 renovation of the capitol concluded that "the building experienced three to five years of wear within a two-week period."

Senate Democratic leader Mark Miller believed the protests were working. "The governor is in real trouble," Miller told my staff. "The people of the state have turned against him."

When we first informed the Republican president of the senate, Mike Ellis, of our plan to reform collective bargaining, he looked at me and said point-blank, "Governor, you can't do this."

The senate chamber was half empty because senate Democrats fled across the border to Illinois to stop us from passing our reforms. For many this was the biggest thing they had done in their lives. They had become folk heroes on the left and regulars on MSNBC. It soon became clear they were never coming back.

Democratic members of the assembly brought their desks outside to hold "office hours."

With senate Democrats still hiding out in Illinois, we found a way around their obstruction and passed Act 10. As word spread that the senate was acting, social media exploded with calls to storm the capitol.

Thousands of protesters descended on the building and began banging on the doors and windows, chanting, "Let us in! Let us in!"

The protesters soon overwhelmed capitol police. Once inside, they began unlocking doors and bathroom windows until a sea of thousands had flooded the capitol, chanting "This is what democracy looks like!" A mob formed to search for the Republican senators who had dared to defy the will of the unions.

When the assembly passed Act 10, protesters in the gallery above screamed "Shame!" On the floor below, the assembly Democrats exploded—yelling, screaming, throwing water, cups, and paper at their Republican colleagues. Speaker Robin Vos said "it was impossible to tell a protester apart from a legislator."

On March 11, 2011, I signed Act 10 into law at the dining room table of the governor's residence. But I was not simply going to sign the law in private, as if hiding from the crowds. We would hold a formal signing ceremony in the capitol later that day.

I would have understood if Act 10's supporters had decided to skip the signing ceremony. But they wanted to be there. They were proud of what we had accomplished. Democratic senator Chris Larson warned that day, "Everyone who is a party to this travesty is writing their political obituary." I was not the least bit worried. I knew our reforms were going to work.

On the day of the recall election, it was still too close to call. Our chief strategist, R. J. Johnson, told me, "It could go either way. I just can't predict." Despite the uncertainty, I felt at peace. I was ready for whatever God had planned for me.

When NBC called the election just before nine p.m., a roar went up. We'd been expecting a long night, possibly even a recount fight. Instead, we won by an even bigger margin than the first time. I hugged my family. They had endured so much over the past year and a half—personal attacks, protests in front of our house, and round-the-clock security. Instead of splitting us apart adversity had drawn us closer.

As I addressed the crowd, I saw a sign hovering over a sea of supporters: "You can't recall courage!" The election was way bigger than me. Our victory sent a powerful message from Madison to Washington that if political leaders have the courage to tackle tough issues, they will have people standing with them.

I'm proud to own a 2003 Harley-Davidson Road King with more than twenty thousand miles on it. Few things are better than the freedom of the open road.

CHAPTER 22

"You Can't Recall Courage"

The final stretch before the recall election was extremely stressful. We had pulled slightly ahead of Mayor Barrett but not by a wide enough margin to provide us with any real comfort. I was conscious of the fact that no governor had ever survived a recall in our country before. To win, we would have to do more than simply defeat my opponent—we would have to defy history.

Tonette was nervous as well. This wasn't like our race in 2010, when we could just feel the victory coming. Moreover, the protesters had been right about one thing: The whole world *was* watching. Everything we stood for was on the line. In the final weeks, we campaigned across the state together as a family. Tonette and the kids had endured so much— the protesters outside our home, the hecklers, and the death threats. After everything they had been through, I wanted to win it for the three of them.

I was also keenly aware of the impact losing this race would have on Wisconsin—and the country. The election had gotten a lot bigger than who the governor of Wisconsin would be for the next two years. Paul

Ryan had said it best in his speech at the Wisconsin Republican convention: "Courage is on the ballot on June 5th."

Paul was right. If we prevailed, it would send a powerful message not only in Madison but also in state houses across the country—and ultimately through the halls of Congress—that if political leaders tackle tough issues, they will have people standing with them. If we prevailed, it would tell every elected official in America that if they are bold, if they do the right thing, their courage and boldness will be rewarded.

If we lost, however, I was convinced it would set the cause of courage in politics back a decade, if not a generation. The opponents of reform were trying to send a message across the country that if you take on the unions, you lose your job. The consequence of defeat would have been disastrous not just for Wisconsin but also for the nation. That is why we had to win. We could not lose.

The Barrett campaign understood the stakes as well—and they were throwing everything possible at us to see what would stick. Mayor Barrett had stopped talking about Act 10 altogether. It was ironic—collective bargaining had supposedly been the reason for the recall, but my opponent was not even running on what he claimed this election was all about.

Instead, Barrett portrayed me as a conservative "rock star" (a line of attack that did not work much better for Barrett than it did when John McCain tried it on Barack Obama in the 2008 election). He said I wanted to turn Wisconsin into a "prototype for the tea party." He accused me of starting a "civil war."[1]

The one thing Mayor Barrett never did was offer a positive vision of his own to move Wisconsin forward.

He got some traction when he attacked us on jobs. A string of monthly jobs reports suggested that Wisconsin had lost 33,900 jobs in 2011. Barrett put up ads declaring that under my administration Wisconsin was dead last in the country in job creation. He accused me of having taken my eye off the ball on what should have been our number one priority in order to pursue an "ideological agenda"[2] (later, voters would learn that our opponent had the facts wrong).

It was a powerful attack, and it was starting to work. But then Mayor Barrett made a strategic error. He suddenly stopped talking about jobs and started running multiple ads attacking me over a "John Doe" investigation into misconduct by some of my former aides in Milwaukee County. I pointed out that Tom Nardelli, my chief of staff at the county, had (per my approval) initiated the investigation because of concerns we had about an individual who volunteered with the county. Then I reminded the voters that as an Eagle Scout, "I live by the standards of integrity I got from my parents."

It was my belief that Barrett was focusing on the John Doe investigation out of desperation because he could not talk about Act 10. "They keep moving to anything else except what this recall is supposedly about, because our reforms are working," I said. At one of our debates, I stated: "So everybody's clear, the mayor doesn't have a plan. All he's got is attacking me."

Mayor Barrett didn't get any traction with his "John Doe" attacks. And the following year, the Milwaukee County District Attorney's Office announced that it was were closing the three-year-long investigation. I was cleared. After the DA announced his decision, a Wisconsin Democratic Party spokesman was so incensed he went on Twitter and compared me to serial killer Jeffrey Dahmer.[3]

"What do @GovWalker and Jeffrey Dahmer have in common?" he tweeted.

He then answered himself. "@GovWalker had better lawyers than Jeffrey Dahmer in beating the rap. Clear that he committed crimes."

It just showed the depth of their bitterness. They so wanted it to be true that they nearly lost it when the truth contradicted their attacks.

As Mayor Barrett's "John Doe" attacks fizzled during the campaign, we turned the jobs issue around on him. In April, we pointed out that nearly all the net job losses in the state the previous month had come from one place: Mayor Barrett's Milwaukee. Wisconsin was reported to have lost forty-five hundred in March 2012, and forty-four hundred of those were in Milwaukee.[4]

"The City of Milwaukee, under Mayor Barrett's failed policies, is an anchor weighing on Wisconsin's ability to create jobs," we declared in a statement.

We also knew the jobs statistics Barrett had been citing, which purported to show that Wisconsin had lost jobs during my first year in office, were not accurate. The monthly jobs reports were based on survey data taken from a small statistical sampling of Wisconsin businesses (about 3.5 percent). But every quarter, the Bureau of Labor Statistics (BLS) in Washington puts out more precise jobs numbers based on comprehensive census data from each state. Unfortunately, the final BLS report for 2011 that would have undermined Barrett's charges was not scheduled to come out until three weeks after the recall election.

The Obama Labor Department was not going to speed up the release to help us out. But there was nothing in the law that prevented *us* from releasing the census data the state of Wisconsin had provided to the federal government. So we released the data, which showed that, after losing 134,000 jobs in the three years before I was elected, the state had actually added 23,000 jobs in 2011. The unemployment rate in Wisconsin had dropped to 6.7 percent (compared to 8.2 percent nationally and the peak of 9.2 percent before I took office).

In May, we ran an ad touting the new jobs numbers. I looked into the camera and said:

I've got some bad news for Tom Barrett but good news for Wisconsin. The government just released the final jobs numbers and as it turns out, Wisconsin actually gained, that's right, gained more than 20,000 new jobs during my first year in office. Add the jobs created this year, and the total goes to over 30,000. Mayor Barrett, you said this election's about jobs; I couldn't agree more. Our reforms are working and we're moving Wisconsin forward.

That effectively took jobs off the table.

Barrett tried to make the election about the past. We made the election about the future. We defined the race as a choice between going forward or backward. Our message was: We made tough decisions to close a $3.6 billion budget deficit—and did it without raising taxes, without massive layoffs, and without harming education or public services. Now thanks to those choices, Wisconsin had turned a corner. We were moving in the right direction, but we were not done yet—we needed more time.

In the end, I felt confident that the negative attack ads from our opponents could not overcome the power of positive results. As I've often said, good policy is good politics, and I believed our election would prove it.

In the end, we raised some $37 million (more than 70 percent of our donors gave us $50 or less). We made some 4.5 million voter contacts during the campaign—using traditional and electronic messaging. We had a strong ground game, a strong record, and a strong, positive, optimistic message. I was confident we would prevail.

But on Election Day, it was still too close to call. After Tonette and I went to cast our ballots, I asked R. J. Johnson, our chief strategist and my friend for more than twenty years, how he felt.

"It could go either way," he said. "I just can't predict."

Despite the uncertainty, I felt at peace. We had done everything we could to make our case. I was ready for whatever God had planned for me.

On Election Day, I headed to Jefferson Elementary School in Wauwatosa to cast my ballot. In most of my previous races, I had just walked into the polling station and voted, but when I arrived that morning there was a long line that went out the door and down the street. As I took my place in line, it seemed like every TV outlet in the world was there to capture the moment. I apologized to the poor guy in front of me who now had what seemed like a hundred cameras bearing down on him. Fortunately, he did not mind—he was a supporter.

After voting, Tonette and I took a last barnstorming tour of the state, and then went to the Waukesha County Expo Center with a group of our personal friends—the Genals, Harmons, Langes, Pankratzes, and Meidels—five families we had known since our kids were in junior kindergarten together. With them and the members of my security detail, who had become like family, we settled in to await the results.

As the polls closed, the tension was intense. Voter turnout had been large. In places like Madison and Milwaukee, that typically spells bad news for a Republican. Yet we had also heard that there had been long lines in small towns throughout the state. We hoped that was a good sign.

Suddenly a roar went up. NBC had called the election. I was in shock, as it wasn't even nine o'clock yet and we'd been expecting a long night, possibly even a recount fight. My campaign staff pulled me out into the hall. My good friend Reince Priebus, our national party chairman (and former Wisconsin party chairman), gave me a big hug, then handed me his iPhone. Mitt Romney was on the line with his congratulations.

Moments later, I was whisked into our "war room," where the campaign team was monitoring election results from across the state. A huge cheer erupted as I entered the room. It was less than an hour after the polls closed and I was still in shock. It was surreal that the race should be over so soon. I looked for R.J. Normally, he's the last to celebrate a victory because he is still nervously examining the last election returns. When he gave me a smile and a hug, I knew it was true: We had won.

Not only had we won, we had made history. No other governor had ever won a recall election.

I searched for Tonette. She was in a holding room with our friends.

I burst in and said we had won and now needed to get ready to give a victory speech. In disbelief she kept saying, "It can't be. It's too early. Are you sure?" So I took her over to see R.J.

"Is it real? Did we win?" she asked.

"You got it," he said.

She threw her arms around him and sobbed. All the pressure of the past eighteen months came spilling out. Then R.J. started crying too. Soon there wasn't a dry eye in the room.

After enduring one hundred thousand or more protesters, tens of millions of dollars in ads, and massive attacks from the left, we had won—and by an even bigger margin than the first time.

I was enormously gratified, but I also knew that the election was way bigger than me. It was all about whether big-government special interests or the hardworking taxpayers were in charge of the state. That day, the hardworking taxpayers won.

As I took in our victory, I thought about Dan Kapanke. Dan had to face the voters in August 2011, just a few weeks before the new school year began and a few months before property tax bills arrived showing the first reductions in over a decade. If only he had been on the ballot today, after it was clear that our reforms had worked, he might have held on to that senate seat.

Tonette, standing with Matt and Alex, introduced me to the huge Wisconsin crowd and to all of the others from across the nation (and around the globe) who were watching our victory party. My family had endured so much over the past year and a half—personal attacks, protests in front of our house, and round-the-clock security. My only doubt about this job was the toll it had taken from my family.

Through God's grace, instead of splitting us apart adversity had drawn us closer. As I walked out onto the stage that night, I thanked God—and hugged my family as if the moment would last forever. I didn't want to ever let them go. Turning to the crowd, I couldn't believe how many people were there, filling not only the Waukesha County Expo Center but the overflow areas outside the arena.

Hovering over a sea of supporters, I saw a sign: "You can't recall courage!" I knew that despite this historic victory, I would need a lot more of it in the difficult days to come.

No one actually believed we would follow through on our promises of reform when I was first elected in 2010. Surely, they thought, the pressure to cave in to the status quo would be so intense that we would crumble, like so many other politicians before us. The same pundits also predicted we'd lose the recall, just as every other governor subjected to the challenge had in American history.

I knew that if our children were to inherit a Wisconsin and a nation as great as the one I grew up in, the reforms we had begun had to be kept intact. We could not fail. With the help of so many great Americans, I was deeply thankful that we were able to get the truth out to the voters of Wisconsin, and prevail against the odds.

In the end, our opponents had spent millions on what amounted to a "do over" of the 2010 election. We won this time by seven points, a bigger margin than in the 2010 election. We won sixty of the state's seventy-two counties, one more than in the 2010. And we won 205,509 more votes in the recall election that we had in 2010.

And that was in a *June* election.

My running mate, Rebecca Kleefisch, became the first lieutenant governor in American history to face a recall election, and thus the first to win such an election. Republicans held on to three senate seats but lost one: Van Wanggaard. His defeat meant that the Democrats temporarily regained control of the state senate, but it was a symbolic victory. The legislature was out of session until after the November election, and the GOP took back control five months later, regaining the majority with two seats to spare.

In exit polls, 52 percent of voters in the recall said they supported our handling of collective bargaining reform. Far from plummeting, as some expected, my support among *union* households actually grew slightly, from 37 percent in 2010 to 38 percent in 2012.

When the recall effort started the previous November, it had the support of 58 percent of voters.[5] By the time the race was over, exit polls also showed that 60 percent of Wisconsin voters disapproved of the recall, saying it should be reserved only for politicians guilty of official misconduct. A majority of our citizens believed it never should have happened—even some who voted *against* me.

In his concession speech, Tom Barrett was met by jeers from the crowd when he said he had called to congratulate me and pledged to work together on the challenges facing our state. A woman actually came up and slapped him in the face for conceding.

I appreciated his gesture, and he and I would later team up on a bipartisan initiative to stimulate entrepreneurship and business growth in Milwaukee.[6]

In the war room just before my speech, Tonette had pulled me aside. She told me I should walk out on that stage, look out at the crowd, and say: "This is what Democracy looks like!"

I smiled. It was a really great line. After hearing tens of thousands of people chanting that very phrase outside my window for months, it would have been enormously satisfying to deliver it. The crowd would have gone wild, and it would have led the news. Perhaps, after all we had been through, I could have indulged myself for one small moment. But then I remembered that devotional reading after the prank call on "the power of humility." I wanted to use my speech as a chance to end the acrimony, and unite our state once again. I decided not to say it.

Instead, I reached out to the Democrats and told them, "We are no longer opponents. We are one as Wisconsinites." And I announced that I was inviting all the members of the state legislature, Republican and Democrat alike, to a cookout at the governor's mansion (it was Tonette's great idea).[7] Nothing brings Wisconsinites of all political stripes together like beer and brats. I invited not just the lawmakers and their spouses, but their staffs as well. People had stopped talking to each other in the capitol, and I felt it was important for everyone to start rebuilding the personal relationships that had been frayed by the recall fight.

A week later, nearly four hundred people—lawmakers from both parties, with their families and staff—attended what became known as the "Beer and Brats Summit." It was a beautiful June day in Wisconsin overlooking a great lake. Sprecher Brewery, a Milwaukee company, made a root beer with a special label that said "Governor Walker's Beer and Brat Summit," and people asked me to sign their bottles for them. I donned an apron and took charge of the grill. Representative Peter Barca, the Democrats' assembly leader whose jaw had nearly dropped on that cold February day when I explained our plans on collective bargaining, came over with his wife. We had a good talk as I flipped the links. He has Italian roots like Tonette's, so we joked about how well I was cooking the Italian sausages. After the event, he told reporters that he thought the summit was a success. "I do think it was a positive step, no question about it," he said.[8]

I was gratified that many of the senate Democrats who had fled the state during the fight over Act 10 were there as well. It was a sign of better things to come.

Some people just could not let go, however. A small contingent of protesters showed up outside the gates to protest. "Healing begins with indictment," read one sign.

Among the crowd was none other than AFSCME chief Marty Beil. When a reporter asked him why he was protesting a bipartisan picnic, he answered: "I want people to see that we're not gone. I want punks like [Representative Scott] Suder over here to see so he knows that we're here for when he runs in the fall for reelection. These guys need to know that we're watching them every second of the day and we'll continue to do that."

It was sad. Beil's intransigence, his belligerence, and his attempt to ram union contracts through the lame-duck legislature had set the stage for the fight that ensued. And now, almost two years later, here he was still at it—threatening legislators and calling them "punks."

He had learned absolutely nothing.

People in our state were exhausted by the partisanship and bickering and just wanted it all to end. Right after Election Day, the *Wisconsin*

State Journal had run a helpful article titled "After the recall, how to remove your bumper sticker." ("Nail polish remover, rubbing alcohol or lighter fluid will loosen a bumper sticker," they recommended.)[9]

But before the stickers could come off, we still had one more election to go: the race for president of the United States of America.

CHAPTER 23

III

Misreading the Message of Wisconsin

We did our best to help Mitt Romney in Wisconsin. After the recall, instead of shutting down the victory centers we had set up across the state, we turned them into Romney victory centers. Our staff and volunteers transitioned seamlessly from the recall election to the general election—giving Romney a built-in infrastructure in the state that would not have been there had it not been for the recall. Instead of being burned out from the long fight, our folks were energized by our victory and ready to help Romney repeat it.

In the end it was not to be. President Obama won Wisconsin by almost exactly the same percentage of the vote I had won in the recall.

Romney deserved a lot of credit for picking Paul Ryan as his running mate. Paul is one of the smartest and most courageous people I know in politics. He is also one of the most decent people I know in or out of politics. I was overwhelmed with pride when Paul spoke at the national convention. The national media made a big deal about seeing a tear go down my face during his speech, but I grew up about fifteen miles down the road from Paul and have known him for years. As kids in high school, we had similar starts. We both worked at McDonald's flipping hamburgers in the back. Paul was told by his manager the reason he had to flip hamburgers in the back was because he didn't have the interpersonal skills to work the front cash register. Now here he was addressing the nation as the Republican vice presidential nominee. When Paul spoke that night, it was like seeing a member of the family on the stage, both for me and for Tonette.

We love people like Paul Ryan in Wisconsin because he has the courage to tackle big issues. Paul is exactly the kind of bold reformer America needed on the ticket. Unfortunately, Mitt Romney never made the case for *himself* as a bold reformer. To the contrary, he distanced himself from Paul's reforms. Instead of showing Americans that the "R" next to his name stood for "reformer," Romney let the Obama campaign convince Americans it stood for "rich" and out of touch.

Mitt Romney is a decent and compassionate man—the kind of person who sits by the bedside of a young boy dying of cancer and helps him write his last will and testament so he can leave his treasured possessions to his friends. Which is why it was so frustrating that Romney allowed himself to be portrayed as a defender of the rich and powerful instead of a champion of the poor and vulnerable. An April 2012 Economist/YouGov poll tells the story: Only 35 percent of Americans said they believed that Romney cared about the poor, and just 38 percent said Romney "cares about people like me."[1]

You can't win the presidency when nearly two thirds of the country thinks you don't care about their struggles.

I knew Romney was in trouble two days after I won my recall election when he seized upon our victory to make his case against Barack Obama. The president "says we need more firemen, more policemen, more teachers," Romney declared. "Did he not get the message of Wisconsin?"[2]

Unfortunately, it was Romney who did not get the message of Wisconsin. In one of my first campaign ads for the recall, I had looked into the camera and said: "We saved the taxpayers hundreds of millions of dollars and kept thousands of teachers, firefighters, and police officers on the job." In another, I declared, "Because public employees now contribute to their health and pension benefits, we're able to put more money back into the classroom . . . and keep thousands of police officers, firefighters, and teachers on the job."

Our reforms had *protected* the jobs of firemen, policemen, and teachers. We had avoided the mass layoffs of public workers that local communities were facing in other states across America. We had strengthened local government and improved public services.

The message of Wisconsin was not that the American people want fewer teachers, or police, or firefighters. The message of Wisconsin was that Americans want *leadership*. And in times of crisis, they don't care if it is Democratic leadership or Republican leadership—they will stand with those who offer bold ideas and have the courage to take on the tough issues.

But instead of offering a big, positive vision for the future, Romney was working to make the campaign a referendum on President Obama. His campaign was trying to model itself on the 1980 Reagan campaign, and the devastating question Reagan asked Americans at the end of his debate with President Carter, just days before the election: "Are you better off than you were four years ago?"

The problem was, the Romney team got the 1980 Reagan campaign all wrong. "Are you better off than you were four years ago?" was Reagan's *closing* argument, not his *entire* argument. Reagan did not make the election simply a referendum on Jimmy Carter. He also explained why voters would be better off in four years' time under *his* leadership. He put forward a positive, hopeful vision of a different future for America—an optimistic vision that attracted not only diehard Republicans but independents and "Reagan Democrats" as well. Reagan didn't just say what he was against; he said what he was for.

I firmly believe that elections are about the future and not just about the past. Reagan's election was about the future. Sure, he delivered many memorable quips that stung President Carter. (My favorite: "A recession is when your neighbor loses his job. A depression is when you lose yours. And recovery is when Jimmy Carter loses his.") But the central message of his campaign was a promise to unleash what he called "the greatness of our people, our capacity for dreaming up fantastic deeds and bringing them off to the surprise of an unbelieving world." Reagan often quoted Thomas Paine's famous declaration that in America, "We have it in our power to begin the world over again," and always added, "We still have that power."

Unlike Romney, Reagan connected with the daily struggles of ordinary Americans. In announcing his candidacy, he shared the story of "a Christmas Eve when my brother and I and our parents exchanged modest gifts—there was no lighted tree as there had been on Christmases past. I remember watching my father open what he thought was a greeting from his employer. We all watched and yes, we were hoping for a bonus check. It was notice that he no longer had a job. . . . I'll carry with me always the memory of my father sitting there holding that envelope, unable to look at us. I cannot and will not stand by while inflation and joblessness destroy the dignity of our people."[3]

Reagan did not dismiss 47 percent of the country as a bunch of moochers. Quite the opposite: At the Republican convention in Detroit he appealed to those who wanted nothing more than to get off government assistance and find work. He promised that "for those without skills, we'll find a way to help them get skills. For those without job opportunities, we'll stimulate new opportunities, particularly in the inner cities where they live. For those who have abandoned hope, we'll restore hope and we'll welcome them into a great national crusade to make America great again."

"We have to move ahead," Reagan said, "but we're not going to leave anyone behind."[4]

That is the Reagan message Romney should have emulated.

Today, in the midst of the worst recovery since the Great Depression, there are millions of Americans who are dependent on the government, but who do not *want* to be dependent on government. Instead of scolding them, Romney should have championed them. Instead of saying he could "never convince them that they should take personal responsibility and care for their lives," Romney should have offered a bold vision for how he would help them become independent again through the dignity of work. Instead of trying to convince them that Barack Obama was responsible for their plight, he should have laid out a vision for how he would help improve their circumstances.

Ronald Reagan would never have said, "I'm not concerned about the very poor."[5] Romney later said his comments were taken out of context, but the context actually made them worse. Romney had gone on to say, "We have a very ample safety net, and we can talk about whether it needs to be strengthened or whether there are holes in it. But we have food stamps, we have Medicaid, we have housing vouchers, we have programs to help the poor."[6]

That was the wrong message for the 2.6 million Americans who had slipped beneath the poverty line in 2010–11, and the millions more who feared they were just a couple of paychecks away from falling under that line themselves. They were not looking for Mitt Romney to *strengthen* the safety net; they wanted to hear how he was going to help them *escape* the safety net. They were desperate to find good jobs, get off government assistance, and work their way out of poverty and up into the middle class. Romney never offered a hopeful and optimistic vision of how he would help them get there. Instead of consigning them to the permanent welfare state, he should have explained how he would help the poor not be poor anymore.

Ronald Reagan would never have uttered the words "self-deportation." To the contrary, during his 1980 campaign Reagan declared: "Can we doubt that only a Divine Providence placed this land, this island of freedom, here as a refuge for all those people in the world who yearn to breathe freely?"[7] My sister-in-law's mother and grandmother came from Mexico a generation ago. They've been in America for more than a quarter century. When Romney talked about "self-deportation," what they heard—even though they're here legally—was that Romney wants people like us to leave. Little wonder that Romney lost the Hispanic vote to President Obama 71 to 27 percent.

When he left the White House after two incredible terms, Reagan used his farewell address from the Oval Office to finally describe for the first time what he saw when he talked about America as a "shining city on a hill":

> In my mind it was a tall, proud city built on rocks stronger than oceans, windswept, God-blessed, and teeming with people of all kinds living in harmony and peace; a city with free ports that hummed with commerce and creativity. And if there had to be city walls, the walls had doors and the doors were open to anyone with the will and the heart to get here. That's how I saw it, and see it still.[8]

That is the Reagan message Romney should have emulated.

To win in Wisconsin, and nationally for that matter, Romney needed to do more than criticize President Obama's record; he needed to offer a hopeful and optimistic vision of his own for America. He needed to explain where he wanted to lead the country—and lay out a clear, bold plan to take on both the economic and fiscal crisis our nation faces. Not a fifty-nine-point plan, mind you. Three or four big ideas that people could understand and relate to—a plan that persuadable voters in battleground states could look at and say to themselves, "If I elect Mitt Romney, here's what he's going to do to make my life better." Unfortunately, Romney never did that.

At one point, I decided to bypass the handlers and send Mitt an e-mail. In the first draft, I poured out all my frustrations. Tonette took one look at it and said, "Scott, he's never going to read that. You wouldn't read that if someone sent it to you." She was right. It was just a litany of complaints.

So I reworded it. I began by telling him that, knowing how tough my recall election had been, I could only imagine how challenging a national campaign must be for him and his family. I thanked him for running. I promised him our prayers. And then I offered some unsolicited advice:

> *Voters want a fighter. They want to know that you are going to fight for them.*
>
> *They also need to know that you have a plan to fix the economy. The great news is that you do. The bad news is that most people don't know about it.*
>
> *I know you get a thousand suggestions on how to campaign, but here are three:*
>
> 1) *Repeat your plan over and over and over again. Build the schedule around the plan. . . . The national media may sour on covering it each day, but local media is more important and they will cover it.*
> 2) *Give out more details. Talk about your jobs plan but also talk about a plan to balance the budget. Explain how that is connected to restoring confidence in our economy. Voters are starving for leadership. You are a leader—show it on the campaign trail.*
> 3) *Most importantly, show more passion. You are a super manager but voters also want to know that you are a fighter—for them and their family.*
>
> *Grab the mike and get out from behind a podium and talk directly to voters. Use real examples of people who would benefit from your plan. Have them join you on the trail. Connect to them like you did to the Olympic athletes. You have real passion. Let the voters see it.*
>
> *You can win this election! We are behind you! We desperately need you to win!*
>
> Scott

I never got a response. Toward the end, Romney did start talking more about his plans, but by then it was too little, too late. And when the 47 percent comment surfaced, it washed away whatever progress he had made.

The Obama campaign skillfully, and brutally, exploited Romney's disconnect with the majority of Americans while effectively making the case that the president was moving the country forward.

President Obama and I could not be philosophically further apart, and I deplore the kind of character assassination that the Obama camp used against Mitt Romney. Moreover, the president ran away from his record; I ran on my record.

But in some other respects, President Obama and I ran similar campaigns. We even had the same slogan: "Forward." (Some asked why we copied the Obama-Biden campaign, but the fact is we had it first. "Forward" is the Wisconsin state motto.)

My fundamental message in the recall election was: We want to keep moving Wisconsin forward, not backward. We inherited a fiscal and economic mess, made tough decisions, and got Wisconsin moving in the right direction. We are turning things around, but we still have plenty to do. We need more time to finish the job.

President Obama made essentially the same argument for his reelection.

By contrast, my opponent in the recall, Mayor Tom Barrett, tried to make the election a referendum on me. He never offered a positive vision for his candidacy. His entire message was "Dump Scott Walker"—just as Mitt Romney's entire message in the fall campaign was "Dump Barack Obama."

In other words, President Obama won by using the same successful message we employed in the recall election, while Mitt Romney lost by emulating the failed message of Mayor Barrett.

To make matters worse, while I had just won an election by telling voters in Wisconsin that we had turned a corner thanks to our policies, Romney came to Wisconsin on the heels of our victory with exactly the opposite message. Instead of embracing our success, he was telling voters in Wisconsin that the state was a mess and headed in the *wrong* direction. People said to themselves: "Wait, I just voted for Walker because things were getting better. Now Romney says it's getting worse?"

Romney should have used the success of Republican governors as a tool against President Obama. He could have said: If you want proof that Obama's approach is failing while Republican ideas are succeeding, just look at the states. In states where our ideas are being tried, we see balanced budgets, jobs being created, and economies that are finally turning a corner. In states where the Obama approach is being tried, we see higher taxes, higher debt, and higher unemployment. Do we want America to be more like California, or do we want to be more like Indiana? Do we want our federal government to emulate the failed policies of Illinois, or the successful policies of Wisconsin?

Unfortunately, Romney never did this. It was a huge lost opportunity. Instead of using the success of Republican chief executives to show why we needed a Republican chief executive in the White House, he campaigned in Iowa, Ohio, Florida, Virginia, Pennsylvania, and Wisconsin (key swing states with Republican governors) by telling voters how bad things were. He was so focused on explaining why President Obama should be fired, but never explained why he should be hired.

If he had shown voters he had a bold, reform agenda and a positive, optimistic plan for America, it would have been appealing not only to Republicans but also Democrats and independents who might have said: "I'm not a Republican, but things aren't going so well in America. He's got a plan, he's committed to it, and he seems to have the courage to act on it. Why don't we give him a shot?"

That's what Reagan did but Romney failed to do.

Just as the Romney campaign misread the reasons for the success of Reagan's campaign, today many in Washington are misreading the reasons for the failure of the Romney campaign. They argue that the lesson of 2012 is that Romney tacked too far to the right, and that Republicans have to "moderate" their views if they want to appeal to a country that is increasingly moving center-left.

With all due respect, that's just baloney. Our principles are not the problem. If our principles were the problem, then why are so many Republican governors winning elections by campaigning on those very principles? Since Barack Obama took office, the GOP has gone from controlling both the legislature and governor's mansion in just eight states to twenty-three states today. Not one GOP governor has lost a general election since 2007.

We did not win all those races by running from our principles. We won by *applying* our principles in ways that are *relevant* to the lives of our citizens.

And besides, which principles are we supposed to abandon? Our belief that the private sector, not government, creates jobs? Our belief that smaller government is better government? Our belief that you should not spend more money than you have—and that it is immoral to saddle our children and grandchildren with trillions of dollars in debt they will never be able to pay? Our belief that government dependency saps our economic strength and denies people the dignity and happiness that can only come from earned success? Our belief that higher taxes inhibit economic growth and destroy jobs, while lower taxes and less regulation are the best way to unleash the entrepreneurial spirit of our country?

In 2012, Republicans did a lousy job of presenting a positive vision of free market solutions to our nation's problems in a way that is relevant to people's lives. The problem was not that Republicans ran on principles and failed; it was that Republicans failed to run on our principles.

CHAPTER 24

"We're Still Here"

After the elections of 2012, things became remarkably quieter in the capitol. As law enforcement told us, the money had run out for the professional agitators, so they moved on to other states and other causes.

Around the state things calmed down too, which is good for most people regardless of their politics. Most Wisconsinites took a deep breath and got back to work. It was a relief to go to public events and not have mobs trying to disrupt the simplest of programs. It was nice to get back to some sense of normal.

In January 2013, I delivered my State of the State Address. I told the assembled legislators:

> Two years ago, when I first stood here as your new governor, Wisconsin was facing a $3.6 billion budget deficit, property taxes had gone up 27 percent over the previous decade, increasing every year, and the unemployment rate was 7.8 percent. Today, Wisconsin has a $342 million budget surplus, property taxes on a median valued home went down in each of the last

two years, and the unemployment rate—well, it's down to 6.7 percent. We're turning things around. We're heading in the right direction. We're moving Wisconsin forward.

Outside the chamber, in the capitol rotunda, a small group of protesters had gathered, a dim remnant of the former occupation.

They chanted, "We're still here!"

Yes, they were. But so was I.

The protesters failed to achieve their objectives. They failed to stop Act 10. They failed to take back the senate. They failed to drive me from office. They failed (so far) to overturn Act 10 in the courts. About all they had achieved was to drain millions of dollars out of the pockets of Wisconsin taxpayers.

The costs of the protest were staggering:

- Clean up and repairs to the capitol and capitol grounds required about thirty-five hundred to four thousand hours and cost an estimated $269,550.
- The cost for law enforcement at the capitol was $7,819,665.[1]
- The cost of paying the fourteen Democratic senators who abdicated their constitutional responsibilities while hiding out across the border in Illinois was $589,820 for the twenty-two days they were away.
- The cost of the 2011 senate recall elections was $2.1 million.[2]
- The cost of the 2012 recall elections was $14 million.[3]
- Added up, the fight against Act 10 had cost Wisconsin taxpayers a grand total of $24.8 million.

And that does not include the tens of millions of private money the unions spent on the protests and recalls. The irony is, after spending all that money and putting our state though eighteen months of turmoil, not only did they fail to stop Act 10, they actually helped *us* achieve our objectives.

First, the protests unified wavering Republicans in the legislature and allowed us to pass our reform package largely intact. There were certainly a number of wavering senators in the Republican caucus. All our opponents needed was for three Republicans to vote against the bill. But instead of identifying and targeting the Republicans they thought could be peeled off, the unions attacked them all.

Republican senators arriving for work were cornered by angry mobs yelling "Shame! Shame!" and "F——— you!"[4] The unions sent crowds of protestors to follow lawmakers around the state, picket their homes, harass them everywhere they went, and generally make their lives miserable. Senator Neal Kedzie had a dead fish thrown on his lawn. Senator Van Wanggaard had protesters descend on his home, including a leader of the local teachers union who declared ominously: "We want him to know we have our eyes on him."[5]

It was not just members of the state legislature and me who were targeted. Paul Ryan had protesters following him everywhere he went—town hall meetings, parades, even outside his home—and he was not even voting on the issue. They just targeted him because he was a Republican who supported our reforms. Paul recalls doing an event on Lake Geneva and having protesters with bullhorns driving by in boats, screaming expletives at him; his wife, Janna; and their young children. He said that the first time his kids ever heard the F-word was when they had protesters yelling it at them.

The unions' goal was clear: to intimidate the senators and strike fear into them. But their smash-mouth tactics had the opposite effect. The more the senators were heckled, harassed, cussed at, and spat upon, the more their resolve deepened. Those who might have been wavering became increasingly determined not to give in. Instead of splitting the GOP, the protesters and agitators helped unify wavering Republicans—and that made it possible for us to pass Act 10.

Second, the protesters' antics also turned off Wisconsin voters. The unions and their allies violated one of the key tenets of Saul Alinsky's *Rules for Radicals*: "Tactics must begin with the experience of the middle class, accepting their aversion to rudeness, vulgarity and conflict. Start them easy, don't scare them off."

The Wisconsin protesters did the exact opposite of what Alinksy advises. They epitomized "rudeness, vulgarity and conflict," and in so doing they lost the sympathy and support of many Wisconsinites.

For example, on June 25, I traveled to Devil's Lake State Park to celebrate the one hundredth anniversary of the landmark. Hundreds of people showed up and chanted the whole time. They sent a flotilla of boats on the water with sails painted to read "Walker Sucks!" and "Kill the Bill!" I wouldn't react. Indeed, I got very good at talking over the din no matter what the protesters said and did.

On July 12, we went to Gateway Technical College in Racine to celebrate the centennial of the technical college system. Hundreds of protesters showed up in red union shirts and pushed their way through the crowd, holding signs and chanting epithets. I talked right over them. When the president of the technical college system, Dan Clancy, got up to speak, they kept right on chanting. You'd think they would have had the decency to stop when I was done and allow the students and faculty to have their day of celebration.

On July 18, I traveled to Beloit with Secretary of Tourism Stephanie Klett and Senator Tim Cullen (one of the fourteen Democrats who had fled the state) for the reopening of a visitors center. As I got up to speak, the protesters began chanting and screaming and yelling and banging cow bells—and didn't stop throughout my speech. Senator Cullen came up to the podium and they began cheering. "One of the fourteen heroes!" someone shouted. But Tim said, "I came here as a state senator to do my job and I think the best thing we can do, regardless of how you feel, is to let this program go forward. . . . I think everybody should be more respectful to the secretary and the governor." They yelled back at him, "He doesn't deserve our respect!" And they resumed chanting

"Shame! Shame! Shame!" and "Recall Walker!" Tim told me later that on the way out they called him a traitor for asking them to be polite.

Scenes like that played out over and over again.

Perhaps the vilest example took place on June 8, 2011, when I attended a ceremony in front of the capitol honoring the athletes participating in the Special Olympics. Surely, the protesters would have the decency not to disrupt an event like that. Well, as soon as I began to speak, protesters dressed as zombies marched in front of the podium and stood between me and the Special Olympians, blocking their view. State Treasurer Kurt Schuller—whose daughter had once been a Special Olympics athlete—spoke for many when he declared, "To be confronted by protesters, who will never understand the personal challenges that these Special Olympians face, who decided to politicize a nonpolitical event, shows a complete lack of civility when civility is something we should all be working toward."[6] He was right.

Afterward, talk radio host Charlie Sykes suggested that I should have "gone Chris Christie on them." Chris has a unique gift, but if I had done that, it would have been about the protesters and me. I wanted to keep the focus on the Special Olympics athletes as best I could. It was their day. Besides, the actions of the protesters spoke louder than any denunciation I could have delivered from the lectern. Any normal person watching on TV that day was horrified by their behavior. I think it was a turning point when people in our state began to realize that these people were *not* like the rest of us. It just showed they had no shame.

Another shameless incident took place on August 26, when I visited the Messmer Preparatory School, a successful Catholic school in Milwaukee. I was coming to read to third graders as part of our reading initiative. Before I arrived, Brother Bob Smith, the school president, got a call from the police telling him that someone had tripped the alarms and vandalized the school. Protesters had squeezed super glue into the locks of the school doors. Brother Smith said it was the first vandalism in eleven years at the school. He told a local radio station that before I arrived, protesters outside the school warned him to "'get ready for a riot,' because they were going to disrupt the visit."[7] He said he told them, "You've got little kids who have no clue what you're even talking about, and you make something political when it isn't, that's just flat-out wrong. People ought to start acting like adults."

On November 15, 2011, the first day the unions could kick off their effort to collect signatures for my recall, they bussed about a thousand people to march in front of my house in Wauwatosa, where our sons, Matt and Alex, who still went to public school, and my elderly parents also lived.[8] The next day, Tonette went on Charlie Sykes's radio show and said, "You know, it's one thing to come out here and protest in Madison at the Executive Residence. . . . But to actually really be on our street in front of our house and disrupt our neighbors. I mean, we have two little girls that live next door, young girls. And then we have an eighty-year-old woman on the corner. I can't imagine what they're going through, those young girls. And we feel for our neighbors."[9]

Tonette also talked about the effect the protests were having on our kids. At the grocery store near our home, Alex and my mother had recently been accosted by a protester who came up and screamed, "Excuse my language, but [EXPLETIVE] SCOTT WALKER!" Tonette went on to say, "As a mom, of course . . . it's on my mind all the time that, is today going to be a good day for them? Is someone going to step out and say something to them? Is someone in the grocery store going to say something to them? I would hope that they would leave, everyone would leave the boys and I alone. But we know that that's not going to happen, obviously, with what they've decided to do to start the recall in front of our house."

One of the protesters even targeted Matt and Alex on Facebook. We got tips of protests planned for their football games at Hart Park. And the Wauwatosa police even had to close off our busy street for a while because of all the protesters in front of our home.

Looking back now, it was moments like that which really backfired on the unions. Most people agreed with Tonette that targeting my family and disrupting the lives of our neighbors and their children was going too far. Protesting at a Special Olympics ceremony, or gluing shut the doors of a Catholic school, or disrupting a fund-raiser for disabled children, was going too far. No matter what your political views, here in Wisconsin people simply don't do things like that.

I hope that people also saw that we didn't respond in kind to provocations like these. We were firm in our convictions, and unrelenting in the pursuit of our reforms. But we always affirmed the right of those who disagreed with us to express their views. We met indecency with decency, and respected those who disrespected us.

There was a reason for that. For one thing, that is how my parents raised me. For another, that is also how Tonette and I wanted to raise our sons. I knew the citizens of Wisconsin were watching, but I also had an even more important audience—Matt and Alex. It was important to me that they saw that I never responded in kind to the often vicious attacks directed against me. I was firm and did not budge—but no matter how personal the invective became, I never made it personal.

I wanted more than anything for my sons to understand that you can be committed to your principles, stick to your guns, and do the right thing—but you must be be decent in how you conduct yourself. I wanted to set a good example so they could always be proud of how their dad handled himself.

Sometimes it was hard. One day, I was visiting a school in Stevens Point, and after reading to the kids I met with teachers in the library. A few questions in, one of the teachers stood up and asked me: "Why do you hate teachers so much? Why are you demonizing us?" I was tempted to pull a Chris Christie, but I resisted. Instead, I looked at her and said, "You know, with all due respect, I just don't see that." I pointed out that I was under such scrutiny that almost anything I said wound up on YouTube. "You go home tonight and search YouTube and try and find a single video of me saying anything but positive things about public school teachers in the state of Wisconsin. You're not going to find it."

If anything, I always went out of my way to point out that the vast majority of the more than three hundred thousand government employees in our state were good, decent, hardworking public servants—and to say how much I appreciated them. Indeed, the reason I waited so long to point out the abuses taking place thanks to collective bargaining was that I did not want to do or say anything that could be misconstrued as criticizing public workers.

Over time, I think people in our state saw the difference in the way we conducted ourselves and the way the union bosses conducted themselves. We always took the high road. We just kept repeating our arguments, explaining why we were doing what we were doing, educating people about how our reforms were pro-worker, pro-teacher, pro-student, and pro-taxpayer. We tried our best never to contribute to the hostility and the rancor. And the unions kept behaving like thugs and goons. In so doing, they made themselves appear extreme and radical, and that helped us unify the state behind our reforms.

The third way the protests backfired is that they made what might otherwise have been an arcane debate over the Wisconsin budget into a national issue. The protests generated national and even global news coverage, and energized conservatives across the country. I got letters of support from people in almost every state.

One day, I received a moving letter from a Vietnam veteran in Texas who had received several flying awards. He told me about the day when two union goons had come to see his dad and told him he was going to join the union or else. He praised my courage for taking on the unions, and said there was only one way to appropriately thank me for my courage. He included a small package. Inside was one of his flying medals. I was floored. I display it with great pride in my office today. It reminded me of the impact we were having on people.

In fact, people all across the country wanted to help and be a part of our efforts. They sent donations, made phone calls, and many even came to Wisconsin to knock on doors and get out the vote. We raised over $37 million to fight the recall and received donations from tens of thousands of people, the vast majority of whom gave $100 or less. Our fight in Madison became a national cause.

None of that would have happened were it not for the protesters and their antics that made network and cable news nearly every night. Our supporters were energized not only by the substance of what we had done but also by our standing up to the protesters. If we had been able to pass the bill in seven days, as we had initially planned, I probably would still have been targeted for a recall. But I would have had to fight it without the backing of all the people from across the country who rallied to support us.

The fourth way the protests backfired is that they gave us an unexpected opportunity to make our case to the people of Wisconsin. Without the recall, I would never have had the opportunity to campaign across the state to defend our record. I would never have had a reason to air television ads across to the state explaining the success of our reforms. Thanks to our opponents, every voter in Wisconsin now knows what our reforms were, why we made them, and—most important—that they worked.

In the end, the protests did more to help us achieve our aims than anything we could possibly have come up with in the governor's office.

It just goes to show that the extremism of your opponents is often your greatest weapon in the fight for what is right.

CHAPTER 25

"We Did That Too"

There was one other way the protests over Act 10 helped us: They so overshadowed everything else going on in the state capitol that we were able to pass a raft of other reforms and initiatives that at any other time might have sparked protests and controversy. Instead they went virtually unnoticed.

Outside Wisconsin, few are aware of these reforms. I remember going to a meeting of Republican governors and listening as my colleagues ticked off the various economic, education, pro-life, and public safety reforms they had implemented. I raised my hand sheepishly and said, "As a point of clarification, we did that too." Everyone knew we had taken on the unions, but many were surprised to learn all the other changes we had made in our state.

For example, we passed legislation to prevent voter fraud by requiring voters to show photo identification at the polls—a bill Republicans had worked to pass since 2003. As I signed the bill into law, the protesters chanted "Shame!" and "Recall Walker!" outside my office. They weren't there for the voter ID bill; they were the same union protesters who followed me everywhere to protest Act 10.

We also dramatically expanded school choice in Wisconsin. We lifted the cap on the number of students eligible to participate in the Milwaukee Parental Choice Program so that children won't have to see their futures decided by a lottery. We lifted the income limits on school choice eligibility, so that middle class families can escape failing schools as well.

Then we expanded school choice geographically from Milwaukee to Racine, the next most troubled school district in the state, then to a statewide program. Because students get report cards, we established report cards for schools so that parents can see which schools are succeeding and which ones are failing their students. And we expanded charter schools by allowing any University of Wisconsin System four-year campus to create a charter school.

In our 2011 budget, we stopped funding for Planned Parenthood. Instead, the state now contracts with less controversial organizations (like county governments) to promote health care for women. I also signed legislation prohibiting any health plan offered through an exchange operating in Wisconsin from covering abortion, and a bill that requires schools that teach sex education to stress abstinence as the only reliable way to prevent pregnancy and sexually transmitted diseases. At any other time, these might have been huge fights—but because of the fight over Act 10, they received little notice.

We also enhanced public safety and the Second Amendment rights of our citizens. My predecessor, Jim Doyle, had repeatedly vetoed legislation to allow the carry of concealed firearms. I signed it into law, transforming Wisconsin from one of the more restrictive to one of the freest states in the union when it comes to the right to bear arms. We restored truth in sentencing by repealing the early release program approved by the last administration, and passed "castle doctrine" legislation to protect homeowners who defend themselves and their families with deadly force from intruders who break into their homes. A group of more than six hundred criminal defense lawyers and academics rallied to oppose the bill. There was a time when that might have seemed like a lot, but after seeing one hundred thousand protesters in our state capitol, a coalition of a few hundred opponents seemed meek by comparison.

In normal times, many of these initiatives might have faced organized opposition. But in Wisconsin, the organized left was so worked up over Act 10, they barely registered a mention, much less a protest.

Since the fight over Act 10, we have not slowed the pace of reform in Wisconsin. I continue to follow the advice Mitch Daniels gave me a few weeks after my election. Never stop reforming—always have the next big idea ready.

Because our reforms got spending under control, in each of my first two years in office, property taxes went down, while our budget deficit became a surplus. We used that to push major tax reform and nearly $1 billion worth of tax relief.

Our current budget cuts individual income tax rates for all taxpayers—as well as lowers the tax burden for small businesses and key industries like manufacturing and agriculture. In addition, we added a tuition tax deduction for families who send their kids to private schools, and we froze tuition at all University of Wisconsin campuses for the first time in the history of the system.

This was a down payment on my goal of reducing the tax burden in our state every year I am in office. We plan to cut taxes over and over and over again until Wisconsin is leading the country in economic recovery.

We are expanding school choice even further. After lifting the caps on size and income in Milwaukee and adding a voucher program in my first budget, we expanded vouchers statewide for low-income families. Expanding school choice gives students in failing schools better options. It also strengthens traditional schools by giving officials in struggling schools an incentive to use the tools in Act 10.

We gave every public school administrator in Wisconsin the same freedom and flexibility that charter schools enjoy. They can now change the curriculum, expand the school day, reward good teachers, and get rid of failing ones—all without getting permission from (or dealing with grievances from) the teachers unions.

Many school districts across the state have used those tools to balance their budgets and improve the quality of education. Unfortunately, some refused to use the tools we gave them. Perhaps they are satisfied with mediocrity. Or perhaps they are so beholden to the unions that even when liberated from the grip of collective bargaining, they still refuse to make the changes necessary to improve performance. Whatever the reason, they need an incentive to use the tools in Act 10.

School choice provides that incentive. If officials at weak or failing schools have to compete for students, perhaps they will summon the will to change. We gave these officials the tools they need to turn their schools around. Expanding school choice will give them the impetus to use them.

Our next big initiative is entitlement reform. We are pushing fundamental reform of Wisconsin's three major entitlement programs: Medicaid, unemployment assistance, and food stamps. Our goal is simple: to help as many people in our state as possible move from dependence on government to independence, dignity, and self-reliance.

Medicaid is the fastest growing entitlement in our state budget. And like so many other government programs, my predecessor dramatically expanded Medicaid without providing the money to pay for it. According to the *Wall Street Journal,* Governor Doyle opened up the program to people earning twice the poverty rate, which led to a 73 percent increase in enrollments. But he did not have the money to cover the 99 percent increase in state Medicaid spending. So he capped enrollment in Medicaid, shutting out people below the poverty line who *should* be getting Medicaid coverage, while people above the poverty line received care.[1]

Then, in 2009, he used one-time federal stimulus funds that were supposed to go to infrastructure to cover ongoing costs of Medicaid. Soon the one-time money ran out, but the increased bills kept piling up. So when he left office, he handed us an entitlement program that was growing out of control, without the funds to sustain that growth.[2]

Doyle's Medicaid expansion was bad enough, but then President Obama passed Obamacare, which mandated yet another expansion of Medicaid—one that would have grown the Medicaid rolls in Wisconsin by an additional 32 percent.

The federal government promised to pay 100 percent of the costs for three years (and 90 percent after that). But I had little confidence they would keep their new promises because they were already reneging on their old ones.

In our 2013–15 budget, we had to increase spending on Medicaid by $644 million. Nearly 40 percent of that money—almost $208 million—was for the current costs of Medicaid that the federal government promised to cover but had reneged on, and other federal changes. If Washington cannot fulfill its current commitments, why on earth would we trust Congress and the administration to cover even bigger costs in the future—especially when they are sitting on a $16.7 trillion debt that is projected to reach $20 trillion by the end of Obama's presidency?

One of my first acts as governor was enabling our attorney general to join the lawsuit challenging Obamacare. And while I was disappointed that the U.S. Supreme Court upheld the law, thankfully the Court did rule that the Obama administration cannot force states to accept the Medicaid expansion. From the moment the Court issued its decision, I knew that I was going to turn it down. It would have been fiscally unsustainable and would have added tens of thousands of people to the Medicaid rolls when my goal was to have *fewer* people dependent on the government, not more.

But I also wanted to reduce the number of uninsured people in our state. So instead of just simply rejecting the Medicaid expansion, as some governors did, I looked for a way to achieve that goal without putting more people on government health care. I approached my decision on Medicaid in much the same way I did my decision on collective bargaining. I had my staff examine all the possible alternatives and search for options to save money while making government work better for our citizens. And after two years of study, we came up with an innovative approach that not only rejected the Medicaid expansion but also reduced both the number of people on Medicaid *and* the number of uninsured people in our state.

Under our plan, every person in Wisconsin who is living in poverty will be covered by Medicaid. We removed the caps Governor Doyle imposed on the number of participants, while moving some eighty-seven thousand people living *above* poverty into the private or exchange markets, where they can get insurance premiums for as low as $19 per month.

By doing this, we can give eighty-two thousand people currently living in poverty access to Medicaid they were once denied. By taking this approach, we will reduce overall the number of people in Medicaid while ensuring that, for the first time, 100 percent of those living under the poverty line are covered. At the same time, we will move the vast majority of people in our state into the marketplace and the exchanges. And we will reduce the total number of uninsured in Wisconsin by 244,580 people—a 47 percent decrease.

Some argue that the exchanges, where many of those moved out of Medicaid will get their insurance, are still heavily subsidized. That is true. But it is far better to have people in subsidized exchanges than in Medicaid. In Medicaid, everything is covered by taxpayers at no cost to the individual. In the exchanges, people at least have to pay a premium that corresponds with their level of income and the level of coverage they choose. That is a step away from government dependence. And as their incomes rise, they will transition out of exchanges and into the private market.

Some critics have said that people moving out of Medicaid will have trouble navigating all the choices in the exchanges, and will simply end up in the emergency room. If that's their position, then their problem is with Obamacare, not with our plan. After all, the president is the one who created the exchanges in the first place.

I could have simply rejected the Medicaid expansion. Instead we found an innovative way to have fewer people uninsured, fewer people in Medicaid, more people in the market, and 100 percent of the poor covered for the first time. Under our plan, the people of Wisconsin will have better health care and will be less dependent on government.

Moreover, our Medicaid reforms addressed a fundamental problem with entitlements generally: Too many entitlement programs have expanded beyond their original purpose of helping the truly destitute. In Wisconsin, the expansion of Medicaid to cover people above the poverty line had actually denied many of those below the poverty line access to the program—because there was not enough money. It is this expansion of entitlements beyond their original intent that is bankrupting states and bankrupting our country.

With our reforms, we are reclaiming Medicaid for those for whom it was intended: the poor. We are making the program sustainable now and for the future in order to keep the promises we have made to those who are truly in need—while moving people above the poverty level into the market with their neighbors and fellow workers.

In addition to reforming Medicaid, we are also reforming Wisconsin's unemployment assistance program. Recipients used to have to demonstrate that they were searching for work just twice a week. We raised that to five or more. When some in the legislature complained that five times was too burdensome, I replied that, quite frankly, I considered that too few. I am a preacher's son. If I was unemployed, the voice of my father in my head would be telling me to get out there and look for work *six* times a week—and to take off Sunday to pray that I would find work the following day. So with all respect, I don't think five days a week is an unrealistic expectation.

We introduced similar reforms to our food stamp program. Right now, the federal government has a requirement that able-bodied, childless adults of working age have to either work or get employment training in order to receive food stamps. But in the past, forty-six of the fifty states have been granted a waiver from that requirement—including Wisconsin. Not anymore.

At the end of 2012, I notified the federal government that Wisconsin would no longer be asking for that waiver. Instead, we established a training program for the 75,878 food stamp recipients in our state who are childless, able-bodied, working-age adults. Today, these individuals need to be either working part-time or signed up for one of our employment training programs in order to receive food stamps.

The new program is part of a $100 million plan to expand and revitalize workforce development in Wisconsin. Because Act 10 allowed us to move from deficit to surplus, we are now able to increase resources for grants for employers, support for apprenticeships, programs for veterans, and funds for our technical colleges and University of Wisconsin System—all aimed at training citizens of our state for jobs in areas like manufacturing, information technology, and health care.

The new approach is good for employers, who desperately need skilled workers to fill positions in areas like manufacturing and health care. It is good for taxpayers because the temporary cost of work training is less expensive than the cost of long-term government assistance. But most important of all, it is good for our fellow citizens in need because it gives them a chance to develop the skills they need to find good jobs, get off of government assistance, and once again enjoy the dignity of self-reliance and earned success.

Last year, I learned about a young woman named Elizabeth. She was a single mom in Milwaukee who had fallen on hard times and was struggling to make ends meet. So she signed up for food stamps. Because she was a parent, and it was before we changed the waiver process, it was voluntary to sign up for employment training along with food stamps. But Elizabeth, to her credit, decided to take advantage of the employment training we offered. She enrolled at one of our technical colleges, worked hard, and became a certified nursing assistant (CNA).

She was such an inspiring success story that when I announced in my 2013 budget address our initiative to require, and increase funding for, job training as part of reform of Wisconsin's food stamp program, I asked Elizabeth to be there so I could introduce her and point her out in the gallery. She thanked me but said she couldn't come that night. You know why? She had to work that day as a CNA, and then that night she had to attend class where she is studying to become a registered nurse.

Elizabeth used the food stamp program exactly as it was intended—as a temporary hand up, not a permanent handout. She needed government assistance, but she did not want to be on government assistance. She wanted the dignity of work and the happiness that comes only from earned success.

We want to share that dignity and happiness with all the people in our state.

Sadly, it seems some folks in Washington measure success in government by how many people are dependent on the government. I measure success by just the opposite—by how many people are no longer dependent on the government. We want fewer people on government health care, fewer people receiving unemployment, fewer people on food stamps—not because they've been kicked to the curb but because they no longer need the help. We want to empower them with a job in the private sector and the dignity that comes from work.

I don't believe that most people grow up in America hoping that someday they will be dependent on the government. I don't believe that most people come to this country as immigrants hoping for a handout. I believe most people want to live the American Dream. They want to live lives of dignity, independence, and self-reliance. They want the chance to work hard, pursue their dreams, and leave their children better off than they were.

There's a reason why in America we take a day off to celebrate the Fourth of July and not the fifteenth of April. In America, we value independence from the government and *not* dependence on it.

Our reforms are moving citizens in Wisconsin from government dependence to true independence.

We need to do the same for citizens across this great land of ours.

CHAPTER 26

The Lessons of Wisconsin Can Be
Used in the Battle for America

There is a lot conservatives can learn from the battle in Wisconsin that can help us win the battle for America. We did a lot of things right in the fight over Act 10, but we also made a few mistakes. Here are some of the lessons learned from our experience that can help inform the larger debate over the future of our country.

CHANGE THE POLLS, NOT YOUR PRINCIPLES

If you know you are doing the right thing, and the polls say voters disagree, change the polls, not your principles. President Reagan used to look at polls not to determine his positions, but to see where he needed to do more to persuade the public. That's a sign of true leadership.

If I had listened to the polls during the fight over Act 10, I would have backed off of our plan. One poll found that if the gubernatorial election were held again, I would have lost to my opponent by seven points. My approval dropped to 37 percent. But I was so confident our reforms would work that I pressed forward into the political headwinds.

And my confidence was vindicated. Our reforms *did* work. And voters stood with me in the recall election.

I wanted to win, but I also wasn't afraid to lose. I cared more about getting things done than getting reelected. That liberated me to take bold actions I might never have taken if my first priority had been political survival. Too many people in politics today spend their time trying not to lose instead of trying to do the right thing. I often say that politicians need to spend more time worrying about the next generation than the next election. The irony is that politicians who spend more time worrying about the next generation than the next election often tend to win the next election because voters are starved for leadership.

Don't Compromise Your Principles but Do Be Willing to Compromise

Another important lesson is that while it's important not to compromise your principles, do be willing to compromise.

My original plan for Act 10 was to eliminate collective bargaining altogether for all government workers. But when my staff pointed out that police and firefighters could go on strike, possibly endangering public safety, I didn't hesitate to exempt them.

Similarly, when Republican senators wanted to reform collective bargaining rather than eliminate it, we compromised again—finding a way to accommodate their concerns while preserving the goals of our legislation. The changes actually improved our bill because they put the unions' fate in the hands of their own members. Teachers and other public employees would choose whether the union could negotiate on their behalf and whether they paid union dues—not the government.

And when the senate Democrats fled the state, I was willing to compromise yet again—offering them a number of substantive concessions if they would come back to Wisconsin and do their jobs. In the end, the senate Democrats didn't take our offer, and we found a way around their obstruction. But simply by offering concessions, we showed the citizens of our state that we were willing to compromise—and exposed the fact that the Democrats were not.

The media and unions portrayed me as uncompromising, but the fact is we compromised a lot. We just refused to compromise our principles. I was willing to be flexible, and to make changes to the bill, so long as the final legislation achieved our overarching goals.

Don't Accept the False Choices Presented to You

With a little ingenuity, you can break the mold and find a better way forward.

When I first took office, we faced a $3.6 billion deficit and two bad choices: raise taxes or dramatically cut government services. Neither of those options was acceptable to me. I had promised to cut taxes, not raise them. And I was not going to slash spending on the poor, throw thousands of people out of work, or devastate education and public services.

By talking to smart people like Mitch Daniels, doing our homework, and examining all the alternatives, we came up with an innovative approach that allowed us to balance our budget while protecting taxpayers, protecting the poor, protecting schools, protecting local governments, protecting teachers and government workers—all while actually improving education and strengthening public services.

We rejected the false choice between raising taxes and cutting government services. There is really nothing revolutionary about this. In the private sector people do it all the time. If you own a business that is struggling, you don't double the price of your product or cut its quality in half. You find ways to run your business more efficiently and deliver a better product than your competitor at lower cost. With Act 10, we simply applied that same principle to state government. It wasn't easy, and it certainly was not without controversy. But it worked.

We also rejected false choices when it came to President Obama's Medicaid expansion. Once again we were presented with two bad options: Accept a massive expansion of Medicaid (knowing that the federal money would eventually dry up and Wisconsin taxpayers would be left on the hook) or reject the expansion (and leave hundreds of thousands of our citizens uninsured). We rejected that false choice and found another way.

Together with Dennis Smith, my secretary of the Department of Health Services, I spent two years studying the issue and examining all the possible alternatives. In the end, we came up with a solution that reduced the number of people on Medicaid, reduced the number of uninsured in our state by 244,580, and moved tens of thousands off government health care and into the market while ensuring that, for the first time, everyone living in poverty was covered. We improved health care for our citizens while decreasing government dependency.

If we can do it in Wisconsin, it can be done anywhere. Conservatives need to stop playing by the rules set by the left. With creativity and a little innovation, we can redefine the debate on our terms.

A Big Crisis Is a Chance to Do Big Things

Another lesson is that times of crisis present a chance to do big things that otherwise might not be possible.

For years, my predecessor had used accounting gimmicks and temporary fixes to paper over our state's fiscal problems. When we came to office, the bag of tricks was empty. We faced an unprecedented fiscal crisis—a $3.6 billion deficit with no way to close it. Rather than simply tinkering around the edges, we took bold action not only to balance our budget in the short term but also to put in place long-term structural reforms that will help us balance state and local government budgets for years to come.

If it had not been for the depth of the fiscal disaster we inherited, our reforms would never have passed—even with a Republican majority. The only reason we were able to make the changes of this magnitude was because of the magnitude of the deficit and the lack of any viable alternatives. Passing Act 10 would have been the right thing to do under any circumstances—but it might not have been *possible* under any other circumstances.

It is an unfortunate fact of life that some people are willing to make tough choices only when there are no easy ones available that will work. That's why we see so many difficult problems kicked down the road for future generations. So when circumstances present you with the chance to take big, bold, decisive actions that would otherwise not be possible, seize it.

You Can Reform Entitlements and Survive

What we did in Wisconsin with Act 10 was in many ways much harder than what Congress and the president need to do to tackle the federal entitlement crisis.

Most of the proposals for saving Social Security and Medicare affect future retirees, not current recipients. Our reforms affected *current* public workers and retirees. It should be a lot easier to change benefits before people start collecting them than it was to roll them back once they are already being paid out.

Our experience in Wisconsin shows that politicians can make the tough decisions to deal with the massive unfunded liabilities we face, and survive. If we can do it in Wisconsin, it can be done in Washington.

Austerity Is Not the Answer

In times of crisis, people are looking for hope. Too often, conservatives present themselves as the bearers of sour medicine when we should be offering a positive, optimistic agenda instead.

At a time when our national debt is soaring, that can be a difficult challenge. It isn't easy to make fiscal responsibility hopeful and optimistic. But it can be done. We did it in Wisconsin.

We could have responded to our budget crisis in Wisconsin with an austerity budget. We could have simply enacted deep spending cuts and told our citizens that it was time for everyone to cinch up their belts and live with less. We could have laid off tens of thousands of middle-class workers. We could have cut Medicaid for needy families, seniors, and the poor. We could have cut $1.25 billion from schools and local governments, and told parents they needed to accept life with many more kids in the classroom. But where is the optimism in that?

Instead we found a hopeful, optimistic alternative to austerity. With the passage of Act 10, we made tough choices, but they were choices about how to save money by making government operate better. We found a way to make government not just smaller but also more responsive, more efficient, and more effective. And because we did, we were able to cut government spending while still *improving* education and public services. We turned our deficit into a surplus, but we rejected the sour politics of austerity.

We're doing the same thing with our entitlement reforms. Our critics say that I must hate poor people because I'm making it harder to get government assistance. The opposite is true. I love the people of my state so much that I don't want them to be permanently dependent on the government. I don't want to make it harder for them to get government assistance; I want to make it easier for them to get a *job*. We are requiring able-bodied citizens to work or receive job training if they receive food stamps. But we are also increasing funding for that training as part of a plan to expand and revitalize our state's workforce development.

I want to help my fellow citizens who have fallen on hard times, and are temporarily dependent on government, to get the skills they need so they can once again support their families and control their own destinies. Today, there is a perception that Republicans simply want to cut things. I take a backseat to no one when it comes to cutting spending and fiscal responsibility. We cut spending and turned a massive budget deficit into a sizable surplus. But austerity is not hopeful or optimistic. Moving people from government dependence to true independence is— and in the long run, it saves money too.

THE BENEFITS OF BOLDNESS

The only reason we have the resources to expand job training today is because of Act 10. If we had not reformed collective bargaining and turned our $3.6 billion deficit into a half-billion-dollar surplus, there would be no money available to reform food stamps by increasing job training . . . or to reform Medicaid to cover everyone living in poverty . . . or to cut income tax rates in Wisconsin. It is only because we took on the unions and freed Wisconsin from the grip of collective bargaining that we are now able to fund our priorities and return money to the taxpayers in the form of lower property taxes and lower income taxes.

The lesson is that benefits of boldness often go far beyond the immediate effects of the action you are taking. Act 10 not only allowed us to fix our budget, improve education, and strengthen public services—it has also allowed us to unleash a host of other reforms that will benefit the citizens of our state for decades to come.

WIN THE CENTER WITH LEADERSHIP

There is a myth out there that the only way to win the center is to move to the center. If that were true, Barack Obama would not be president today—and I would not be governor of Wisconsin.

There are independent, reform-minded voters in every state. In times of crisis, they want leadership. They don't care if it is Republican leadership or Democratic leadership. If you step forward and offer a reform agenda that is hopeful and optimistic, they will give you a shot. And if you have the courage to follow through and keep your promises, they will stick with you. (It is still amazing to me that politics is one of the few professions where keeping your word makes you "courageous." Everywhere else in life, keeping your word is expected. Somehow it is exceptional in politics.)

In Wisconsin, we have a phenomenon known as Obama-Walker

voters. When I was first elected to lead Milwaukee County, a deep blue Democratic enclave, no one thought I would survive very long. My election was a fluke, the pundits said, and if I wanted to stay in the job I would have to do what so many Republicans in urban areas do and move to the middle. Instead, I governed as a conservative reformer and didn't flinch—and won three consecutive elections with a larger percentage of the vote each time. In 2008, the year President Obama won Milwaukee County with 67.5 percent of the vote, I won with nearly 60 percent.

As governor, I have continued to pursue bold, conservative reforms. And in the 2012 gubernatorial recall election, one out of six voters who cast their ballots for me also planned to vote for President Obama. Exit polls showed that these Obama-Walker voters constituted 9 percent of the electorate.[1] And today, polls show that about 11 percent of Wisconsinites continue support both me and President Obama.

There are probably no two people in public life who are more philosophically opposite than President Obama and me. Yet more than one in ten Wisconsinites approve of us both.

To make a conservative comeback, we need to be able to win these Obama-Walker voters, and their equivalents in other states. The way to win over those in the middle is not by abandoning your principles. To the contrary, the courage to stand on principle is precisely what these voters respect. If you back away from your principles, you not only lose your base, you also lose the one thing that attracted these independent voters to you in the first place. The way to win the center is not to waver. The way to win the center is to champion bold, positive reforms that make people's lives better—and to show that you have the courage to follow through on these reforms.

The way to win the center is to *lead*.

CHAMPION THE VULNERABLE

Liberals want to portray conservatives as defenders of the rich and powerful.

Unfortunately, we often make it too easy for them to do so.

I recall doing a television interview one day about our entitlement reforms, and I was getting really fired up talking about how nobody comes to this country wanting to be dependent on the government. Whether they arrived here on a raft, or were born here in a barrio, people all want the same thing: self-determination, independence, opportunity, and the chance for their kids to do even better than they did—the American dream.

After the interview was over, and I was preparing to leave, the woman who had prepared me for the show came up to me in tears and said in broken English: "That's me." At first I didn't understand what she meant. She told me, "I'm from Cambodia. I came here to live the American dream. You were talking about me."[2]

Conservatives need to champion people like her. We need to champion immigrants who come here seeking a better life. We need to champion those born here in poverty who want nothing more than to escape it. We need to heed the call Ronald Reagan delivered in his farewell address at the Republican National Convention in 1992: "With each sunrise we are reminded that millions of our citizens have yet to share in the abundance of American prosperity. Many languish in neighborhoods riddled with drugs and bereft of hope. Still others hesitate to venture out on the streets for fear of criminal violence. Let us pledge ourselves to a new beginning for them."[2]

Republicans need to reclaim their position as the party of upward mobility and opportunity for all. We need to lay out a positive vision for an America where every one of our citizens—no matter what their race, creed, origin, political party, or station in life—has a chance for a better future. We need to offer innovative, free market alternatives to the permanent welfare state.

That requires more than saying the right things. It requires showing up in inner-city schools and talking about expanding school choice, reading initiatives, and our plans to reform education so that everyone among us will have the mental tools to build a better life. It requires showing up at community colleges and job-training centers, and talking about our plans to help people escape dependency and get the skills they need for the jobs of the twenty-first century. It requires visiting local chambers of commerce, particularly in struggling neighborhoods, and talking to small-business owners about our plans to create jobs and opportunity in places bereft of hope.

Voters want to know we are fighting for them. We need to fight for the vulnerable among us. Just as important, we need to fight cronyism and corruption. One of the reasons we took on collective bargaining in Wisconsin is because it was inherently corrupt. Collective bargaining allowed the union bosses to effectively sit on both sides of the bargaining table when contracts are negotiated—putting their interests ahead of those of teachers and students and taxpayers. It was cronyism, plain and simple. We dismantled it.

We need to take on and dismantle cronyism and corruption wherever we find it—whether it is President Obama's "green energy" program that gave billions in taxpayer dollars to his political cronies or the billions of dollars in government benefits, taxpayer subsidies, and corporate welfare that special interests receive from Washington each year and do not need.

BE DECENT

During the fight over Act 10, our opponents compared us to Hitler and slave masters. And those were just the Democratic senators. Today it seems that whenever the left is losing a political battle, they villainize their opponents.

We see this phenomenon in Washington as well. During the debt limit standoff, President Obama declared, "What's motivating and propelling at this point some of the House Republicans is more than simply deficit reduction. They . . . are suspicious about government's commitments, for example, to make sure that seniors have decent health care . . . [and] about whether government should make sure that kids in poverty are getting enough to eat."[3]

The president wasn't simply questioning the wisdom of the House Republicans' policies, he was also questioning their motives. He was saying Republicans want to take health care away from seniors and food out of the mouths of poor children.

Sadly, this is not uncommon. We suffered far worse in Wisconsin, but we never responded in kind. When I served in the state assembly I used to tell new members not to personalize their differences, because their opponents today may be their allies tomorrow. And during the fight over Act 10, no matter what the other side threw at us, I never responded in kind and always affirmed the right of our opponents to protest and have their say.

Decency is its own reward. But it also serves to contrast you with the extremism of your opponents. They often cannot help but to overreach. We saw that when the union bosses accused Justice Prosser of protecting a pedophile priest. It was an outrageous accusation. It was untrue. And it cost them the election. It cost them control of the state supreme court. And it ultimately cost them victory in their fight to overturn Act 10.

At one point during the protests, Representative Robin Vos was sitting in a bar near the capitol when a protester came up and poured a beer over his head. He was mortified and just wanted to forget that it ever happened. When he told me about it the next day, I urged him to tell the press. The people of Wisconsin needed to know that our opponents poured beer over the head of Republican leaders, shouted at and spit on senators, disrupted a Special Olympics ceremony, and glued shut the doors of a Catholic school I was going to visit.

By contrast, we always took the high road and never contributed to the hostility and the rancor. In the end, the contrast between our conduct and their outrageous behavior helped turn public opinion in our favor—especially among the Obama-Walker voters. There are millions of Americans who are frustrated by the cheap shots and smash-mouth politics that are all too common today. When you come under vicious personal attack, you win more support by responding with decency than you do by responding in kind.

Own Up to Your Mistakes

Another important lesson is that when you screw up, own up to it. When I took that prank call from the fake David Koch, it was one of the most embarrassing moments of my life. I went out before the press and took my beating. I learned from the experience—to be more humble and to make certain I was doing things for the right reasons.

Because I owned up to what I had done, it was harder for our critics to continue exploiting the story and easier for us to move past it. Today, too many political leaders are hesitant to admit mistakes— and that often gives their mistakes a much longer shelf life than they deserve.

At the same time, never apologize for doing the right thing. Some of my advisers wanted me to apologize to the state for the unrest over Act 10. That would have been a terrible mistake. Reforming collective bargaining was the right thing to do. Moreover, we never responded in kind to the provocations of the protesters, or did anything to bring dishonor to our state. Apologizing would have done nothing to win over those who were angry with me. And it would have dispirited those who stood with me—folks who supported me precisely because we stood on principle.

While I did not apologize, I did acknowledge a critical error I made, which was not properly preparing the people of Wisconsin for our reforms. I was so eager to fix the problems we faced, I did not do enough to explain to people what they were or why our solutions were the right course. I've learned from that experience and applied those lessons when announcing subsequent reforms.

NEVER STOP REFORMING

We didn't stop reforming once we passed Act 10 and defended it at the ballot box. We expanded our education reforms and turned immediately to the next big idea: entitlement reform. And once we have reformed entitlements, we will turn to the next big reform, and the next one. We are following the advice Mitch Daniels gave me before I took office: Never stop reforming. Never stop innovating. When you set the pace of reform, voters will see you as someone who is constantly trying to make things better. And your opponents will be forced to respond to your agenda rather than setting one for you.

Plus, it's fun. I enjoy finding creative solutions to difficult challenges.

BE RELEVANT

The people I speak with in Wisconsin are not talking about who will blink first in the latest budget standoff in Washington. They want to know: Will my neighbor down the block who's been out of a job for six months be able to find work? Will I be able to support my family and save enough for retirement and to send my kids to a good college? Will my kids' school perform well enough to help them get into college in the first place? And when my son or daughter graduates, will he or she be able to find a job in our state and be able to stay here, or will he or she have to move away?

Those are the questions that are relevant to our citizens. Republican governors are succeeding because we are focused on answering those questions.

Republicans nationally need to be focused on those kinds of questions as well. We need to talk about things that are relevant to people's lives, such as: Are our children going to be able to afford the debt being passed on to them by the federal government? And how can we improve the economy so that our citizens may find better job prospects and enjoy a better quality of life? "Sequesters," "fiscal cliffs," and "debt limits" are not relevant to people's lives; growth, opportunity, and upward mobility are.

Part of being relevant means going to places where Republicans don't typically show up. When I was a local official, I did very well in areas that were dominated by Hispanic voters. The reason: I was a strong advocate for small businesses and for school choice. Voters in those neighborhoods knew me because I helped small-business owners grow and because I championed the Catholic schools in their area. I spoke in terms that were relevant to these voters and I spoke to them in familiar places.

Speaking in terms that are relevant to everyday citizens isn't always easy. When I first ran for governor, I talked about the fiscal and economic crises we faced in our state and then I laid out my plans to fix them. I was so focused on these issues that it was likely that if a reporter asked my mother's maiden name, I would say, "Fitch, and every Fitch I know believes we need to fix the economy and the budget." The lesson is: Stay relevant.

Win the Fairness Fight

Conservatives spend far too much time trying to move minds without moving hearts as well. We gather tons of empirical data to back up our arguments, only to see the liberals respond with heartbreaking stories about how our policies will supposedly hurt children, the elderly, and the destitute. The heartbreaking stories win.

As the American Enterprise Institute's Arthur Brooks points out, human beings by their nature respond to moral, rather than empirical, arguments. If we find a policy morally repugnant, there is little anyone can say that is likely to change our minds using data, reason, or empirical evidence. When we feel something is wrong, it is just wrong—period.

This is an admirable quality, really. We respond to moral arguments for a reason: That is how God made us. We are inherently moral creatures, created in His own image and likeness. We were designed by our Creator to see the world through the prism of good and evil, of right and wrong. That is why most of us want not only to be a prosperous nation but also a nation that is good, decent, and—yes—fair.

President Obama understands this, which is why he made "fairness" a central message of his reelection campaign. Who is opposed to fairness? Shouldn't everyone get a "fair shot"? Shouldn't everyone pay their "fair share"? The president appealed to the American people's innate sense of fairness. Republicans did not. That is one of the main reasons he won a second term.

If we want to win the policy debates of the twenty-first century, we need to stop allowing our political opponents to claim the moral high ground that we should be occupying ourselves. For example, most Americans believe that conservatives care about balancing budgets, while liberals care about putting more money into classrooms. But in Wisconsin, *our* reforms put more money into classrooms. It was the unions and the Democrats who were ready to see us cut a billion dollars from classrooms, and lay off thousands of teachers, just so long as they could continue to fill their coffers with involuntary union dues. We stopped them, and protected students and teachers from disastrous cuts.

The unions tried to make the battle over Act 10 a fight over collective bargaining "rights." It was a powerful message. No one wants to see anyone's "rights" taken away. Taking away "rights" gets a reflexive moral reaction from people. The unions said we wanted to take "rights" away from teachers, janitors, nurses, prison guards, garbage collectors, bus drivers, crossing guards, and snowplow operators. Most people responded: That wasn't fair.

As a result, support for our reforms plummeted.

We began to recover only when we started making our case against collective bargaining with moral arguments. We told the story of Ms. Sampson, the award-winning teacher who lost her job because of "last in, first out" rules under collective bargaining. Wisconsin voters responded: That's not fair.

We explained how corrections officers and bus drivers abused overtime rules under collective bargaining to make six-figure salaries. Wisconsin voters said: That's not fair.

We explained that public workers had no choice of whether to join a union, and that the government forcibly took as much as $1,400 a year out of their paychecks to hand over to the union bosses. Wisconsin voters said: That's not fair.

We explained how government workers paid nothing for their pensions and next to nothing for their health care, while their employers—the hardworking taxpayers—did not enjoy such lavish benefits. Wisconsin voters said: That's not fair.

As conservatives, we should be able to finish any public policy argument with the words "that's not fair." If we can't do that, we need to go back and rethink how we are making our case.

This is not to suggest that empirical evidence doesn't matter. To the contrary, if people had not seen that Act 10 was working—that schools were better off, local governments were balancing their budgets, and property tax bills were down for the first time in over a decade—we would have lost the recall. Results matter. But it was also critical for people to see not only that our reforms worked but also that they were just and fair.

If we counter the left's arguments simply with logic, reason, and data alone, we will lose the debate over the future of our country. But if we counter them with logic, reason, data, *and* an appeal to the American people's innate sense of fairness, we can prevail.

CONCLUSION

Unintimidated

If you picked up this book, I suspect you are frustrated about the prospects for positive change in our country. Now that you've come to the end, I hope you see why I am so optimistic about the future.

Yes, things do look bleak in Washington today. But if you look beyond our nation's capital, you will see positive change is taking place all around us. Across America, citizens are casting their ballots for fiscal responsibility. Courageous political leaders are taking on the entrenched interests, delivering reforms relevant to the lives of their citizens, and showing that they will not be intimidated by threats and scare tactics.

And voters are rewarding men and women who stand for principle with second terms—or, in my case, the chance to continue my initial term.

I know some are saying that conservatives need to change our principles and moderate our approach if we want to win elections. We've heard that tune before. In the 1980s, British prime minister Margaret Thatcher recounted how, when she first became Conservative Party leader in 1975 at the height of the Labour Party's power, "People said we should never be able to govern again.

"Remember how we had all been lectured about political impossibility?" Thatcher asked. "You couldn't be a Conservative, and sound like a Conservative, and win an election—they said. And you certainly couldn't win an election and then act like a Conservative and win another election. And—this was absolutely beyond dispute—you couldn't win two elections and go on behaving like a Conservative, and yet win a third election.

"Don't you harbour just the faintest suspicion that somewhere along the line something went wrong with that theory?" she said.[1]

Today, we can sound like conservatives and act like conservatives—and still win elections. Those who say we can't don't see what I see in Wisconsin and what my fellow governors in states all across America see. We don't need to change our principles. What we need is more courage.

We need to do more than simply say no to President Obama and the Democrats' big-government agenda. Republicans must offer Americans big, bold, positive solutions for our nation's challenges—innovative policies to reform entitlements, get our debt under control, reduce the size of government, improve education, reduce dependency, and create hope, opportunity, and upward mobility for all of our citizens.

We need to make not just the economic case for our reforms but the moral case as well—showing how conservative policies and ideas will make America not only a more prosperous but also a more just and fair society.

Above all, we must show Americans that we are more concerned with the next generation than just the next election.

If we do all these things, Americans will stand with us.

I know because they stood with me.

Just as the union bosses tried to intimidate us in Wisconsin, President Obama and the Democrats in Congress are now trying to intimidate conservatives into backing off the cause of reform. Just like the protesters who occupied the capitol in Madison, they believe that we will cave under pressure and give in to their demands for higher taxes to fuel continued fiscal profligacy.

We need not fear their threats. From my experience in Wisconsin these past three years, I can say one thing with confidence: Americans will back politicians who have the courage to make tough, but prudent, decisions.

Whenever I get down on what is happening in America today, I think back to our founders. As a kid, I loved learning about the history of our country. Maybe I was a bit of a geek, but I thought of our founders almost like superheroes—bigger than life.

It would have been wonderful to visit our nation's capital and other historic sites on the East Coast, but growing up as the son of a pastor in a small town, I didn't have a whole lot of money. For us, a family vacation entailed driving as far as our used Chevy Impala station wagon would take us, and back.

So in the fall of 2011, I had the opportunity to visit Philadelphia for the first time and I got up early and visited Independence Hall.

When I set off for what had once been the Pennsylvania state house, I half expected to see the colonial equivalent of the Hall of Justice. Instead, what I saw was a small, simple room full of desks and chairs much like the ones we sit in today.

You see, the founders weren't superheroes. They were ordinary people just like us who had the courage to do something extraordinary. They didn't just risk their political careers. They didn't just risk their businesses. They literally risked their lives for the freedom we hold so dear today.

What has made America exceptional is that throughout our history, in times of crisis—be it economic or fiscal, military or spiritual—there have been men and women of courage who have stood up and decided it was more important to look out for the future of their children and their grandchildren than their own futures.

To win the fight for America's future, we must summon that courage anew. We must offer a better vision for America: a country that lives within its means, empowers its citizens to build better lives, and leaves its children better off than we were. A country where courageous leaders make the hard choices necessary to balance budgets, improve education, and make government smaller, more efficient, and more effective.

That America may seem distant today, but I assure you it is within reach. And the path to this America does not begin in Washington, D.C. It starts in the states.

We can reach our destination so long as we remain unintimidated.

POSTSCRIPT

"Scott, Don't Spend Money You Don't Have"

People often ask me, with tens of thousands of people chanting outside my window, protesters shaking my car and following me everywhere I went, and multiple death threats sent to me and my family, how did I keep such calm?

It wasn't always easy. What gave me the inner strength to go on was my faith. During the worst moments, I often reflected on these passages from Scripture:

> *"Therefore do not worry about tomorrow, for tomorrow will worry about itself. Each day has enough trouble of its own."*
> *—Matthew 6:34*

> *"Who of you by worrying can add a single hour to his life? Since you cannot do this very little thing, why do you worry about the rest?"*
> *—Luke 12:25–26*

> *"My grace is sufficient for you, for my power is made perfect in weakness."*
> *—2 Corinthians 12:9*

I also took strength from my family. I've told you already how Tonette was my rock during the fight over Act 10. I also relied on the love, encouragement, and example of my parents.

Nearly every day I was going through the protests, my mom would send me a text message that read: "L&P from L&P" (which stood for "love and prayers from Llew and Pat").

My mother is so positive and so compassionate. No one seems to bother or faze her. She is the most selfless person I know. When I served in the state assembly, I used to tell new members not to personalize their differences because their opponents today may be their allies tomorrow. That kind of thinking clearly came from my mother.

During my tenure as Milwaukee County executive I had to make some tough decisions that were not always popular. I remember walking in a Veterans Day parade after my first budget was completed. I got wild cheers from most but also an occasional middle-finger salute from a few (Tonette always seemed to notice them). Instead of responding in kind, I would walk over and wave and say, "Thanks for coming out to support our veterans."

I would do the same thing at town hall meetings I held when some would show up with signs or shirts knocking me. One union bus driver came to nearly every meeting from the time I first ran for county executive. Often, I would give him the microphone at the start of the comment portion, and he would attack me. Sometimes the crowd would start booing. I would have to remind them to be polite and that everyone had a right to be heard. So when a hundred thousand people descended on the capitol a few years later, my response was exactly the same—because that is how my mother raised me.

Over the years, my mom always had a knack for reaching out to people at just the right time. Often she would track down old classmates of mine with a card—or, more recently, with a Facebook post. She loves keeping track of people and sending them a note and a photo (she takes millions of them).

When I was a kid, she would make chocolate chip cookies (they are the best because she takes them out just before they are done, so they melt in your mouth) and give me a box to share on the bus after football and basketball games and track meets. Over the years, she has continued to make those cookies, and now she shares them with shut-ins, fire and police stations, and others. During my 2010 and 2012 campaigns, she would make cookies and put together boxes for each of the victory centers around the state. Then she and my father would drive around the state and deliver them to the volunteers.

She's the reason why Alex got the idea to take a plate of cookies out to the protesters when they first showed up outside the Executive Residence.

The office in Sheboygan gave my mom and dad shirts that say, "Scott Walker is Our Son," and they wear them all over the place. They really love meeting the people who support me. My dad is slowing down, but he loves these trips and they really bring out his personality.

My comfort speaking in front of crowds clearly comes from my father, who was a pastor when I was growing up. Often he would call me to the pulpit to give a prayer, lead a responsive reading, or read a Scripture. As I got older, he even invited me to preach for him.

More than speaking, my father taught me how to relate to people. When he would give sermons, he would tell stories that would relate to people in our congregation and in our town. He would mix humor and substance, and the members of our church loved his messages.

Even though my father could talk a lot (a friend once told me he could talk the bark off a tree), I was always surprised to hear how much he knew about people he had just met. Often he could tell me details I did not know about people I had known for years—I'd only scratched the surface.

Dad would talk, but he always drew those around him into his conversations, showing that he really enjoyed getting to know them. For years I've run into people who tell me funny stories about my father—he's really a character—but they all love him. I've heard of folks who met him in line at McDonald's or at the bank or even on the side of the freeway, after he'd pulled over to help them with a flat tire. There are so many stories like that.

One day when I was young, he met a guy from Milwaukee and they got to talking about faith. Well, the next Sunday, my dad comes home and his suit is soaking wet.

"What happened to you, Dad?" I asked.

"Remember that guy I met last week?" he replied. "Well, he asked me to come to his church to see him get baptized and he wanted me to join him—so I just jumped right in with him."

My dad's example of faith, his interest in people, and his compassion for others have inspired me to a life of service. For a brief time in the 1970s, my dad served on the city council in Plainfield, Iowa. It was a small town of about 450, and we lived there until we moved to Delavan, Wisconsin, in 1977. I was so proud of my dad, and I got inspired to help local government. As a young kid I noticed that the city hall in Plainfield didn't have a state flag. So I got a large container, cut a slit in the top, and walked all over town collecting coins. Once it was filled, we bought an Iowa state flag and gave it to the city.

Being a pastor's kid—the "P. K.," as we call it—wasn't always easy. In a small town, the P. K. is under incredible scrutiny. Everyone knows who he is, what he is doing, and how he conducts himself. During the worst of the protests, I told my kids I understood the pressures they felt because of their dad's position in the community and how hard that could be.

Matt and Alex were amazing. Thankfully, they are super guys, so their friends really rallied behind them through all of the protests. Once, when documentary "film" maker Michael Moore called for students to walk out of schools in Wisconsin, Matt and Alex's friends made them a big sign of support filled with signatures of fellow students.

I told Matt when he went off to college that there was nothing there that would be any more of a challenge than the past two years. Tonette and I prayed a great deal with our sons, and that really helped us keep things in perspective. Plus, they enjoyed having my parents around—as well as my brother and his family.

My brother, David, was born on March 2, 1971, in Waverly, Iowa. He was a freshman when I was a senior in high school. When we were younger, it was more of a paternal relationship. Now, as we age, it is equal.

David married my sister-in-law, Maria, and moved with her to Phoenix. In 2003, they had Isabella. In 2007, Eva came along and they decided to move back to Wisconsin.

My parents were constant babysitters for Matt and Alex when the boys were young (we could not have done it without them as my mother was always offering to stay with the boys), so David and Maria were looking to connect their girls to my parents. My mom was very happy.

They put their house on the market, and it sold much faster than they thought. So Tonette offered to have them move in with us. They arrived in June and stayed with us until right before Christmas.

My brother is the banquet manager (and occasional bartender) at the DoubleTree and Maria works at a Sears in Brookfield. Maria's mother, stepfather, and grandmother live in Madison.

David does not work in politics, but he follows it. He frequently sends me a text or gives me a call about an idea. He offers me some great perspectives because he is talking to people all of the time. Many a Friday night I get a call from him when he has the bride and groom at a wedding on the line because they are fans. Like my father, he really listens to people and gets to know them. Then he tries to help them.

David's is a typical middle-class family. He is a good and decent fellow who gets along with anyone. My brother is a good reality check. During the height of the protests, it was David who reminded me that he paid more than $800 per month for his health insurance and the little bit he could set aside for his retirement. He said he would love to have the deal I was offering public employees. It put things in perspective.

Our grandmother Eleonor Fitch had a tremendous impact on me too. She and my grandfather Ray Fitch raised my mom on a farm where they didn't have indoor plumbing until my mother went to high school. My grandfather (Boppa) died in 1974. My grandmother (Nana) lived on until 2008. She worked several part-time jobs (Avon lady, babysitter, and insert stuffer at a newspaper) and watched every penny. My brother and I would laugh as she would take us to McDonalds with all of her coupons and count out every penny from her coin purse. She didn't buy anything on credit. When she bought a TV or a table or even a car, she saved up for it.

I always remember her saying, "Scott, don't spend money you don't have."

It a lesson that I apply every day as governor of Wisconsin.

ACKNOWLEDGMENTS

Most important, thanks be to God for His abundant grace and everlasting love.

Throughout the book, I mention my appreciation for my amazing family. Now, I would like to thank my extended family.

First, a salute to Major General Don Dunbar and the ten thousand men and women of the Wisconsin National Guard. It is my sincere honor to serve as your commander in chief.

There is also a special place in my heart for all of the Gold Star families I've met over the years. I wear two wrist bands to honor their loved ones.

Next, I am blessed with amazing staff. Eric Schutt is the leader of my official office. He is brilliant and has remarkable interpersonal skills. Eric and Mike Huebsch are the driving force behind our good work in state government. We have an outstanding team in the governor's office— Rich Zipperer, Scott Matejov, Brian Hagedorn, Cindy Polzin, Jocelyn Webster, Julie Lund, Tom Evenson, Wendy Riemann, Waylon Hurlburt, Kimber Liedel, Eileen Schoenfeldt, Michael Brickman, Eric Esser, Casey

Himebauch, Al Colvin, Andrew Davis, Karley Downing, Teri Hatchell, Patrick Hughes, Caitrin Smith, Madeline Henry, Daniel Suhr, Bob Nenno, Brian Hummel, Ryan Hughes, Alex Fhlug, Alex Boyd, Colton Haas, Kody Kvalheim, Hannah Vogel, Elizabeth Hizmi, Ethan Schuh, Tiffany Black, Chelsey Hamilton, Rachel Kaminski, Mary Ann Lippert, Cheryl Berdan—and so many more. It includes others like Chris Schrimpf, Ryan Murray, Cullen Werwie, Andrew Hitt, Ashlee Moore, Lisa Kulow, Bill Kloiber, Annie Andres, Jason Culotta, Nicole Simmons, and Nancy Hayer, who served during the first few years.

Dorothy Moore walked into our office in 2002 and never left. She looks out for me each and every day. She trained a very capable team including Alicia Bork and Jennifer Grinder—as well as Angie Hellenbrand.

In addition, we also have an equally talented cabinet. It begins with the hardest working lieutenant governor in the country—Rebecca Kleefisch—and continues with Mike Huebsch, Kitty Rhodes, Stephanie Klett, Cathy Stepp, Ben Brancel, Reggie Newson, Reed Hall, Peter Bildsten, Eloise Anderson, Wyman Winston, Dave Ross, Rick Chandler, Mark Gottlieb, Ted Nickel, John Scocos, Ed Wall, Phil Montgomery, and Greg Gracz—as well as Dennis Smith. A big thank-you to them all.

Dave Erwin is the Capitol Police chief and was the head of the Dignitary Patrol Unit. The others in the DPU who keep me and my family safe are Jason Zeeh, Jack McMahon, Shelly Hutter, Rick Fitzgerald, Joe Lowe, Mike Galvan, Mark Dolin, Eric Dante, Andrew Martin, and Luke Kraemer. Thanks to them and all of the Capitol Police Department officers at the residence and capitol.

In the political world, R. J. Johnson and I have worked together for more than two decades. He and Keith Gilkes laid out the plan to win our 2010 election and they both have keen political instincts. Keith is a great leader. Stephan Thompson, Jill Bader, Joe Fadness, Patrick Hogan, Mary Stitt, and Dan Morse were part of that great team that did more than win—we laid out a road map for reform. My current campaign team—including Jonathan Wetzel, Colleen Coyle, Taylor Palmisano, and Matt Censky, as well as Kate Donor, Camille Moughon, and Laura Gralton (Jennifer Bannister too)—is building on that proud tradition.

Mike Grebe is the ultimate statesman and I am proud that he serves as the chair of my campaign. My friend Reince Priebus really delivers and is a super leader. Brad Courtney is a longtime friend (his wife, Barb, is a good friend too) who always steps up to the challenge. John Hiller and I first met in college, and he helped lead our transition team—twice.

Jim Villa was my first chief of staff at the county and is always keeping track of what I'm up to these days. Tom Nardelli took over for Jim and did a good job "keeping the trains running on time." Sadhna Lindvall, Rod McWilliams, and Fran McLaughlin helped us get our message out. Steve Mokrohisky provided excellent counsel.

Along the way, I was pleased to recruit Linda Seemeyer to help run the county. Others followed, including Bill Domina, Sue Black, Steve Agostini, Rob Henken, Chuck McDowell, Bob Dennik, Tom Carlson, Domingo Leguizamon, Karen Jackson, Dashal Young, Cory Hoze, Hattie Daniels-Rush, and Cindy Archer—to name a few. We improved local government and learned that true reform required dramatic changes in state law. Cindy helped implement those changes early in my term as governor.

Chuck Wikenhauser, Jack Takerian, Stephanie Sue Stein, John Hayes, Lisa Jo Marks, Brenda Cannon, Paula Lucey, and Ron Malone were all valued members of our team at the county too.

I was also blessed to have excellent staff over the years in the capitol: Lynn Casey Wilk, Ed Eberle, Mark Grapentine, Melissa Gilbert, and Greg Reiman.

My thanks to the many fellow governors and other elected officials who lifted me up early in my first term. They, along with folks like Fred Malek, Phil Cox, Bob Wood, Kevin Keane, and Nick Ayers, were a real inspiration.

Former Wisconsin governor Tommy Thompson frequently checks in with me. He worked so hard to improve Wisconsin, and I try to follow his example in that regard every day.

The members of the Wisconsin State Assembly and State Senate deserve incredible praise for their courage. I mention it in the book, but it is worth remembering the abuse these lawmakers got during the debate.

Special thanks to Senate Majority Leader Scott Fitzgerald, former speaker Jeff Fitzgerald, current speaker Robin Vos, Senator Alberta Darling, and Representative John Nygren.

In addition to hanging with my family or watching sporting events, one of my favorite ways to relax is riding my 2003 Harley Davidson Road King. I love to ride with Dave and Patti Davis, Vicki and Tony Sanfelipo, Cheryl and Rich Kuchenbecker, John and Sue Schaller, Scott Pochowski, Beth Lohmann and Steve Pericak, JT, Dog, Turkey, and plenty of others. I pray that they all continue to ride safe!

One of my greatest refuges has been our church. Pastor John and Betsy Mackett and Pastor Mark and Val Werner—as well as good friends Becky and Barry Geary are all part of a wonderful support network at Meadowbrook Church in Wauwatosa.

We also have an incredible group of friends. Our kids met in junior kindergarten (they're now in college) and we've remained friends since then. Tonette and I really love Anne and Gene Genal, Nancy and Keith Harmon, Laura and Chris Lange, Ruth and Mark Meidl, and Claire and Dick Pankratz. We do a fair amount of social events with them and our great friends Candee and Ray Arndt. We love the pond parties at Crystal and Jim Berg's home and hunting with Jim and Tom Balistrieri. Thanks for keeping us real and focused on our family and friends!

My agent, Glen Hartley, is the best in the business. Bria Sanford is an incredible editor, and I am grateful to her, Adrian Zackheim, and all the talented folks at Penguin. Ed Gillespie, Charlie Sykes, Dennis Smith, and Brian Riedl read drafts of the book, and their insights were invaluable. Craig Shirley shared his unique knowledge of the history of the

1980 Reagan campaign. Justin Lang provided incredible research, and together with Ian Peterson, Heather Malacaria, Emly Cashel, Jill Mattox, and Keith Miller ably transcribed dozens of hours of interviews. And I am grateful to the family of my coauthor—Pam Thiessen and their children Max, Jack, Eva, and Lucy.

Special thanks to Marc for really spending the time to understand me and my family and what really took place in Wisconsin. It is quite an honor to have such a gifted scholar share my passion for reform and help me put these ideas into the format of a book.

And finally, a personal thanks to the voters of Wisconsin for your faith in me—not once but twice—to serve as your governor. I will not let you down!

NOTES

Introduction: "If It Can Happen in Wisconsin, It Can Happen Anywhere"

1. www.washingtonpost.com/blogs/the-fix/post/the-worst-economic
   -recovery-america-has-ever-had-scott-pelleys-soon-to-be-starring-2012-election
   -role/2012/08/03/6206cb22-dd7a-11e1-8e43-4a3c4375504a_blog.html.

2. http://money.cnn.com/2013/06/24/pf/emergency-savings/index.html.

3. http://cbo.gov/sites/default/files/cbofiles/attachments/43907-Budget
   Outlook.pdf.

4. Rutger's Heldrich Center Study Finds Three in Four Americans Touched
   Personally by Great Recession, February 7, 2013. http://news.rutgers.edu/
   medrel/news-releases/2013/february-2013/rutgers-heldrich-cen-20130207.

5. www.purdue.edu/president/about/index.html.

6. http://articles.washingtonpost.com/2013-01-17/opinions/
   36410313_1_mitch-daniels-limited-government-bureaucracies.

7. www.nj.gov/governor/news/news/552013/approved/20130628e.html.

8. www.christiefornj.com/about.

9. www.humanevents.com/2012/07/20/susana-martinez-changing
   -new-mexico-and-looking-ahead/.

10. www.michigan.gov/snyder/0,4668,7-277-57579--,00.html.

11. www.spokesman.com/stories/2011/mar/18/otter-signs-teacher-pay
    -bargaining-bills/; www.spokesman.com/stories/2013/apr/20/otter
    -signs-as-law-limits-on-teachers/.

12. http://host.madison.com/news/local/govt-and-politics/wisconsin-budget
    -surplus-projected-to-grow-to-million-revenue-to/article_ec6cc518-666a
    -11e2-ac09-0019bb2963f4.html.

13. "Protesters out in force nationwide to oppose Wisconsin's anti-union bill,"
    Los Angeles Times, February 26, 2011.

14. http://articles.washingtonpost.com/2012-06-04/Opinions/
    35462098_1_Democrat-Tom-Barrett-Scott-Walker-Wisconsin-Voters.

Chapter 1: "This Is What Democracy Looks Like"

1. Interview with Mike Huebsch.

2. http://tpmdc.talkingpointsmemo.com/2011/03/wisconsin-sheriff-pulls
   -deputies-from-capitol-says-they-wont-be-palace-guard.php.

3. www.publicpolicypolling.com/main/2011/05/walker-would-lose-to
   -feingold-or-barrett-in-recall.html.

4. www.time.com/time/nation/article/0,8599,2058601,00.html.

5. www.nationaljournal.com/economy/fallout-from-wisconsin-20110311.

6. www.uwsc.wisc.edu/BP32PressRelease1_WIpols_FINAL.pdf.

7. www.gallup.com/poll/116500/presidential-approval-ratings-george
   -bush.aspx.

8. www.politico.com/static/PPM152_110221_wi_memo.html.

Chapter 2: "Go Ahead and Do It!"

1. www.jsonline.com/news/milwaukee/44156882.html#stakes.

2. www.wpri.org/WIInterest/Vol11No2/Sykes11.2.pdf.

Chapter 3: "See What You've Gotten Yourself Into?"

1. www.jsonline.com/news/statepolitics/assembly-expected-to-back-
   constitutional-amendment-on-transportation-fund-raids-es8og5c-
   190863431.html.

2. www.jsonline.com/news/statepolitics/115501969.html.

3. http://walker.wi.gov/Documents/Act_10_Success_Recap.pdf.

Chapter 5: "Bring It On"

1. www.huffingtonpost.com/2010/11/08/jim-doyle-highspeed-rail-_n
   _780614.html.

2. www.youtube.com/watch?v=vMAKW-VzY-c.

3. http://static.maciverinstitute.com/uploads/2010/12/Screen-shot
   -2010-12-06-at-9.08.22-AM1.png.

4. www.channel3000.com/news/Walker-Renews-Calls-For-Union
   -Concessions/-/1648/8312034/-/tvpliqz/-/index.html.

5. www.jsonline.com/news/statepolitics/111463779.html.

6. www.wrn.com/2010/12/union-head-fires-back/.

7. http://host.madison.com/wsj/news/local/crime_and_courts/
   article_6274d8ee-beb8-11de-9b20-001cc4c03286.html.

8. www.jsonline.com/news/statepolitics/111922624.html.

9. http://quorumcall.wispolitics.com/2010/12/decker-no-vote.html.

10. www.wrn.com/2010/12/senate-deadlocks-on-contracts/.

11. http://quorumcall.wispolitics.com/2010/12/jauch-shreds-decker.html.

12. www.wrn.com/2010/12/senate-deadlocks-on-contracts/.

13. http://archive.org/details/MartyBeil-RussDeckerIsAWhore.

14. www.jsonline.com/news/statepolitics/111922624.html.

15. http://host.madison.com/news/local/govt-and-politics/contracts-for
    -state-employees-remain-in-limbo/article_e9ed9046-07cc-11e0-9aac
    -001cc4c03286.html.

Chapter 7: "Let's Bring Them a Plate of Cookies"

1. www.cbo.gov/sites/default/files/cbofiles/attachments/01-30-FedPay.pdf.

2. http://krugman.blogs.nytimes.com/2011/01/08/assassination
   -attempt-in-arizona/?src=twt&twt=NytimesKrugman.

3. www.motherjones.com/mojo/2011/01/grijalva-giffords-shooting-tea
   -party-palin.

4. www.politifact.com/wisconsin/statements/2011/feb/22/lena-taylor/
   wisconsin-state-sen-lena-taylor-d-milwaukee-says-h/.

5. www.weeklystandard.com/blogs/reductio-hitlerum-all-rage-among
   -unionist-protesters-wisconsin_550333.html.

6. www.wpri.org/blog/?p=1613.

7. www.nationalreview.com/corner/301931/jesse-jackson-walker-old
   -south-politician-robert-costa.

8. www.time.com/time/nation/article/0,8599,2058601,00.html.

9. www.washingtonpost.com/wp-dyn/content/article/2011/01/13/
AR2011011301532.html.

Chapter 8: Occupy Madison

1. Interview with Robin Vos.

2. www.thedailypage.com/media/2012/05/13/Quagliana%20report
%20051011.pdf.

3. www.nytimes.com/2011/02/26/us/26madison.html?_r=0.

4. http://host.madison.com/entertainment/dining/restaurant-news
-ian-s-pizza-to-move-across-state-street/article_71d6e070-4372-11e1-a830
-001871e3ce6c.html.

5. Stein, Jason, Patrick Marley. *More Than They Bargained For: Scott Walker,
Unions, and the Fight for Wisconsin*. Madison, WI: University of Wisconsin
Press. Kindle edition (locations 1658–1660), 2013.

6. www.mediaite.com/tv/fox-interviews-wisconsin-democrat-rep-who
-rescued-gop-senator-mobbed-by-protesters/.

7. www.jsonline.com/blogs/news/116427424.html.

8. www.jsonline.com/blogs/news/116422204.html.

9. http://online.wsj.com/article/SB10001424052748704657704576150111817
428004.html.

10. www.nytimes.com/2011/02/22/us/22union.html?pagewanted=all&_r=0.

11. www.jsonline.com/blogs/news/116289674.html.

12. www.youtube.com/watch?v=zjFbMDp5Pg8.

13. http://host.madison.com/wsj/news/local/education/university/uw
-sanctioned-doctors-for-writing-sick-notes-for-protesters/article
_0869a5c6-7f47-11e1-a7f7-0019bb2963f4.html.

14. http://host.madison.com/news/local/health_med_fit/state-board
-sanctions-more-doctors-for-sick-notes/article_50360d1e-44b7-11e2
-9a76-0019bb2963f4.html.

Chapter 9: A Racket, Not a Right

1. http://chippewa.com/news/local/praise-
flows-as-the-th-returns-to-wisconsin/
article_b3101532-3c9a-11e0-9eae-001cc4c03286.html.

2. http://crooksandliars.com/john-amato/excellent-wi-firefighter-afl
-cio-ad-bl.

3. http://gazettextra.com/news/2011/feb/16/cities-rush-settle-contracts
-legislature-approves-/.

4. www.wrn.com/2011/03/racine-rushing-through-union-contracts/.

5. www.politifact.com/wisconsin/statements/2011/mar/03/scott
-walker/gov-scott-walker-says-local-public-unions-rushed-t/.

6. http://articles.washingtonpost.com/2012-06-01/opinions/
35459305_1_government-employees-teachers-union-second-most
-important-election.

7. http://blog.nj.com/njv_paul_mulshine/2009/09/steve_sweeney_might
_fight_for.html.

Chapter 10: "Scott, Why Are You Doing This?"

1. www.jsonline.com/news/wisconsin/45104107.html.

Chapter 11: "The Power of Humility, the Burden of Pride"

1. http://cmsimg.fdlreporter.com/apps/pbcsi.dll/bilde?NewTbl=1&Site=U0&
Date=20120107&Category=FON01&ArtNo=201070803&Ref=PH&
Item=1&Maxw=640&Maxh=410&q=60.

2. http://s1092.photobucket.com/user/duguy/media/Top.jpg.html.

3. www.nationalreview.com/corner/288211/meet-ian-murphy
-christian-schneider.

4. http://buffalobeast.com/fuck-the-troops/.

5. www.jsonline.com/blogs/news/116751499.html.

Chapter 12: Meet Ms. Sampson

1. http://host.madison.com/wsj/news/local/govt_and_politics/article
_24af32d4-13f4-11df-86b2-001cc4c002e0.html.

2. http://host.madison.com/news/local/govt_and_politics/cashing-in-city
-paid-million-in-overtime-last-year/article_ae24d6ae-7277-11df-a0f7
-001cc4c002e0.html.

3. www.postcrescent.com/article/20130119/APC019803/301190082/
Corrections-overtime-drops-10M-2012.

4. www.postcrescent.com/ic/iteam/DOCOTbypayperiod.pdf.

5. http://journaltimes.com/news/local/article_6a940044-5e23-11df-91a0
-001cc4c03286.html.

6. http://journaltimes.com/news/local/govt-and-politics/collective
-bargaining-change-means-more-work-options-for-jail-inmates/
article_97bd5d58-a243-11e0-b2f9-001cc4c002e0.html.

7. www.waow.com/Global/story.asp?S=11891208.

8. http://abcnews.go.com/Health/milwaukee-schools-ban-viagra-teachers
-union-sues-discrimination/story?id=11378595.

9. www.fox11online.com/dpp/news/140-green-bay-teachers-looking-to-retire.

10. www.jsonline.com/news/education/96349689.html.

Chapter 13: Enter the Thunderdome

1. Interview with Jeff Fitzgerald.

2. Interview with Robin Vos.

3. Stein, Jason, Patrick Marley. *More Than They Bargained For: Scott Walker, Unions, and the Fight for Wisconsin*. Madison, WI: University of Wisconsin Press. Kindle edition (locations 3429–3431), 2013.

4. www.620wtmj.com/blogs/charliesykes/117064153.html.

5. www.postcrescent.com/viewart/20110228/APC0101/303010023/
Wisconsin-Rep-Gordon-Hintz-apologizes-comments-made-Assembly
-floor-following-budget-vote.

Chapter 14: "1 Walker Beats 14 Runners"

1. http://host.madison.com/news/local/govt-and-politics/walker-blames
-senate-minority-leader-for-ongoing-budget-stalemate/article_2fc9a1d2
-48d1-11e0-90e1-001cc4c03286.html.

2. http://dailycaller.com/2011/02/21/top-ten-ways-to-tell-if-you
-might-be-a-member-of-a-public-sector-union/.

3. www.wkow.com/story/14219065/senator-mark-miller.

4. http://wispolitics.com/1006/large/110308_Alternative_budget_adjust
ment_memo.pdf.

5. www.jsonline.com/blogs/news/117755883.html.

6. www.jsonline.com/blogs/news/117854499.html.

Chapter 15: The Proxy Fight Begins

1. http://online.wsj.com/article/SB100014240527487038063045762365839
66428502.html?mod=WSJ_Opinion_LEADTop.

2. Ibid.

3. www.brennancenter.org/analysis/judicial-public-financing-wisconsin -%E2%80%94-2011.

4. http://wispolitics.com/1006/110324_Troy_Merryfield_Statement__1_.pdf.

5. www.jsonline.com/news/statepolitics/118694454.html.

6. www.jsonline.com/blogs/news/119347799.html.

7. http://online.wsj.com/article/SB10001424052748704503104576250822733679638.html.

8. www.jsonline.com/news/statepolitics/119410124.html.

9. http://online.wsj.com/article/SB100014240527487038063045762365839664285 02.html.

10. http://online.wsj.com/article/SB1000142405274870380630457623278004 7736062.html.

11. http://host.madison.com/news/local/education/teachers-union-layoffs -could-be-bellwether-for-other-public-employee/article_6ee3f158-c7a0 -11e0-aba0-001cc4c002e0.html#ixzz2ZVOxBk7I.

12. http://online.wsj.com/article/SB100014240527023048213045774364624 13999718.html.

13. http://watchdog.org/95888/public-union-membership-plummets-two -years-after-wi-act-10/.

14. http://washingtonexaminer.com/wisconsin-public-sector-unions -report-drastic-membership-declines/article/2526421.

15. www.maciverinstitute.com/2013/04/after-scott-walkers-reforms -public-sector-union-membership-plummets/.

16. www.jsonline.com/watchdog/noquarter/lawsuits-benefits-are-only -for-members-afscmes-rich-abelson-says-7m9kmej-204014551.html.

17. www.jsonline.com/watchdog/noquarter/lawsuits-benefits-are-only -for-members-afscmes-rich-abelson-says-7m9kmej-204014551.html.

Chapter 16: "This Is War!"

1. www.wisconsinhistory.org/dictionary/index.asp?action=view&term _id=15563&search_term=recall.

2. www.amazon.com/Leadership-Promises-Every-Day-Devotional/dp/ 140411324X/ref=sr_1_1?ie=UTF8&qid=1374242810&sr=8-1&keywords= leadership+promises+for+every+day+a+daily+devotional.

3. www.620wtmj.com/blogs/charliesykes/117726263.html?blog=y.

4. Interview with Dan Kapanke.

5. www.youtube.com/watch?v=yA771GNyXjM.

6. www.politifact.com/wisconsin/statements/2011/aug/04/nancy-nusbaum/candidate-nancy-nusbaum-says-state-sen-robert-cowl/.

7. www.wkow.com/global/story.asp?s=11021488.

8. www.channel3000.com/news/Reality-Check-Ad-Targets-Recall-Challenger-s-Driving-Record/-/1648/8303510/-/15t30ua/-/index.html.

9. www.politifact.com/wisconsin/statements/2011/jul/24/wisconsin-family-action/wisconsin-family-action-says-wisconsin-rep-fred-cl/.

10. www.wiscnews.com/portagedailyregister/news/local/article_fbd2b8aa-9632-11e0-94ed-001cc4c002e0.html

11. www.youtube.com/watch?v=lbs67zbJ6G8&feature=endscreen&NR=1.

12. www.nytimes.com/2011/08/11/us/politics/11wisconsin.html?_r=0.

Chapter 17: You're Welcome, Madison!

1. http://city-journal.org/2012/22_1_scott-walker.html.

2. "Health insurance changes to net big savings for school district," *Ozaukee Press*, March 21, 2012.

3. "Preliminary PW-S budget erases $1.9 million deficit," *Ozaukee Press*, June 15, 2011.

4. "Appleton schools retains WEA Trust for insurance," *Appleton Post Crescent*, June 22, 2011.

5. Editorial, "The Good, Bad About AASD Health Insurance," *Appleton Post Crescent*, July 5, 2011.

6. http://lacrossetribune.com/news/local/madison-matters-wea-is-forced-to-adapt/article_a59f406e-8774-11e1-a7b7-001a4bcf887a.html.

7. http://eagnews.org/wp-content/uploads/2013/04/First-Years-of-Freedom-report.pdf.

8. www.fdlreporter.com/article/20110802/FON0101/108020361/City-manager-2012-budget-will-tough?odyssey=tab|topnews|text|FON-News&gcheck=1

9. "Green Bay School Board OKs $235.6 million budget," *Green Bay Press Gazette*, September 27, 2011.

10. http://host.madison.com/news/opinion/editorial/sky-isn-t-falling-on-public-schools/article_2b1236a0-1e86-11e1-9681-0019bb2963f4.html.

11. www.city-journal.org/printable.php?id=7771.

12. www.jsonline.com/blogs/news/117731088.html.

13. http://online.wsj.com/article/SB10001424052970204301404577170740792232880.html.

14. http://eagnews.org/wp-content/uploads/2012/04/Milwaukee-Contract-Analysis.pdf.

15. www.jsonline.com/blogs/news/210406821.html.

16. www.wiscnews.com/portagedailyregister/news/article_479e9224-fad6-11e0-b74b-001cc4c002e0.html.

17. www.wiscnews.com/news/local/govt-and-politics/article_5b7536f8-01bc-11e1-b105-001cc4c03286.html.

18. http://host.madison.com/news/local/govt-and-politics/new-work-rules-set-in-as-contracts-lapse/article_da55410c-bb86-55a6-8ffa-71bb933fe4be.html.

19. www.jsonline.com/news/statepolitics/127269673.html.

20. www.jsonline.com/news/statepolitics/127269673.html.

Chapter 18: Ending the "Lemon Dance"

1. http://educationnext.org/a-culture-of-complaint/.

2. Interview by AEI research assistant Justin Lang with Joe Halaiko, HR Director at Messmer.

3. http://books.google.com/books?id=Y8po-8b9XroC&pg=PA110&lpg=PA110&dq=collective+bargaining+in+milwaukee+schools+fuller+mitchell+hartmann&source=bl&ots=2T5Mso_GBy&sig=ZOf3LsfIoktcZ4GBCFd_kvUkcAk&hl=en&sa=X&ei=KV9wUfzZNbez4AOjuYGoCg&ved=0CEoQ6AEwAw#v=onepage&q=collective%20bargaining%20in%20milwaukee%20schools%20fuller%20mitchell%20hartmann&f=false.

4. http://educationnext.org/a-culture-of-complaint/.

5. http://m.npr.org/news/front/154995772?singlePage=false.

Chapter 19: "Does Anyone Remember What This Recall Was All About?"

1. www.maciverinstitute.com/2011/10/walker-hopes-to-follow-engler-model/.

2. http://floyddems.blogspot.com/2006/03/daniels-approval-rating-drops.html.

3. www.nationalreview.com/articles/280382/john-kasich-vs-public-unions-robert-costa.

4. www.jsonline.com/news/opinion/127339738.html.

5. www.youtube.com/watch?v=8rAEM-QJFHk.

6. www.wisn.com/Kenosha-Teacher-Receives-Threats-Over
   -Walker-Ad-Involvement/-/9374034/8043924/-/m1mmpv/-/index.html#ix
   zz2SWalOtep.

7. http://eagnews.org/pro-reform-wisconsin-teacher-stands-her-ground
   -despite-harassment-from-union-members/.

8. www.flickr.com/photos/althouse/7318183974/.

9. http://journaltimes.com/news/local/numerous-union-grove-shops
   -threatened-with-union-boycott/article_aba5a224-5b8c-11e0-88b7
   -001cc4c03286.html.

10. www.todaystmj4.com/news/local/119031454.html.

11. http://online.wsj.com/article/SB10001424052748703806304576232780047736062.html.

12. www.620wtmj.com/blogs/charliesykes/117764004.html?blog=y.

13. www.620wtmj.com/blogs/charliesykes/117764004.html?blog=y.

14. http://online.wsj.com/article/SB10001424052748703806304576232780047736062.html.

15. www.weeklystandard.com/blogs/wisconsins-property-taxes-drop
    -first-time-12-years_637099.html.

16. http://online.wsj.com/article/SB100014240527023044327045773480801243221186.html.

17. www.jsonline.com/news/statepolitics/democratic-hopefuls
    -split-on-union-issues-bg505he-147470205.html.

18. www.jsonline.com/blogs/news/150760775.html.

19. http://online.wsj.com/article/SB100014240527023035521045774383041888861694.html.

20. www.rasmussenreports.com/public_content/politics/general_state_sur-
    veys/wisconsin/wisconsin_poll_support_for_budget_cutting_not_for_
    weakening_collective_bargaining_rights.

21. https://law.marquette.edu/poll/wp-content/uploads/2012/05/MLSP6
    _Toplines.pdf.

22. http://online.wsj.com/article/SB100014240527023047076045774263229441410102.html.

23. www.weeklystandard.com/articles/wisconsin_645900.html.

24. www.motherjones.com/politics/2012/04/scott-walker-recall-wisconsin
-democrat-union.

Chapter 20: P.O.T.U.S. Is M.I.A.

1. http://www.jsonline.com/blogs/news/117073853.html.

2. www.realclearpolitics.com/video/2011/02/17/obama_on_wisconsin
_collective_bargaining_law_an_assault_on_unions.html.

3. www.nytimes.com/2011/02/19/us/19union.html.

4. http://money.cnn.com/2012/08/22/news/economy/federal-worker-pay
-freeze/index.html.

5. www.huffingtonpost.com/2011/02/17/dnc-expands-mobilization
-protests-ohio-indiana_n_824743.html.

6. http://abcnews.go.com/Politics/president-obama-national-democrats
-mobilize-state-employee-protests/story?id=12949812.

7. www.washingtonpost.com/blogs/plum-line/post/exclusive
-wisconsin-dems-furious-with-dnc-for-refusing-to-invest-big
-money-in-walker-recall/2012/05/14/gIQAj6lxOU_blog.html.

8. www.dailykos.com/story/2012/05/11/1090745/-Tom-Barrett
-gets-an-Obama-campaign-assist-in-Wisconsin-recall-against-Scott
-Walker.

9. www.huffingtonpost.com/2012/05/31/tom-barrett-scott-walker_n
_1561152.html.

10. http://politicalticker.blogs.cnn.com/2012/06/05/barrett-says-obama-visit
-would-have-been-distraction/.

11. http://freebeacon.com/cutter-wisconsin-recall-has-nothing-to-do-with
-presidential-election/.

12. https://law.marquette.edu/poll/wp-content/uploads/2012/05/MLSP6
_Toplines.pdf.

13. www.cbsnews.com/8301-503544_162-20036133-503544.html.

14. www.jsonline.com/news/statepolitics/approvers-of-obama-and
-walker-are-indemand-swing-voters-nr74kio-172986401.html.

15. http://m.jsonline.com/news/statepolitics/political-opposites-barack-obama
-scott-walker-are-ratings-twins-u39v9ak-208019701.html.

Chapter 21: What Wisconsin Looks Like if We Lose

1. http://online.wsj.com/article/SB100014240529702045559045771649442 79702590.html.

2. www.jsonline.com/blogs/news/147753025.html.

3. www.chicagotribune.com/news/opinion/ct-perspec-0321-states -20130321,0,4367919.story?dssReturn.

4. http://archive.org/details/FOXNEWSW_20130228_230000_Special _Report_With_Bret_Baier#.

5. www.nytimes.com/2013/02/07/us/governor-of-illinois-tells-legislators -pension-costs-put-state-at-critical-juncture.html.

6. www.moodys.com/research/MOODYS-LOWERS-STATE-OF-ILLINOIS -GO-RATING-TO-A2-FROM—PR_234787.

7. http://online.wsj.com/article/SB100008723963904439215045776434018 68728684.html.

8. www.nbcchicago.com/blogs/ward-room/emanuel-teacher-raises-ctu -124050004.html.

9. www.nbcchicago.com/blogs/ward-room/chicago-mayor-rahm -emanuel-collective-bargaining-teacher-strike-169680186.html.

10. http://blogs.suntimes.com/sweet/2011/02/rahm_emanuel_said_wiscon sin_go.html.

11. http://online.wsj.com/article/SB10001424127887323916304578401023993657866.html.

12. http://capitolfax.com/StateContractSummaryAFSCME31.pdf.

13. www.suntimes.com/news/education/15235099-418/winners-and-losers -in-teachers-strike-rahm-emanuel-is-both.html.

14. http://online.wsj.com/article/SB100014240527487037308045763133532 41550130.html.

15. http://online.wsj.com/article/SB10001424127887323916304578401023993657866.html.

16. http://capitolfax.com/StateContractSummaryAFSCME31.pdf.

17. http://chiefexecutive.net/will-wisconsin-rise-again.

18. http://chiefexecutive.net/wisconsin-is-the-17th-best-state-for-business-2013.

19. http://chiefexecutive.net/best-worst-states-for-business.

Chapter 22: "You Can't Recall Courage"

1. www.politico.com/news/stories/0512/76778.html.

2. www.nationaljournal.com/blogs/hotlineoncall/2012/04/barrett-calls
-for-end-to-civil-war-in-first-wisconsin-recall-ad-11

3. www.jsonline.com/watchdog/noquarter/top-democratic-aide
-compares-scott-walker-with-jeffrey-dahmer-3990353-194403111.html.

4. www.jsonline.com/business/metro-milwaukee-lost-4400
-jobs-in-march-state-reports-q855m0a-148913245.html.

5. http://online.wsj.com/article/SB10001424052970203611404577046160573675088.html.

6. www.wisn.com/marketplace/milwaukee-jobs/Walker-Barrett
-team-up-to-boost-entrepreneurship/-/9375170/19505776/-/q704hf/-/
index.html#ixzz2ROy7AH5e.

7. www.startribune.com/video/157442285.html#/157442285/video/1/hpmfv.

8. www.washingtontimes.com/news/2012/jun/12/madison-wis
-wisconsin-gov-scott-walker-cant-avoid-/

9. http://host.madison.com/news/local/govt-and-politics/elections/after
-the-recall-how-to-remove-your-bumper-sticker/article_bf044c7c
-b0df-11e1-85cd-0019bb2963f4.html.

Chapter 23: Misreading the Message of Wisconsin

1. http://cdn.yougov.com/cumulus_uploads/document/62c5cvpx77/
econToplines.pdf.

2. www.rawstory.com/rs/2012/06/08/romney-obama-didnt-get-the
-message-of-wisconsin-about-cutting-teachers-firefighters/.

3. www.reagan.utexas.edu/archives/reference/11.13.79.html.

4. www.reagan.utexas.edu/archives/reference/7.17.80.html.

5. www.washingtonpost.com/blogs/plum-line/post/romney-ill-never-con-
vince-obama-voters-to-take-responsibility-for-their-lives/2012/09/17/
0c1f0bcc-0104-11e2-b260-32f4a8db9b7e_blog.html.

6. www.washingtonpost.com/blogs/the-fix/post/romney-im-not-concerned
-with-the-very-poor/2012/02/01/gIQAvajShQ_blog.html.

7. www.presidency.ucsb.edu/ws/?pid=25970.

8. http://reagan2020.us/speeches/Farewell.asp.

Chapter 24: "We're Still Here"

1. http://media.jsonline.com/documents/capitolsecurity.pdf.

2. www.jsonline.com/news/statepolitics/130197198.html.

3. www.jsonline.com/news/statepolitics/recalls-this-year-cost
   -taxpayers-more-than-14-million-3h6s664-169814556.html.

4. http://host.madison.com/ct/news/local/health_med_fit/vital_signs/
   article_14946c20-448b-11e0-9529-001cc4c03286.html.

5. http://online.wsj.com/article/SB100014240527487044766045761582831 9
   8424372.html

6. www.jsonline.com/news/statepolitics/123554474.html.

7. www.620wtmj.com/news/local/128458763.html.

8. http://wauwatosa.patch.com/articles/about-1-000-rally-against-walker
   -near-his-tosa-turf-but-some-stand-by-him.

9. http://Freedomeden.Blogspot.Com/2011/11/Tonette-Walker-Protest
   -At-Wauwatosa.html.

Chapter 25: "We Did That Too"

1. http://online.wsj.com/article/SB100014241278873239519045782882507 2
   3189588.html.

2. www.maciverinstitute.com/2011/11/the-expansion-of-badgercare/.

Chapter 26: The Lessons of Wisconsin Can Be Used in the Battle for America

1. http://www.jsonline.com/news/statepolitics/approvers-of-obama-and
   -walker-are-indemand-swing-voters-nr74kio-172986401.html.

2. http://reagan2020.us/speeches/RNC_Convention.asp.

3. www.commentarymagazine.com/2013/01/15/barack-obama-negotiator/.

Conclusion: Unintimidated

1. www.margaretthatcher.org/document/106941.

INDEX